AF865307

Praise for
SECOND WAVE

"Drawn from secret case files and bristling with riveting detail, *Second Wave* is an extraordinary account of al Qaeda's terrifying plot to smuggle explosives—and possibly a weapon of mass destruction—into a busy American seaport. With his unparalleled access as a former prosecutor, Lebowitz takes readers along on an unforgettable journey as US officials try to piece together the plan for a 9/11 'sequel' against a backdrop of CIA black sites and Guantanamo Bay's notorious Camp 5 prison. The book's chilling finale is a warning to Americans about coming dangers as new US leaders abandon counterterrorism as a priority, weakening safeguards that have helped prevent another major attack against the homeland."

—**Joby Warrick,** author of *Black Flags: The Rise of ISIS*, winner of the 2016 Pulitzer Prize for General Nonfiction

"A fascinating book written by an expert participant in the pursuit and prosecution of the masterminds of the 9/11 attack and potential follow-on attacks. . . . An exciting yet disturbing account of the antagonists and protagonists, the mistakes and successes and the lessons learned that we must not forget. . . . Many accounts cover the 9/11 attacks, but Lebowitz exposes al Qaeda senior leaders' unimaginable intent, a second strike against the US homeland with a weapon of mass destruction. . . . What is most chilling is his description of the convergence of the visceral hatred of hardcore terrorists and the banality of useful idiots who enabled the successful 9/11 attacks and the planning for the second wave. . . . Lebowitz not only warns that, twenty-five years after the original attack, we need to remain vigilant, but he also warns that the price we pay today for adequate security pales in comparison to the butcher's bill we will certainly pay if we allow history to repeat itself."

—**Lieutenant General Stephen Fogarty,** US Army (Ret.); former commander of US Army Cyber Command and US Army Intelligence and Security Command

"Every American needs to read this book to understand the complex dark world of counterterrorism. Lebowitz shines a spotlight into the secret corners of sleeper agents, hostile intelligence agencies, spies, and terrorists plotting to detonate dirty bombs on US soil. Is the threat still viable? Read this book and draw your own conclusions."

—**Fred Burton,** former counterterrorism special agent and *New York Times* bestselling author

"A hidden chapter of the War on Terror that reads like a thriller but is chillingly real. *Second Wave* is gripping, revelatory, and urgently relevant, exposing how close America came to a catastrophic follow-up to 9/11 and why we must remain vigilant in the never-ending struggle against terrorism."

—**Michael P. Scharf,** former dean of Case Western Reserve University School of Law (2013–2024) and president of the American Branch of the International Law Association

"Leaving nothing out from the heroics and hubris, Lebowitz's unparalleled combination of access, participation, insight, and storytelling skill will leave readers with a better understanding of how the United States government both succeeded and failed to meet the high ideals and expectations of its hallowed Constitution and those who swore an oath to support and defend it. . . . Lebowitz's work is also a telling indictment of how national security priorities can shift so abruptly between administrations as to leave a country weaker and less secure. We should be grateful for the author's dogged efforts to bring this story to light 'to ourselves and our posterity.'"

—**Daniel Maurer,** associate professor of law, Ohio Northern University; author of *Crisis, Agency, and Law in US Civil-Military Relations*; Lieutenant Colonel, Army (Ret.)

"Some books inform you. This one will shake you. . . . Michael Lebowitz spent years as a prosecutor inside the War on Terror—in the courtroom, in Guantanamo, in the classified files no one was supposed to see. What he found was a post-9/11 nuclear plot so dangerous that the US government fought for years to keep it secret. *Second Wave* is one of the most important untold stories of our generation: meticulously researched, impossible to put down, and overdue by twenty years. If you only read one book about the War on Terror, make it this one."

—**Dr. Tony Brooks,** US Army Ranger, author of *Leave No Man Behind*

"Through years of intensive research and dogged determination, Lebowitz has produced a study that reminds us of the extreme dangers our nation has faced, and the lengths to which our government has gone to keep them secret."

—**Clay Mountcastle, PhD;** Director, Virginia War Memorial

SECOND WAVE

INSIDE AL QAEDA'S POST-9/11 ATTACK PLAN AND AMERICA'S SECRET EFFORT TO STOP IT

MICHAEL LEBOWITZ

DIVERSION
BOOKS

Diversion Books
A division of Diversion Publishing Corp.
www.diversionbooks.com

Copyright © 2026 by Michael Lebowitz

All rights reserved, including the right to reproduce this book or portions thereof in any form whatsoever. No part of this publication may be reproduced or transmitted in any form or by any means, electronic or mechanical, including photocopying, recording, or any other information storage and retrieval, without the written permission of the publisher.

The views expressed in this publication are those of the author and do not necessarily reflect the official policy or position of the Department of Defense or the US government. The public release clearance of this publication by the Department of Defense does not imply Department of Defense endorsement or factual accuracy of the material.

Diversion Books and colophon are registered trademarks of Diversion Publishing Corp.

For more information, email info@diversionbooks.com.

First Diversion Books Edition: August 2026
Hardcover ISBN: 979-8-89515-165-5
e-ISBN: 979-8-89515-166-2

Design by Westchester Publishing Services
Cover design by Jonathan Sainsbury // 6×9 design

Printed in the United States of America
1 3 5 7 9 10 8 6 4 2

Diversion books are available at special discounts for bulk purchases in the US by corporations, institutions, and other organizations. For more information, please contact admin@diversionbooks.com.

The publisher does not have any control over and does not assume any responsibility for author or third-party websites or their content.

For Charlie, Jake, Justine, and Jessica.
Hoping for a better world.

CONTENTS

CHAPTER 1

NUCLEAR THREAT

Finally on the ground in Bangkok, mentally preparing for his once-in-a-lifetime business meeting, a bespectacled man wearing the high-end attire appropriate for a business titan walked confidently through the parking garage toward the car that would take him to the Shangri-La Hotel.

Masked men suddenly surrounded him. They put a bag or hood over his head. They slammed him onto the ground, or maybe it was the trunk of a car. He struggled to break free, but he was overpowered, then cuffed at the wrists and the ankles. Despite his heavy weight, he was lifted and tossed into some kind of vehicle. One of the men lay on top of him, pinning him down.

He screeched in pain.

"My shoulder! My shoulder!" he screamed. They quickly muzzled his mouth.

Darkness. Silence. Pain. Disorientation. The vehicle was moving, but where were they taking him?

He could barely breathe. His shoulder continued to hurt. He thought he might have a heart attack. But he was unable to plead for help.

So he forced his mind to be analytical. This is an American operation, he told himself. Who else would be so brazen? Being kidnapped by Americans is better than any number of alternatives in this War on Terror. And he was a New Yorker, after all. America was based on the rule of law. He'd handle everything they'd throw his way, resolve the matter, and return to his family.

At some point the vehicle stopped, and he was moved, put in a chair. Someone gave him liquid nourishment, maybe Ensure. And a shit bucket.

He sat there for hours staring into darkness, but it felt like days.

Eventually, they stood him up and guided him onward as he shuffled along. He sensed he was now outside and then was led up a ramp, a vibrating ramp. They pushed his head down, placed him on his knees on a floor. The vibrations intensified. The feeling was familiar.

He was on an airplane.

* * *

After 9/11, CIA officials confirmed that al Qaeda was continuing a years-long mission "to pursue its strategic goal of obtaining a nuclear capability." For Usama bin Laden, acquisition of weapons of mass destruction (WMDs) was a "religious obligation," part of his Jihadist war against the West. By 2003, Khalid Sheikh Mohammad, the mastermind behind the 9/11 attack, confirmed to CIA interrogators that al Qaeda remained interested in developing a nuclear weapons capability. But the organization's intent wasn't abstract. The 9/11 mastermind revealed that he knew someone who "suggested where these weapons might be obtained." That man was a Pakistani. He was well connected. Sophisticated. Most frightening of all, this mysterious man owned a shipping business with an office in New York. To investigators after 9/11, the nuclear threat wasn't just a possibility. It was happening.

* * *

The small cells with their thick, heavy metal doors only intensified the sense of foreboding. Unbreakable windows adorning each cell door vanquished privacy. Fluorescent lights stood in for the scorching Caribbean sun. Such was life for the detainees of Guantanamo Bay's Camp 5. The US government called it a detention facility. Virtually everyone else called it a prison.

A plaque outside this maximum-security facility offered a mission statement: Honor Bound to Defend Freedom. Since 2002, this was where foreign terrorists went after being plucked from far-off places in the War on Terror. The US government justified Guantanamo Bay as the place for "the worst of the worst." In some cases, that was true. The men who plotted the 9/11 attacks and, before that, the USS *Cole* bombing were taken to Guantanamo—or GTMO—as the military called it. But those men—the true "worst of the worst"—were housed at a top-secret camp located at a different part of the island base.

Camp 5 was mostly for terrorists a tier or two lower than those who were deemed "the worst." Foot soldiers mostly. These inmates included a personal chef to top al Qaeda leaders, someone who stored bomb-making materials, a man who oversaw an improvised explosive device cell, and many others who were along for the ride. But there were some who had played more significant roles. There was a top bodyguard to Usama bin Laden named Sanad al-Kazimi. Another guy facilitated new recruits' attendance at terrorist training camps. An al Qaeda bombmaker named Hassan bin Attash, who personally built suicide vests, was captured and hauled off to Camp 5.*

Cell blocks in Camp 5 served as neighborhoods and developed their own culture. Shackled detainees were allowed to interact in common areas if they behaved. Each detainee had his own story. Many had families on the other side of the world. They talked to each other about them.

Of course, conflicts emerged. Fights over television programming would flare up on occasion. Sometimes detainees would try to take their anger out on the guards.

Camp 5-Delta was the name of one of those cell blocks, and one of its detainees stood out from among the rest. He was much older, and he lorded over the other residents and guards on the block like a stately nobleman deigning to meet his subjects. He was the one I came to see in early 2011 as a prosecutor operating on behalf of the Department of Defense. Before entering the compound, I asked my Army escort about the man, referring to him by name.

"Who?" asked my escort, a young Army sergeant who barely looked old enough to drink.

I had been working on a criminal case against this man for about two years. He was the lynchpin to al Qaeda's nuclear ambitions. He was connected to top Pakistani nuclear scientists. He was close with Pakistani

* Hassan's brother, Khallad, was an al Qaeda operative with a prosthetic leg who led a pre-9/11 trial run to ascertain that terrorists could sneak razor knives onto US airliners. Khallad was incarcerated down the road with the "worst of the worst" contingent.

intelligence officials known for their terrorist sympathies. The fate of the world literally rested on whether this man could deliver on his bravado regarding nuclear weapons before the plot could be foiled. He was directly connected to many of the big names of enemy combatants under investigation in the War on Terror: Usama bin Laden, Khalid Sheikh Mohammad, Majid Khan, Ali Abdul Aziz Ali. His case had become an obsession for me.

But his *precise* role remained a well-guarded secret, knowledge of it limited to a few perfunctory public statements and provocative revelations that investigators gathered over time. As the scope of the post-9/11 War on Terror expanded year by year, this businessman commanded the attention of virtually all US government agencies—from counterintelligence and law enforcement to the Department of Homeland Security and the military. Congress and the White House were also involved. His name was everywhere and yet nowhere: What was his ultimate role in the conspiracy?

I had officially traveled to Guantanamo Bay to meet with FBI and military investigators. But I unofficially sought a tour of Camp 5 for the specific purpose of seeing this man.

My Army escort that day appeared to be oblivious to his real name and his real story. "We don't use names here," he informed me.

Shifting tactics, I said, "ISN 1094," using the internment serial number given to the detainee upon his arrival at Guantanamo Bay.

"Oh, the old guy," the escort replied with a nod that told me he knew more.

I tried to get some details, but the sergeant wasn't forthcoming. He told me he wasn't allowed to say much, with camp protocols and all. But with a sly look, he did offer me one gratuitous tidbit. "1094's a sneaky fucker."

* * *

At the time of my visit to Guantanamo, the fact that the US had faced the prospect of a second attack possibly even worse than 9/11 was still mostly shrouded in secrecy. In the aftermath of 9/11, by 2003, port security was flagged in the media as a potential national emergency. Intelligence officials believed explosives were already en route to the US. A wealthy, seemingly untouchable Pakistani-American industrialist appeared central to the plot. It was a gripping story involving a web of key players on both sides of the War on Terror. But many events tied to the port security scare have since been classified. The story touched CIA, FBI, and military equities too sensitive to expose without risk.

I had been assigned to serve as a prosecutor in the case against five men accused of plotting the 9/11 attacks, and I had been poring over hundreds of thousands of pages of information. It was a mix of classified and unclassified material. Buried within these documents was a name that frequently surfaced and caught my attention.

Digging deeper, I learned about a plot to smuggle shipments of explosives into the US for what was to be al Qaeda's post-9/11 operation. And for the next decade, I read through tens of thousands of classified and unclassified documents chronicling the many nuances of the plot. This included reams of Guantanamo Bay transcripts and media reports. The research evolved into personal interviews with many of the al Qaeda members referenced in this book, as well as interviews with US law enforcement, military, and CIA officials with direct involvement in the investigation and manhunt. I also faced off in the Guantanamo Bay courtroom against the five men accused of plotting the 9/11 attacks.

I have taken pains in this book to run a full gamut of horror and hubris, bravery and heartbreak.

The events and characters related herein represent a profound moment in American history that our government has resisted being made public.

Current and former government employees like me are required to submit manuscripts for official prepublication review to ensure that no proprietary or classified information is inadvertently released. I first submitted the manuscript for review in 2019. In 2021, the book was stamped "Not Cleared due to Full Objection." The Department of Defense and the CIA declared that many of the details and much of the history contained in this book were too dangerous to reveal.

Even worse from my point of view, they did not tell me that the book was rejected until 2024. If it weren't for an earnest government employee who took it upon himself to investigate, this story would still be locked away. That employee communicated the following assessment to me:

> Mr. Lebowitz/Mike—I have scoured all domains multiple times and can find no paper trail notifying you of the results of your review. This

> is very unusual because [an unnamed official] was habitually precise in her handling of all her cases, and if she had a closure would have notified the author and thereby laid the foundation for a Reconsideration or an Appeal. At any rate, I cannot find a response letter and can find no evidence that one was sent that you may have missed.

That note suggested to me that the Department of Defense and the CIA wanted this book to disappear. Only in 2025, after another year of negotiation, was the book finally approved for publication by the powers that be; albeit some names would need to be changed, and a few factual details had to be omitted. But essentially, the entire story can now be told.

CHAPTER 2

THE BIG FISH

It was early 2003 at the Bagram Air Base in Afghanistan, and the prison was abuzz. A "big fish" might be coming. Although details were still a bit murky, military personnel were told to expect the imminent arrival of an HVD—the acronym for *high-value detainee.* But there was a catch. This particular HVD had not yet been captured.

The Bagram Collection Point featured lots of metal fencing covered in barbed wire. Concrete barriers helped shield the base from periodic mortar attacks. Watchtowers loomed from above. Uniformed soldiers and civilian contractors scurried across dust-covered roads and pathways nestled between the fencing and concrete.

Rumors over the HVD's identity were widespread. Thousands of low-level members of al Qaeda and the Taliban were being cycled through Bagram's makeshift detention facility, a flow that occurred virtually every hour of the day, seven days a week. Military personnel escorted detainees, many of whom had been snatched off the battlefield through raids or combat missions, or otherwise simply handed over by Afghan rivals into an abyss of uncertainty. The arrivals rarely inspired any significant intrigue. But this time was different.

Young Army guards—some still in their late teens—began prepping cinder-block interview rooms and a confined living space for the big fish. Meanwhile, the rumors persisted through that old-fashioned game of "telephone." An Army private heard from a civilian contractor who was briefed by an FBI agent and her CIA liaison that the HVD was an "old guy."* The vast majority of detainees were in their twenties and thirties.

"Is it bin Laden?" a few soldiers wondered aloud, barely able to hide their excitement.

"Older," that Army private replied.

"No way it's bin Laden," others chimed in, those with some inkling that members of al Qaeda's senior leadership during this time were being transferred to secret CIA detention facilities scattered across the globe. Those secret locations were known as "black sites." Bagram was many things, but this section of the sprawling base was not run by the CIA—nothing like a black site.

Why was an HVD coming to Bagram's military detention facility? HVDs were ordinarily under the CIA's purview.

While HVDs were mostly al Qaeda and Taliban leadership, the HVD classification also included individuals trusted by the al Qaeda leaders in planning and implementing their deadly terrorist attacks. This was nearly two years after the September 11, 2001, attacks. Al Qaeda plots were still an ongoing threat. The CIA needed to learn everything about these ticking time bomb plots, sometimes employing harsh and controversial means that many considered to be torture.

During that summer of 2003, while the young soldiers at Bagram were preparing for the arrival of their very own HVD, CIA officers were skulking around the military detention zone in their jeans and polo shirts. And so were a gaggle of FBI agents and military investigators. Regardless of affiliation, they were all on alert and preparing to greet this most curious HVD. But one question persisted among the soldiers: "Why are *we* getting him?"

* * *

Bagram wasn't the only place buzzing. Preparations for the big fish were also quite lively back in Washington, DC. The CIA, FBI, the Pentagon, and even the White House were all involved. The HVD needed to be captured and interrogated—and fast.

---

* Military investigators on the ground during that time later explained the buzz to the author.

Recent arrests and interrogations of other HVDs led to speculation by investigators that hidden shipments of al Qaeda's massive explosives were already steaming toward US ports. The explosives themselves were believed to be disguised as mundane consumer goods. Upon arrival, terrorist accomplices would be waiting to unload the explosives as part of a massive conspiracy to murder countless Americans. The amount of explosives at this early stage was thought to be enough to fill several large trucks—enough to blow up a bridge, a building, or to distribute to suicide bombers strategically located throughout the country for multiple, smaller attacks.

Word about the plot was starting to leak. Majid Khan, a recent graduate from Owings Mills High School in Maryland, had just been captured in a raid in Pakistan. Khan was linked to senior al Qaeda leadership, including the alleged 9/11 architect, Khalid Sheikh Mohammad (a.k.a. KSM). Investigators believed Khan had knowledge of the explosives, possibly with mass destruction potential, being smuggled through the ports. Perhaps even more concerning was Jose Padilla, a US-based al Qaeda operative and likely participant in the distribution of these explosives believed to be planning to set off a radiological bomb—or "dirty bomb."

All this was good, reliable, and frightening information. Port security became national news. Port authorities in New York, Los Angeles, and elsewhere were placed on heightened alert. But exact details of the threat remained elusive. Al Qaeda didn't exactly own its own shipping company. How would they navigate the logistics of international maritime trade? If the reporting was accurate, then someone with money and experience with the nuances of global shipping was involved. Someone not on the radar. A terrorist sympathizer perhaps operating under the cover of being a legitimate businessman.

In March 2003, just months before all the commotion at Bagram, investigators caught a potential break. Majid Khan was now detained in one of the CIA black sites. As Khan began undergoing coercion by torture known as Enhanced Interrogation Techniques (EITs), he started to talk. By all accounts, Khan's early days in CIA custody were marked by an agonizing regime of EITs, followed by interrogations, or "debriefings," as the CIA refers to them.

Between the EITs and debriefings, CIA officers assigned Khan with what the CIA called "homework." Like the term implies, Khan was tasked with writing down helpful information during his downtime at "home"—his dimly lit cell. A special pen was provided, one specifically designed to prevent Khan from using it to harm himself or others. A heavily redacted report noted that Khan was "the crucial first link in the chain." The same report referred to a "building block" process, where "information from one detainee can be used in debriefing another detainee."

Khan would later recall:

> After being detained, I told my captors about the people I had met, the things I had been asked to do. . . . I told them everything I knew about everything they asked. I did everything I could do to cooperate and hoped to be released. But I wasn't released. Instead, the more I cooperated and told them, the more I was tortured. . . . I remember an older American man—a US interrogator—who would tell me they were not "buying my story . . . you're peeing on my shoes and telling me it's raining."

At some point in these early days of confinement, Khan provided a name. And then he startled his CIA handlers with the disclosure of an unforeseen second name. It was a father and son duo with some sort of nebulous business links in New York. But was Khan telling the truth? Or were the names an untrustworthy by-product of torture?

It wasn't much, but at least they had a lead. Later that month, the mysterious father and son were mentioned at another black site. And then another. They were names that barely registered with intelligence cognoscenti. But there clearly was a link between this duo and al Qaeda's leadership chain. Most striking for the agents, the father and son appeared to possess the financial and corporate legitimacy to facilitate the clandestine shipments of explosives.

Among these agents, it was already considered just a matter of time before the next attack. But as investigators learned more about these new, well-heeled suspects, one tidbit of information further shocked investigators in their offices throughout Washington, DC. This father and son might be Americans.

With al Qaeda's massive explosives possibly on the way to American ports and two American businessmen somehow involved, agents of various stripes in offices and in the field were scrambling to put together a case.

CHAPTER 3

A FAMILY BUSINESS

"Charles Stern" was used to watching mammoth cargo ships come and go from New York Harbor.* International shipping was his business, after all, and Stern and his business partner ran the import/export company International Merchandise Group (IMG). The company was a passion project conceived by the two men, who shared a burning desire to succeed despite the odds. Like countless others, Stern and his partner were chasing the American Dream.†

Raised in a poor Orthodox Jewish household in Brooklyn, Stern watched as his father worked several jobs to support his large family. The younger Stern dreamed of something better, frequently making his way to the ports where thousands of enormous ships came and went, stocked with metal containers. Stern would watch as the dockworkers loaded and unloaded the cargo, almost as if it were a choreographed dance. It appeared to be a hard life, but a decent life.

But what about the ships and the cargo? Stern would discover that the real money was in shipping. He wanted in.

---

* The name "Charles Stern" is a pseudonym used here for legal and national security reasons. Several other names in this book have also been altered to comply with classification restrictions, legal counsel, or government clearance requirements.

† Stern's out-of-place association with al Qaeda's plot to smuggle explosives in the US—including possible nuclear or radiological—was a constant source of intrigue for many of the FBI agents assigned to the case over the years. Stern's role in the story was detailed through numerous FBI agent interviews with the author.

In the early 1980s, at a Manhattan coffee shop, he met his kindred spirit—a thirty-something-year-old Pakistani immigrant who was educated, spoke fluent English, and was as tenacious and success-driven as he was. The two instantly clicked and talked for hours. They opened up to each other about their business ideas, which they discovered constituted a shared dream of getting rich by importing and exporting textiles. Stern and his new friend exchanged contact information and agreed to meet again soon. That man, Saifullah Paracha, soon became Stern's business partner—a relationship that lasted for nearly twenty years.

Stern and Paracha were both husbands with young children at home. To support their growing families, they worked day and night to build IMG, scrapping for every contract they could get. Although this paid the bills, they weren't content. They had their eyes set on a larger prize. They wanted to be middlemen managing imports and exports for the major corporations and multinationals. Paracha was especially intrigued by the prospect of obtaining contracts to ship clothing sold by Kmart.

As the two maneuvered and fought to obtain contracts over time, they became more than just business partners. Stern and Paracha bonded as friends. Stern referred to Paracha by his nickname, Saif. They looked out for each other. Their families frequently socialized together. Young Uzair Paracha was often underfoot as the adults worked, making Stern laugh with his jokes. Stern would then make funny faces back at Uzair, causing Saif's toddler to crack up with giggles.

Saifullah had always shuttled back and forth between New York and Pakistan. But by 1986, he and his wife, Farhat, agreed that it was important for the children to be connected to their homeland in Pakistan. Farhat was particularly homesick. She missed her family and their traditions. Saifullah wasn't as keen on returning to Pakistan; much of his family was in New York. His brother was a US citizen. But Saifullah relented. He understood the call of home for his wife. His reservations about living in Karachi mostly involved his business and his friend.

Stern assured Saifullah that their business would not suffer in the least. They agreed that Stern would run things in New York, and Saifullah would work to dominate the shipping market from Pakistan. It would be a truly international business. Saifullah also assured his partner that he had had every intention of traveling to New York on a regular basis. The two men agreed that with this new arrangement, the business would not only survive but surely flourish.

Still, if IMG was going to secure big-name contracts, it had to look and play the part. To this end, Stern secured office space in Manhattan's haute Garment District. The contracts and the money continued to roll in. IMG was soon shipping clothing for companies like Walmart. Stern and Paracha became millionaires. Indeed, the 1990s were boom years for IMG and its founders. Their families were able to reap the rewards of travel and enjoy luxurious lifestyles.

While Saifullah often traveled to New York to conduct business, Stern also flew to Karachi on a regular basis. He was always welcomed into the grand Paracha home. Nobody seemed to care that a yarmulke-wearing Orthodox Jew was spending time in their house, which was adorned with intricate Islamic artwork. Instead, the Parachas and Stern often engaged in polite debates and conversations about religion. They discussed politics, too. It was fun and stimulating. Saifullah and Stern were both socially liberal, but generally realistic about the ways of the world. Their points of view rarely differed much. To the Parachas, Stern was family.

The IMG family enterprise hit a rough patch immediately after 9/11. Various disruptions and shipping impediments caused IMG's business to slow down, and the cofounders scrambled to secure a $2 million loan to keep things afloat. Between the two of them, now experienced businessmen, IMG was able to survive, but not without some changes, including the company name, which the two agreed to change within the United States from IMG to Chenco.

Stern accepted the fact that Saifullah had some other business endeavors in Pakistan. Stern had side projects as well, so there was no animosity. Stern was aware that Saifullah had recently begun dabbling in the Karachi real estate market, investing heavily in the construction of a seaside apartment complex called Cliftonia. Saifullah was also involved in a cement business and a media company called Universal Broadcasting. Stern marveled at Saifullah's intense desire to make as many connections as he could. This instinct for building relationships played a key role in the breadth of his business activities.

During one of Stern's final trips to Saifullah's Karachi office around 2001, Stern saw for himself the operations of Universal Broadcasting's makeshift media company. This included some strange characters who mainly kept to themselves behind closed doors and shuttered blinds. Most of these people did not engage in conversation or otherwise interact with Stern. However, one man briefly caught his attention.

Introduced to Stern by the name of Mir, the man came across as particularly dismissive and contemptuous of others. Stern didn't harp on this until two years later, when he was shocked to see a picture of Mir flashing across his television screen. A news report identified Mir as Khalid Sheikh Mohammad, the alleged mastermind of the 9/11 attacks, known in intelligence circles by his initials, KSM. He was also named as a suspect in the murder in Pakistan of *Wall Street Journal* reporter Daniel Pearl, who was forced to acknowledge his Jewish heritage before being beheaded in front of a video camera. For Stern, this was chilling indeed. He, an Orthodox Jewish man, realized that, while in Pakistan, he had come face-to-face with a man believed to be one of the most notorious anti-Semitic mass murderers in recent history. But back in 2001, Stern just regarded the man known as Mir as an asshole.

Meanwhile, Saifullah's other business pursuits were top of his own mind, and he tried to limit his role in the main company, Chenco. But he could keep it in the family. Even with the new name and expanding scope of operations, Chenco's founding partners agreed in late 2002 that Uzair would be named CEO. Saifullah's eldest son had just graduated from Karachi's Institute of Business Administration (IBA) and now expressed his desire to follow in his father's footsteps. Uzair would travel to New York and work out of Stern's office space in the Manhattan Garment District. Stern understood that Uzair would not only do work for Chenco but also represent Saifullah in some of his other business ventures.

In February 2003, Uzair traveled to New York with a bag full of glossy marketing materials for the Cliftonia apartment complex. Uzair soon explained to Stern that he intended to market the upscale housing project to Pakistani expatriates living in the US. Uzair also confided that he was preparing to propose to his New York–based girlfriend. He even showed Stern the ring.

Stern was fond of the boy and was happy to have him around. After all, Stern had watched Uzair grow up into the man he had become. He was proud of him. Stern, for his part, had fulfilled his own dream. He was a successful import/exporter. In the 1990s and early 2000s, the two mutually beloved families did not know that their relationship would soon take a sudden, heartbreaking turn.

* * *

In 1997, government investigators learned a horrifying truth. A man named Usama bin Laden, considered merely a terrorist financier, was much more dangerous than they thought. Bin Laden led an organization called al Qaeda, made of various committees, and two intertwined committees—known as the "military committee" and "media committee"—were planning operations against US interests worldwide. Al Qaeda's most ominous mission? To obtain nuclear material.

Government analysts "found connections everywhere."

The following year, Pakistan shocked the world by testing a nuclear weapon. The State Department waffled on how to react to a nuclear-armed Pakistan. Extensive sanctions could have brought "total chaos" to the country, which would have created fertile ground for Islamic radicals based in Pakistan and neighboring Afghanistan. Some of those radicals belonged to the group actively seeking nuclear material: al Qaeda.

As intercepted correspondence captured him saying, bin Laden was intent on carrying out a "Hiroshima" against the United States.

In 1999, the government analysts, a small group tucked away at offices in New York and Virginia, received more stark reporting. An al Qaeda camp in Afghanistan called Darunta was being used for chemical weapons development. Reports also indicated that al Qaeda operatives were seeking to amass nuclear material at a site in Herat, Afghanistan.

In 2000, it was revealed that one of the Pakistani government's top weapons developers was leading the most dangerous nuclear smuggling ring ever disclosed. President Clinton cautioned Pakistani President Musharraf about the dangers of nuclear proliferation. "I offered him the moon when I went to see him, in terms of better relations with the United

States, if he'd help us get to bin Laden and deal with another issue or two," Clinton recalled. Despite the stakes, Clinton was reticent to press the bin Laden issue with Musharraf, reportedly because members of Pakistan's Inter-Services Intelligence Directorate were present. The CIA by this time was well aware that many Pakistani intelligence officials held sympathies for terrorist groups.

* * *

Pakistan was only two days old when Saifullah Paracha was born. It was August 17, 1947, and the world around him was in upheaval. This era was known as Partition—when India and Pakistan split into predominantly Hindu and Muslim nations respectively, while simultaneously gaining independence from Britain. Millions were in the process of being killed in riots or otherwise displaced. Bloodshed was everywhere in young Saifullah's world.

Like many children in rural Pakistani families, Saifullah was born into extreme poverty. The youngest of nine siblings, he and his family mostly slept on the dirt floor of their tiny home. Food was scarce as they scraped by. Rice was the predominant staple in their diet.

Saifullah's hometown—the village of Mangwal—was one of numerous, mostly anonymous rural enclaves that were being ripped apart during Partition. Previously, the majority of Mangwal's residents were Sikhs. The remaining villagers were Muslims, with a minuscule number of Hindus mixed in. But once Partition occurred, the Sikhs and Hindus fled for the relative safety of India. It is estimated that Mangwal lost about 70 percent of its population during Partition. Only the Muslims remained.

Despite the dwindled population and lack of opportunity, Saifullah somehow managed to blaze a path to success. He pulled himself out of poverty through sheer determination, guile, and his self-driven work ethic. Years later, law enforcement personnel couldn't help but view Saifullah's success with a sense of awe.

"It's almost impossible for someone to do what Paracha did," said a Pakistani-American female FBI agent known to Saifullah as "Mae." She added, "Paracha is a force of nature."

A court document from a 2020 lawsuit (*Paracha v. Trump*) described Paracha's rise in the business world from his humble Pakistani roots:

> Saifullah Paracha is a western-educated businessman. He was born in a rural village in Pakistan and, though raised in poverty, successfully pursued an education . . . Mr. Paracha received a permanent resident visa from the United States consulate in Pakistan; over the next several decades, Mr. Paracha travelled frequently between Pakistan and the United States. Mr. Paracha is a practicing Muslim, and . . . has cosmopolitan and moderate sympathies. Mr. Paracha and his wife, Farhat, sent their children to private Catholic schools in Pakistan. The family travelled frequently, to the United States and elsewhere, and "enjoyed a comfortable life similar to that of many westerners." . . . He took business trips to Malaysia, Saudi Arabia, Iran, Iraq, Sweden, the United Kingdom, China, and India; he traveled for leisure to Japan, Yugoslavia, the Philippines, and the United Arab Emirates.

Indeed, Saifullah was an enigma. Not only did he achieve heights in Pakistan that should have been unattainable for a man with his background, but he had successfully carved out his own place in the American Dream. Saifullah was rich, happy, Westernized, and well liked. His family was thriving. Paracha was even very open about the fact that his good friend and business partner was an Orthodox Jew.

Saifullah's early key to success was through education. He easily mastered his studies and developed a shrewd business sense at a young age. Soon, Saifullah made his way into Karachi. He fell in love with the bustling city and all its potential. Saifullah quickly realized that he was the type of man who was essentially a dime a dozen in Karachi—competing with millions of others for the same jobs. He wanted more than just to be another faceless villager doing menial work in the big city. He envied and idolized the cosmopolitan movers and shakers. Saifullah was certainly not a burger—a term used to describe someone privileged and Westernized—i.e., a rich young Pakistani.

But he wouldn't mind being one.

Saifullah eyed the United States as his big ticket to financial success. If he could make it in America, he could return to Pakistan with a leg up over the competition. He convinced himself that the nascent computer industry was poised to take off. In 1971, Saifullah applied and was accepted into the computer science program at the New York Institute of Technology. That fall, he moved to New York on a student visa.

Life in New York was not what he expected. Instead of being a faceless villager in Karachi, Saifullah was now a nameless foreigner in New York City. Like many immigrants and foreign students, Saifullah gravitated toward the familiar. In this case, it was family members living in the city.

After months toiling away with his studies, Saifullah became restless. He was excelling in school, just as he had excelled in nearly everything else he put his mind toward. But by 1974, the passion was just not there. To Saifullah, computer science would get him a job, but then what? A decent life for sure, but no power, no real challenge. There was no opportunity to conquer the world as a computer scientist working for a salary and paychecks, he thought. If he continued on his current track, Saifullah was destined to be what he saw as ordinary. He refused to degrade himself that way.

Despite being in the US on a student visa, Saifullah decided to drop out of school. He convinced his brother—who also was in New York—that they should go into business for themselves. They raised some money together and took over a travel agency called Global Travel Services. The agency focused on travel arrangements for Pakistanis shuttling back and forth to the United States.

Saifullah thrived in this new role. He was making money. More importantly, he was his own boss. As an added benefit, by directly working with so many Pakistanis and Pakistani-Americans, Saifullah was making countless valuable connections within that community. Whenever they needed to travel, they called Saifullah Paracha. He was becoming indispensable among his fellow countrymen of a certain class and standing.

Saifullah's first success in business coincided with success on another front. He met his future wife. Like Saifullah, Farhat studied in Pakistan before traveling to the US to improve her life. At NYU, Farhat was earning a master's degree in sociology. She was smart, kind, opinionated, and fiercely independent. She respected traditional Pakistani customs and was certainly in touch with Islam. But at the same time, she unabashedly voiced her liberal views. She was pragmatic and sophisticated. Farhat was unlike anyone Saifullah had ever met. He fell in love deeply and almost immediately.

For her part, Farhat found Saifullah funny and kind, yet no pushover. She respected his drive. Saifullah had a toughness about him that she inferred was from his upbringing back in Mangwal as the youngest of ten children. Saifullah showered Farhat with affection, sparing no expense in his efforts to woo her. Like her beau, Farhat was already smitten.

Saifullah and Farhat married in 1979. The following year, on January 7, 1980, the couple had their first child—Uzair. Eventually, three more children would be born—Muneeza, Mustafa, and Zahra. The family was close-knit and loving. Saifullah was the clear patriarch; a jovial, stocky man who relished his role as head of the house. He was also a talker. Saifullah pontificated on just about everything. When out at a restaurant, it was common for Saifullah to call the manager to the table so he could provide unsolicited advice. Saifullah gregariously spoke to anyone who would listen. He loved meeting new people. That was his passion. And while he could be verbose at times, most appreciated Saifullah as a harmless, fun guy. Saifullah was a true pillar of his community, both in New York and Karachi.

Saifullah's road to success within the United States was not without potholes. Perhaps the biggest obstacle occurred in the late 1970s. This is when Saifullah nearly found himself deported. He was so busy building his company and making connections that he failed to address his visa status. He had arrived in New York on a student visa. But as the 1970s progressed, he had subsequently dropped out of school and purchased his own travel agency. Saifullah was certainly a productive member of society. But he wasn't a student anymore. Around 1978, the oversight caught up with him. The old Immigration and Naturalization Service (INS) sent him a notice that he was to be deported.

Saifullah did not back down. He retained an immigration lawyer and instructed him to fight the deportation, which was put on hold while the matter was litigated through the courts. In 1980, Saifullah's lawyer argued the case in front of an immigration judge, making the plea to allow Saifullah to remain in the country. In the meantime, Saifullah continued to build his life and career and did not consider the ramifications of deportation. He didn't think it would happen. After all, he had studied up on the law and was certain that his case was sound. He was rarely wrong. But in this instance, Saifullah miscalculated. His lawyer lost the case, and Saifullah was ordered to surrender for deportation in a few months' time.

At that point, Saifullah moved quickly. He discovered a loophole that would effectively nullify his deportation. All he had to do was leave the country of his own volition. And that's what he did. In 1980, Saifullah returned to Karachi. His deportation was rendered moot, and the US government did not consider him to be a deportee. His file remained clean. With the American Dream still so irresistibly attainable, Saifullah continued to work the system.

Saifullah and Farhat immediately submitted paperwork to obtain lawful permanent resident (LPR) status. The process was surprisingly easy, and they were granted their green cards. Each of their children also received legal status in the country. Saifullah and Farhat were free to travel and work in the United States without further fear of removal.

LPRs are non-citizens who are lawfully authorized to live permanently within the United States. They may accept employment without special restrictions, own property, and even join the military. LPRs also are eligible to apply to become US citizens. Saifullah and Farhat took full advantage of their newfound legal status. For the next twenty years, they shuttled back and forth between Pakistan and New York. Uzair received early childhood education from the Rainbow Montessori School in Brooklyn. Saifullah eventually purchased the posh house down the street from Donald Trump in Jamaica Estates, Queens. And of course, Saifullah and Charles Stern founded IMG, the import/export company they established in the heart of Manhattan's Garment District.

While in Pakistan, Saifullah never forgot his poor upbringing in Mangwal. He joined several prominent Pakistani philanthropic organizations. As part of these endeavors, Saifullah championed the construction of a hospital in Punjab province near his childhood village. In the mid-1990s, he was named chairman of the Council of Welfare Organizations, an umbrella group overseeing several charities. Between the charities and his business empire, Saifullah rubbed elbows with countless people from all walks of life, including the ruling elite. And for every person he met, Saifullah faithfully recorded their names and contact information in a seemingly innocuous Casio electronic organizer that was gifted to him from Charles Stern back in 1999.

As for religion, Saifullah made sure that he was regularly seen at the mosque. He chose to pray with a conservative religious organization called Tanzeem-e-Islami under the tutelage of cleric Dr. Israr Ahmed. The organization's conservative tenets appeared to contrast with Saifullah's (and Farhat's) lifestyle, particularly where their eldest son was a burger and Saifullah's business partner and friend was an Orthodox Jew.

Tanzeem-e-Islami, under Dr. Ahmed, opposed what it called "modern secular curriculum" in universities. The group also expressed hostility toward the United States. Dr. Ahmed preached against Western values and vices, claiming that such values were corrupting Pakistan. And he was not shy about supporting Jihad against the West, although he was careful to avoid direct calls for terrorist activity.

Saifullah was quite active with Tanzeem-e-Islami. He hosted numerous events and led discussions with its members. Nobody appeared to doubt his religious convictions.

Religious commitment aside, Saifullah lived life to the fullest. He worked hard and ate well, paying little attention to his health. Saifullah became somewhat obese, which was typically overshadowed by his gregarious, jovial personality. As he got older, he developed several ailments, including diabetes, high blood pressure, psoriasis, arthritis, and gout. He managed these issues with a regimen of medication. It was something someone of his stature and means could certainly handle. Unbeknownst to Saifullah at the time, his health would later become a matter of international intrigue and controversy. But in 2001, at age fifty-four, his ailments were just manageable side effects of getting older and a lifestyle that reflected his success.

Meanwhile, his LPR status was beneficial in less obvious ways. It might have even saved Farhat's life. In 1996, Farhat was diagnosed with cancer. The family rushed to New York to ensure that Farhat received the best hospital care. They spent nearly a year living in New York and Connecticut. Eventually, Farhat's cancer went into remission. By this time, Saifullah was already at the top of his game in terms of status and wealth. By beating cancer with his wife, he felt invincible.

* * *

Saifullah's hands trembled as he made the call. He was not planning on calling Uzair, but he had to warn him. It was early March 2003, several years since he and his wife had seemingly beaten back fate. Uzair was in New York. The boy might be in danger.*

Just moments prior, Saifullah had been watching television in his palatial Karachi home. To that point, everything was business as usual. Uzair had been named CEO of Chenco and was planning on proposing to his girlfriend. The other kids were doing well in their studies. Farhat was cancer-free. Moreover, an investor named Mustafa had pledged 200,000 euros for the Cliftonia real estate project. Life was good. And then Saifullah watched the news.

A terrorist was captured in Rawalpindi, Pakistan. But it wasn't just any terrorist. It was Khalid Sheikh Mohammad—KSM—the arch terrorist who investigators believed had planned the 9/11 attacks, perhaps the world's most wanted man after Usama bin Laden. Security forces had apparently raided an al Qaeda safe house, resulting in the capture. Appearing disheveled and dirty, KSM's image was broadcast throughout the world.

The news was deeply disconcerting for Saifullah. To him, KSM was Mir, a man who had been in his life since mid-2001. Mir had been to his Karachi office on numerous occasions. There was documentation linking the two men. Money. Discussions. Business. In fact, the Cliftonia investor Mustafa—the one who pledged 200,000 euros—was an associate of Mir. Worse, Mustafa had introduced Saifullah to another one of their associates: a young man named Majid Khan.

It could be nothing, Saifullah rationalized. He hadn't spoken to Mir since sometime in 2002. Mir, for whatever reason, had designated Mustafa—who appeared to be in his mid-twenties—as his point person for Saifullah. That relationship had continued to the present without any issues. Saifullah probably had nothing to worry about. He wasn't a terrorist or a member of al Qaeda.

The business with Majid Khan could be troublesome for Uzair. The four of them—Saifullah, Uzair, Khan, and Mustafa—had met for dinner several months earlier. They had a follow-up meeting at Snoopy's Ice Cream

---

* Interviews between the author and FBI agents, as well as Saifullah's attorneys, captured the mood.

Parlor in Karachi. There, Mustafa asked Saifullah to assist Khan with a matter involving what was then called the Immigration and Naturalization Service (INS) in the United States. Saifullah agreed, encouraging Uzair to take the lead in helping Khan. Uzair and Khan then sped off on a motorbike. Who knows what they discussed after that. Saifullah then turned to more important business he had with Mustafa, mainly the Cliftonia project. If Khan was an associate of Mustafa, and Mustafa was an associate of Mir, Saifullah wondered if Uzair might be caught up in the Mir/KSM capture. Uzair, after all, was in New York. Would Mir/KSM implicate him? Saifullah had to warn his son. He made the call.

In New York, Uzair wasn't sure what to think. The father and son discussed KSM's capture. Saifullah offered some relatively vague information about Khan's and Mustafa's association with KSM. Uzair didn't seem surprised about the al Qaeda connection. But Uzair was in possession of documents belonging to Khan. This included Khan's Maryland driver's license, his Owings Mills High School identification card, and a Bank of America credit card. These documents, which were sitting in his room in Brooklyn, were part of Uzair's assigned task related to Khan's dealings with the INS. Uzair asked his father what he should do about Khan's documents. Should Khan's driver's license and credit cards be tossed into the trash? Saifullah rejected that idea.

"Don't do anything yet," Saifullah replied. He advised Uzair to simply keep the documents hidden until he could get a handle on the situation. Saifullah added that he needed to make some more calls.

The next phone call was to Mustafa. Nobody answered the phone, and Saifullah hesitantly left a message. There was some concern that Mustafa may have been picked up by the security services. Saifullah stared at his phone, ruminating over his relationship with Mir and his associates. He couldn't help but wonder how these events would impact the Cliftonia project. A significant amount of time and money was already invested in the complex.

Saifullah didn't have to wait long for the phone to ring. It was Mustafa. He was safe.

Saifullah grilled Mustafa. He wanted to know more about Mir, and how Mir's capture would affect the current business. Mustafa remained calm. He basically told Saifullah that there was nothing to worry about. He was going to lie low for a while, but all would turn out okay. Whether out of hope or denial, Saifullah went against his better judgment and trusted Mustafa's words. Life would carry on.

Meanwhile, around the same time that Saifullah was speaking to Uzair and Mustafa, others were talking. In a black site, Majid Khan discussed Saifullah and Uzair Paracha. Khan talked about Uzair's role in handling Khan's driver's license and credit card. Khan also elaborated on what the two young men discussed on the motorbike after they left Snoopy's Ice Cream Parlor. Perhaps more disturbingly, Khan acknowledged that Uzair's role was part of a broader scheme to get Khan back into the United States for one specific purpose: Khan was going to be an al Qaeda sleeper agent. Eventually, Khan—at KSM's behest—would be activated to detonate bombs at numerous soft targets on the East Coast, including gas stations. All he needed were the explosives and detonators.

KSM was talking, too. He was opening up about Khan and the Parachas and Mustafa.

A formerly top-secret CIA correspondence from March 2003 provides insight into the thinking at the Agency during this period:

> HVT interrogator set the stage for the meeting by telling KSM that we have Majid in custody and that we know there is more to the story of KSM's relationship with Majid than what KSM had reported. KSM reluctantly nodded affirmatively and was left to await interrogation team. . . . We would note, however, that KSM's version of events differs primarily in that he portrays Majid as quite the eager young recruit who went so far as to propose operations inside the US. . . . We request that [CIA Headquarters] provide . . . with background and requirements for Majid . . . to help us vet KSM's story as we suspect that their joint "gas station operations" is the tip of the iceberg for what all Al-Qa'ida may have in mind.

In mid-March 2003, FBI Special Agent Janelle Miller was in Islamabad, Pakistan. When the call came in, she found herself rushing to pack her bags. She had been working with Pakistani intelligence officials as part of the War on Terror, and this phone call on a secure, top-secret phone line changed everything. Agent Miller learned about the father and son, Saifullah and Uzair Paracha.*

Details about the duo were still scant within FBI circles, but the CIA couldn't keep the Paracha information to itself. Saifullah and Uzair might be involved in shipping al Qaeda explosive devices—including potential nuclear or radiological weapons—to the US, and there were those who believed these explosives might already be en route to their targets. Moreover, CIA leadership understood that the Parachas might have United States citizenship, or at the very least hold lawful permanent resident (LPR) status, colloquially known as green cards. Either way, they were believed to have some sort of US status. As such, the FBI needed to be consulted right away.

Agent Miller knew what to do. First things first: learn everything she could about Saifullah and Uzair Paracha. And she had to work fast. From her base in Pakistan, she sought to gather as much information as she could before rushing off to New York.

For starters, Agent Miller confirmed that Saifullah—the father—was in Karachi, Pakistan. But Saifullah was not a typical terrorist operating from the shadows. His name appeared to be all over the place—philanthropy, business, and high society—yet never associated with al Qaeda. Despite her efforts, Agent Miller couldn't find anyone in Pakistan who suspected that Saifullah was anything other than a legitimate businessman. As far as the government of Pakistan was concerned, Saifullah was no terrorist.

In fact, Saifullah was well known and well regarded within the upper echelons of Pakistani society. He was prominent and rich. He was also extremely well connected within the Pakistani political class. Saifullah was even friendly with Hamid Gul, the head of Inter-Services Intelligence (ISI), Pakistan's equivalent to the CIA. It would not be easy simply to pick up Saifullah at his house for interrogation. A court document later summarized Saifullah's privileged status:

---

* Years later, Agent Miller and her FBI colleagues recalled to the author the exigent challenge they faced.

> In addition to these business ventures, it is undisputed that Mr. Paracha was an active philanthropist who was particularly interested in building schools and hospitals in Pakistan and, later, in Afghanistan. . . . Mr. Paracha was an active member of the Council of Welfare Organizations ("CWO"), a charitable organization "made up of successful Pakistani businessmen and political leaders," who shared a goal of "provid[ing] support in Pakistan and the region regarding education, health, justice, and food support." As a respected man in his community, Mr. Paracha had substantial social status and political connections. For example, he travelled with or maintained relationships with Saudi Arabia's minister of petroleum, the President of Afghanistan, the President of Pakistan, the head of Pakistan's intelligence service, the mayor of Karachi, and various other political and educational leaders in Pakistan.

Agent Miller realized that any contact with Saifullah was essentially off-limits, as there were too many political considerations at play. If Uzair—the son—was in Pakistan, he probably would have been off-limits as well. The US government would have had to engage in painful and lengthy negotiations with the Pakistani government with no guarantee of ever achieving access to the Parachas. Given the potential severity of the danger involved, significant concessions to the Pakistanis would likely have to be offered. The situation would have been a mess.

Fortunately for the FBI, Uzair had departed Pakistan a few months earlier and was now in New York. Still, Agent Miller didn't celebrate this news. Uzair's location was a double-edged sword. Certainly, the FBI could avoid Pakistani obstruction, but it became apparent that Uzair had traveled to New York to work for his father's import/export business.

Shipping. Explosives. Nuclear materials. Seaports. The agent was acutely aware that her fears regarding port security might be manifesting themselves at that very moment through the movements of the son. Time was of the essence, and Saifullah would have to wait. Only a short while after first hearing the name Paracha, Agent Miller boarded a plane to New York. She wanted nothing more than to have a long chat with Uzair Paracha.

CHAPTER 4

ECHOES OF 9/11

Back in New York in March 2003, as Uzair was getting off the phone to hide Khan's documents, FBI Special Agent Janelle Miller was in her office at the Joint Terrorism Task Force. She had just returned from Pakistan where she had learned as much as she could about the Parachas, father and son. Now that she was home, she was anxious to have a chat with Uzair, whom she had come to suspect, along with his father, of being involved with an al Qaeda conspiracy. The logistics were coming together, as information continued to flow.

As she reviewed new intelligence, Agent Miller learned something else about the father—something that frightened her. Apparently, Saifullah had "recommended to an al Qaeda operative that nuclear weapons should be used against US troops and *suggested where these weapons might be obtained*." For Agent Miller, an already exigent circumstance became even more so. Pakistan had recently become a nuclear power. Government officials had been warning that al Qaeda was seeking nuclear materials and that a network of Pakistani scientists sold nuclear technology and expertise to Libya, Iran, and North Korea. Moreover, Agent Miller already knew that Saifullah was associated with the highest levels of Pakistani government. Could there be a connection?

There was now information linking the Parachas to an al Qaeda sleeper agent in need of explosives, nuclear weapons proliferation, an import/export business, and the mastermind of the 9/11 attacks. The FBI could not wait much longer. Unfortunately, Saifullah was untouchable so long as he remained in Pakistan. But Uzair was only several blocks away. He certainly needed to be brought in for questioning. In the meantime, Agent Miller continued to learn more about the players, some of whom were being tortured at that very moment.

* * *

Uzair had been regarded as a "burger" ever since the years when he was attending school in Karachi. He was privileged and Westernized.

Indeed, Uzair was the quintessential burger. "He had a goatee when this was considered to be an epitome of a burger kid's outlook," a former classmate, who studied with Uzair at the upscale B.V.S. Parsi High School in Karachi, told a newspaper several years later. "I remember he had friends who were girls and maybe a girlfriend. In a middle-class boys' school, this was an inspiration and achievement!"

Uzair was the eldest of four children, a child of the '80s (born in 1980, in fact) and came into his own in the 1990s. His father, Saifullah, was enamored with his firstborn. Whenever Saifullah made one of his frequent trips abroad for business or philanthropy, he reminded Uzair that the boy was the man of the house. To this end, Saifullah showered Uzair with gifts of privilege—cars, fancy clothes, and education. The family also lived in an exorbitant house within a gated community in Karachi. Maids and landscapers made sure the house was well maintained. Islam was always present—this was, after all, Pakistan—but religion was not a priority inside or outside the home. Instead, Muslim Eid celebrations and feasts were simply good excuses to get the family together to catch up and have fun.

Although Uzair was clearly a burger, there is no record of anyone accusing him of being troublesome or overtly elitist. He was just a Western-oriented rich kid doing what burger kids did. Uzair was a star cricket player in high school and college. He enjoyed watching Hollywood films and reading books, especially novels and the classics. His bedroom in Karachi was stocked full of CDs. Like his father, Uzair was clearly an extrovert; he always clamored to go out with his friends. In college, he parlayed his outgoing social nature into several gigs as an emcee for parties and talent shows. At times, particularly after a family member was diagnosed with cancer, Uzair called in favors from his many friends and contacts to collect donations for the Shaukat Khanum Memorial Cancer Hospital in Karachi. Uzair's many favorable attributes were quite likely to set him up for his future career as a marketer and businessman.

"I always thought that if he would do anything bad that would be related to an overdose of booze or drugs which are considered to be the symbols of our liberal elites, but it was completely the other way round," a former classmate later lamented. "Islamic extremism and him?"

Throughout the 1980s and 1990s, the Paracha family—Saifullah; his wife, Farhat; and children Uzair, Muneeza, Mustafa, and Zahra—traveled regularly from their home in Pakistan to their home in New York. They made this trip nearly every year and stayed for more than a month at a time. Travel to the United States was easy. Everyone in the family held LPR status, meaning they could come and go as they pleased. In fact, LPRs are generally permitted to live in the US full-time if they wished. In New York, Saifullah tended to his many business ventures while Uzair and the rest of the family soaked up the culture, often shopping for high-end products.

Saifullah paid state property taxes every year. Their house was in the Jamaica Estates section of Queens. The neighborhood was upscale and conformed with the status and sense of entitlement that Saifullah was seeking to impress upon his children, particularly Uzair. Just down the street—a three-minute walk away—was Donald Trump's house.

Proximity to prominent people such as Trump was probably not a coincidence. From the moment Uzair was born, Saifullah made sure that his son had the best clothes, the best accommodations, and the best education. Yet Saifullah wasn't being indulgent just for the sake of being indulgent. As would be proven time and again in the years ahead, Saifullah always had a reason for his actions. He was grooming Uzair for success. And success in Saifullah's mind involved access and relationships. It was who you knew. To make these relationships, one needed to act the part.

Access to influential people was Saifullah's drug of choice. Starting in 1999, Saifullah carried an electronic Casio organizer everywhere he went. The device contained countless names and phone numbers of prominent people with influence in all facets of society. Every addition to the organizer validated his success. Saifullah later described the Casio with obvious pride:

> I have about 3,000 names and various information regarding India in it. Pakistan has nuclear weapons and military and aircraft. I kept it for my immediate references. I had 3,000 names and addresses of all my

> friends and relatives around the world. I even have vital phone numbers: Pakistan President, Pakistan Prime Minister, who was known to me in Pakistan. The ministers and the mayors were my friends. They visited me in my home. I had all their numbers.

Saifullah could never have enough contacts. He always wanted more. He wanted Uzair to know of his contacts and cultivate them, as well.

Near the turn of the century, however, the full-family treks to New York abruptly ended. Only Uzair was traveling to New York. Saifullah, for his part, sought to renew his LPR status through the mail instead of in person. Around the same time frame, in 2000, it just so happened that Saifullah traveled to Afghanistan and was granted an audience with Usama bin Laden.

* * *

Back at Bagram, Agent "Ruby Caine"* wasn't sure what to think. Ruby was an Army sergeant assigned to the Criminal Investigative Task Force (CITF), which had been created by the Department of Defense in 2002, the previous year. CITF agents were tasked with investigating matters pertaining to detainees of the War on Terror. One prominent function of CITF agents was to conduct detainee interviews. They were not authorized to conduct harsh interrogations—certainly no torturous EITs were allowed. CITF interviews were expected to be performed by the book.

Ruby was at the forefront of CITF activities. She had engaged in several interviews with low-level terrorism suspects. Nearly all these detainees were considered to be foot soldiers of some sort—certainly they had nothing to do with larger plots or conspiracies. Some may have had little or nothing to do at all with al Qaeda or the Taliban. Ruby went all in during these interviews. If the detainee had any information that could be helpful to the US government, she was going to get it.†

---

* The name "Ruby Caine" is a pseudonym used here for legal and national security reasons.

† Several former CITF personnel described to the author Agent Ruby's notoriety in detail.

Ruby's zeal was starting to get noticed by her superiors—exactly what she wanted. Ruby wanted to get deeper into the game. She wanted to conduct interviews like the FBI or even the CIA. And she wanted to do this on equal footing. When word trickled down that a big fish might be on his way, Ruby made it very clear that she was ready for the assignment. It was the big time. She understood HVD-level individuals rarely—if ever—transited through Bagram's military detention zone.

Still, Ruby knew that CITF did not have much of a reputation with the FBI or CIA. For starters, the organization was too new. Its investigators were generally viewed as second-rate, the entire force cobbled together as one of the many knee-jerk political reactions to the 9/11 attacks. Even among the more pragmatic FBI agents, CITF involvement in substantial investigations was preferably relegated to the fringes of the case. In this way, CITF seemed to always play second fiddle.

In 2003, a secret email circulated within the FBI. The subject line? IMPERSONATING FBI AT GTMO. An FBI official wrote the following to alert colleagues in the field:

> Of concern, DOD interrogators impersonating Supervisory Special Agents of the FBI told a detainee that [nefarious suggestions redacted]. . . . These tactics have produced no intelligence of a threat neutralization nature to date and CITF believes that techniques have destroyed any chance of prosecuting this detainee. If this detainee is ever released or his story made public in any way, DOD interrogators will not be held accountable because these torture techniques were done [by] the "FBI" interrogators. The FBI will be left holding the bag before the public.

Ruby refused to let any of this get in her way. She wasn't an NCIS or Army CID investigator like many other CITF agents. She was a soldier trained in military intelligence. She had worked her way into CITF the hard way, through grit and determination. By mid-2003, she had proven her chops. If there was a big fish to be interviewed, she wanted in on it.

But the story surrounding this peculiar HVD kept changing, and the FBI was not very forthcoming with CITF. Ruby knew that the HVD was believed to be an old guy. He might be an American. And he may or may not be coming to Bagram.

Was the interview on or off?

Ruby heard some vague chatter regarding a political fight over the CIA's legal authority over Americans.

So, Ruby could do nothing but wait and lobby her supervisors to get a crack at the HVD should he arrive at Bagram's military zone. She didn't know it then, but Ruby would eventually leave her mark on the case in a wholly unexpected way.

* * *

CIA officers had a seemingly endless list of questions for all their high-level detainees. If Saifullah Paracha was viewed as a "big fish," then Khalid Sheikh Mohammad's capture was the counterterrorism equivalent of catching Moby Dick—because of the leading role investigators believed KSM had played in planning the 9/11 attacks. It was certainly significant that the CIA was interested in finding out from KSM whatever he knew about Saifullah and Uzair Paracha. Perhaps even more importantly, the CIA needed to know if any explosives or nuclear devices were on their way to New York. CIA officials were determined, and indeed had authorization from the highest levels of government, to get this information by virtually any means necessary.

KSM was a thinker, an ideas man. An engineer by trade, he was educated at a small North Carolina college in the 1970s, an experience that was marred by what he perceived to be racism and bigotry against Muslims and others. KSM left North Carolina and was content to never return. And with lingering bad feelings about the US, he had a special affinity for his cousin Ramzi Yousef, who was convicted for masterminding the 1993 World Trade Center bombing that killed six people and injured more than one thousand.

It seemed that KSM would have little to nothing in common with the Parachas, who were social and economic climbers without any extreme religious views or violent tendencies. But like the Parachas, KSM was known to think very highly of himself. He liked to refer to himself as "Muktar," which roughly translates to "the brain" or "the mayor." One of his first terrorist plots, conceived in the mid-1990s, revolved around the idea of organizing several hijackers tasked with joining him in taking control of several passenger planes. The hijackers would then order the pilots to land at specific airports in big cities in Asia. KSM himself would exit one of the planes and host a news conference explaining his actions and the organization's demands. Obviously, that nascent plot evolved into something much more sinister.

KSM and the rest of al Qaeda maintained operational security extremely well; meaning, like the mob, it compartmentalized its terrorist operations so only a few select individuals knew what was really going on. Abu Hafs was the right-hand man of Usama bin Laden. When KSM first broached the idea of hijacking planes to use as missiles against American targets, he needed Abu Hafs and bin Laden to sign off on the plan. This happened in 1999. A year later, in January 2000, Nawaf al Hazmi and Khalid al Mihdhar became the first hijackers to enter the United States. KSM learned valuable lessons about competence (or lack thereof) and adaptability from Hazmi and Mihdhar. The two would-be hijackers were set to attend pilot training near San Diego. They could not master the English language, nor could they get the hang of flight school. Hazmi and Mihdhar were ultimately pulled out of flight school and instead designated as what were termed at the time "muscle hijackers."

The failures of Hazmi and Mihdhar served as a practical lesson to al Qaeda leadership, particularly KSM. He realized that to effectively infiltrate the US, al Qaeda ideally needed a core group of Western-educated covert commanders who could understand and blend into American society. For the 9/11 plot, the Westernized command structure included those hijackers tasked with piloting the jetliner. The rest of the hijackers, who would gradually filter into the US, were designated "muscle hijackers" due to their role in subduing the passengers and crew rather than piloting. Ultimately, the lessons learned with respect to Mihdhar and Hazmi paved the way for the rise of lead hijacker, Muhammad Atta.

Just as the two would-be pilot hijackers were flunking out of flight school, a group of Arab nationals decided to abandon their university in Hamburg, Germany. Among this small group of classmates was Ramzi Binalshibh, from Yemen, and Atta, an Egyptian. Their goal was to fight against the Russians in Chechnya. In early 2000, these engineering students snuck off to Afghanistan to receive military training. For KSM and bin Laden, their arrival was perfectly timed. Al Qaeda needed committed Jihadists who could speak English and endure the rigors of flight school. Equally important, al Qaeda needed men who could obtain visas into the US. A further requirement was that each recruit had to be willing to become a martyr—in this context, meaning each would commit suicide as part of an act of mass murder—for the cause. For KSM, it was very difficult to find recruits who met all these criteria. To him, the arrival of the Hamburg classmates was divine providence.

Initially, Binalshibh was tasked to be the commander of the group. Atta was set to be his deputy. As a Yemeni, even back then it was more difficult for Binalshibh to obtain a US visa. Despite being accepted into a Florida flight school, Binalshibh failed to receive a visa. Desperate to get into the country, Binalshibh went so far as to convince the flight school to draft a letter on his behalf. After five attempts at securing a visa, Binalshibh finally gave up. Atta ascended to the leadership position. Binalshibh went on to serve as a key conduit between Atta and KSM.

Atta was an angry and ruthless man. Some of his Hamburg roommates described him as a painfully rigid Islamist with an aloof, off-putting personality, known for having complete contempt for any female who showed even a hint of immodesty. One witness who knew him in Hamburg suggested that Atta was so vehemently anti-female that some believed he was both compensating for and seeking to repress homosexual tendencies. Regardless, Atta embraced his role as the lead hijacker. And through it all, KSM pulled the strings from afar.

After the 9/11 attacks, the US began its campaign against al Qaeda operatives. Abu Hafs, bin Laden's right-hand man and military commander, was among the first senior leaders to be removed from the battlefield—killed in November 2001 when a missile flattened his compound in Afghanistan. Despite the tactical victory, some intelligence personnel lamented the lost opportunity to interrogate Abu Hafs. Efforts were made to capture other senior leaders by conducting elaborate raids throughout the world. If they were senior enough, or at least believed to be senior enough, these new detainees were designated as HVDs and transferred to CIA custody. The CIA would then implement the debriefing process, which sometimes involved EITs, with torture seen as a means to an end.

The CIA achieved many successes, and the month of March 2003 marked quite a few. Early in March, Majid Khan was captured. Khan was believed to be an al Qaeda operative tasked with carrying out terrorist plots on behalf of al Qaeda. He was the first al Qaeda operative to associate Saifullah and Uzair Paracha with the terror group. Several weeks later, KSM was captured in a raid in Rawalpindi, Pakistan.

The CIA had many questions, but not necessarily about the 9/11 attacks. Instead, the CIA wanted to know where and when the next attack would be occurring—what was by then called the "Second Wave." There were multiple threats coming from al Qaeda operatives and individual cells. But KSM had proven to be the most vicious. KSM had the vision and the connections to lead a second wave of attacks that were on par with—or deadlier than—9/11. KSM's association with the wealthy family that just happened to own a shipping company became an all-consuming priority for investigators.

CIA officers implemented the EIT program on KSM soon after his capture, forcing him to endure techniques such as waterboarding, extreme stress positions, and sleep deprivation. All of this occurred under the watchful eye of medical professionals. KSM initially stated that by the summer of 2001, he "was too busy with the 'planes operation' (9/11) to continue planning for any second-wave attacks." But the facts would continue to contradict KSM's initial denial. The CIA knew KSM was pursuing nuclear weapons during that time frame. They also soon learned that KSM—in the summer of 2001—was frequently visiting a man who claimed to know how to obtain weapons of mass destruction and ship them to the US.

According to declassified documents, CIA officers first asked KSM about the Parachas on March 24, 2003. Evidently, the Paracha line of questioning was posed after KSM's fifteenth bout of waterboarding. KSM would ultimately be waterboarded 183 times. Paracha was clearly a topic of paramount interest.

"KSM did not volunteer the purported smuggling plot, but rather was asked about it by interrogators," the CIA officers noted in one of their reports. KSM's responses were somewhat muddled. He attempted to downplay the Parachas' role in al Qaeda operations. In some ways, KSM seemed to mock Saifullah Paracha as a poser. KSM knew him for sure. They did some work together in Karachi. But Saifullah was portrayed as a sort of hanger-on, someone who was just happy to be part of the crew or on the fringes. KSM added that Saifullah's eagerness to please rendered him ripe for manipulation. KSM was even more dismissive of Uzair, the burger.

Despite these evasions, KSM revealed one fact that further exacerbated fears about the involvement of the Parachas with al Qaeda. KSM told the CIA officers—again, under torture conditions—that Saifullah Paracha had agreed to use his business as a cover to smuggle explosives. The CIA, in a series of declassified emails and memoranda, summarized the revelation with two sentences as follows:

> KSM identified a mechanism for al-Qa'ida to smuggle explosives into the US via a Pakistani businessman and textile merchant who shipped his material to the US. The businessman had agreed to use this method to help al-Qa'ida smuggle in explosives for follow-on attacks to 9/11.

This information was quickly passed to the FBI in Pakistan and New York. Somewhere in the world, explosives were destined for the United States. The FBI did not know whether those explosives were conventional . . . or something worse.

* * *

Longtime South Carolina Senator Ernest "Fritz" Hollings (Dem) was an insistent and leading voice on upgrading security measures at the nation's ports. He had introduced multiple bills over the years seeking additional funding to bolster infrastructure and prevent vulnerabilities in coastal access. Hollings was not always successful. The money was needed in other places and there were, as always, contentions and competing interests. The eyes of the public and the politicians were focused primarily on transportation—i.e., airlines and highways. Even the safety of railroads was prioritized over the ports. When al Qaeda successfully hijacked jetliners on 9/11, all eyes were on aviation.

Nevertheless, Senator Hollings intensified his fight for port security funding, and people started to listen. In October 2001, the Pew Research

Center reported that 87 percent of Americans said they were still angry about the 9/11 attacks. Throughout the fall of 2001, 73 percent said they were either very or somewhat fearful of another attack. On December 6, 2001, Hollings raised an alarm on the Senate floor.

Hollings did not hold back. He harangued his colleagues: "Our 361 sea and river ports handle 95 percent of US international trade. These ports annually transfer more than two billion tons of freight—often in huge containers from ships directly onto trucks and railcars that immediately head onto our highways and rail systems. But less than two percent of those five million containers are ever checked by customs or law enforcement officials. That is a gaping hole in our national security that must be fixed."

The silver-haired senator with a sharp tongue implored Congress to pass legislation that would fund seaport security at levels comparable to land border security along the Mexico and Canada frontiers. He argued in favor of a new port security bill that specifically addressed the threat of terrorism. "As you can see, we have major vulnerabilities at our seaports," he said. "Most of the security procedures and infrastructure improvements contained in our bill have long been practiced at our airports and land border crossings, yet we have failed to take these preventative steps at our seaports. We have left the security of our seaports to local authorities and private businesses. But making our seaports secure is now an issue of national security—and Congress must immediately address these vulnerabilities."

Despite the urgency, Hollings well understood that after decades of neglect, a complete overhaul of port security would take years. Academic and government studies supported Hollings's contentions. At the time, roughly 80 to 90 percent of global trade moved by sea. Most goods were carried in shipping containers and included merchandise such as toys, household items, office supplies, computers, and clothing, not to mention garbage and hazardous materials. All these items were packed into more than 15 million containers at locations throughout the world. Each year, ships logged more than 200 million visits to global ports, making this the most critical activity of international trade.

Between 9/11 and the spring of 2003, a number of port-related security events were reported. During a Senate hearing on October 25, 2001, Senator Hollings testified that he was alarmed to learn that a suspected al

Qaeda operative had smuggled himself inside an Egyptian shipping container bound for Canada. During a port stop in Italy, the operative was arrested and later escaped while on bail. According to Hollings's testimony, the shipping container had been retrofitted with a makeshift bed and bathroom. The operative also possessed a laptop, satellite phone, airport maps, a power source, three airport security badges for Thailand, Canada, and Egypt, and a certificate from a two-year course in airplane engine maintenance. Senator Hollings described this event as "chilling."

Hollings and his supporters like Senator Dianne Feinstein of California recognized that the lax oversight of the nation's ports represented a major weakness that could be exploited by terrorists not only to wreak havoc on the economy but also to kill people. A 2003 report issued by the Organisation for Economic Co-operation and Development (OECD) further raised alarm. The OECD, an intergovernmental policy organization, contended that even a minor maritime terrorist event occurring in a major port could have disastrous economic repercussions.

The OECD referenced a war game simulation involving the detection of radiological devices hidden inside shipping containers throughout ports in the United States. The simulation revealed that merely the existence and detection of such devices—not even their detonation—would cost about $58 billion for the US alone, with our ports affected for months in the aftermath of such a catastrophic event.

In addition to the numbers and simulations, reality was starting to set in and raise concerns. Events in New York City and the nation's capital contributed to extremely tense atmospheres in both cities, even to the point of hysteria. Shortly after 9/11, New York City Hall, the nearly two-hundred-year-old seat of Big Apple government, had been turned into an amalgamated symbol of the city's heightened security: fortified walls, perimeter fencing, concrete barriers, restricted parking zones, and ubiquitous metal detectors. There was also a visible security, law enforcement, and military presence.

Less than two years after 9/11, officials decided to ease some rules on metal detectors at City Hall. Life went on, and the city continued bustling. But at 2:08 in the afternoon on Wednesday, July 22, terror returned to City Hall. Council members dove under desks. A dozen little girls ran screaming from the council chamber. Two men were dead, shot to death inside the room.

One media outlet captured the dire mood inspired by this horrific event: "Life in Lower Manhattan—a place where everyone lives with the memory of the Sept. 11, 2001, terrorist attacks—froze in the hours after the shooting. Traffic stopped on the Brooklyn Bridge; subways came to a halt. . . . The crush of heavily armed police officers flooding the area—just blocks from the World Trade Center site—once again had New Yorkers fearing that a terrorist attack had taken place."

After city officials had loosened metal detector restrictions so that city council members could avoid the long waits and hassle, a man accompanying Councilman James Davis was permitted to bypass security. The man turned on the councilman and shot him before perishing in a shoot-out with police. It was not a terrorist attack, but it proved how easily violence could pierce the rituals of public life.

In post-9/11 Washington, DC, city bureaucracy was under intense pressure from multiple directions. Old threats in the capital meshed with new ones. In late 2001, anthrax had been mailed to a number of prominent individuals, including members of Congress. Five people were killed and seventeen others were sickened in what the FBI calls "the worst biological attacks in US history." And for three weeks in 2002, snipers terrorized people going about their daily lives—pumping gas, shopping, and mowing the lawn—along the beltway that encircles Virginia, Maryland, and Washington, DC.

Meanwhile, the Second Wave plot and al Qaeda's efforts to obtain weapons of mass destruction continued. Law enforcement and the intelligence community were trying to keep up. In 2003, changes were still being implemented. "The 9/11 attacks signaled a change in the very nature of terrorism," said Elaine Kamarck, a senior fellow at the Brookings Institution. "Instead of being linked to concrete political goals, the new Islamic version welcomed mass casualties and did not shy away from killing noncombatants . . . [Usama bin Laden's strategic worldview] wasn't considered normal in the world of counterterrorism. In the aftermath of 9/11, pressure built for change, and policymakers started creating new organizations."

The first major change occurred in November 2001. The Transportation Security Agency (TSA) took federal control over airport security from what had previously been contracted out by the airlines. In March 2003, the Department of Homeland Security was officially established as a cabinet-level agency. But other important changes had yet to be implemented. Information sharing mechanisms such as the National Counterterrorism Center and the Office of the Director of National Intelligence would not be created until 2004. The 9/11 Commission Report describing vital recommendations to avoid the next terrorist disaster would not come out until 2004. As such, the Second Wave was being investigated during a dangerous time of transition. Old methods were being cast aside while new approaches were not fully realized. The job was going to be difficult and, for some, treacherous.

During this period, it was becoming clear in the intelligence community that terrorists had become aware of those holes in our port security. As KSM confirmed under CIA interrogation, al Qaeda was reaching out for expert assistance on targeting our ports with a potential attack far more lethal and destructive than 9/11.

Shortly after Majid Khan and KSM identified the Parachas during their CIA debriefing sessions, a New York cab driver named Sayed Abdul Malike found himself on the FBI's radar. He had searched for bomb-making instructions on the internet. That alone was not an unusual occurrence; numerous al Qaeda sympathizers were found to be using the internet for such purposes. But Malike had done something else: He had begun researching methods of disrupting the ports. At one point, Malike was spotted casing the Port of Miami—taking photos and pumping sailors for information. Malike then returned to New York, where he sought to purchase five bulletproof vests, night vision goggles, C-4 explosives, Viagra, Valium, and sleeping pills, along with bulletproof plating and a camera for his vehicle.

Malike was ultimately not found to be connected to any larger plot involving al Qaeda leadership. But perception was powerful and reflected the keen interest of investigators in all cases related to al Qaeda. During this time frame, Iyman Faris, an Ohio truck driver, was believed to be targeting bridges at the direction of al Qaeda and was arrested in March 2003. The American Jose Padilla had also been detained; he was suspected of plotting with senior leadership to detonate a radioactive bomb. By now law enforcement suspected that such a bomb would come through the ports, and everyone knew that the ports were not adequately protected. If the issue of port security was already dire in the spring of 2003, the trickle of information about Saifullah and Uzair Paracha was enough to cause panic among those who were privy.

Perhaps not coincidentally, government-funded projects involving port security finally began to be implemented. These measures traced back to Hollings and his Maritime Transportation Security Act of 2002. An agency within the Department of Energy, the National Nuclear Security Administration (NNSA), later developed a program called the Megaports Initiative, which sought to screen containerized cargo for nuclear and radiological materials as the cargo moved through the global maritime shipping networks.

The Coast Guard also moved to create maritime intelligence fusion centers located in Norfolk, Virginia, and Alameda, California. These fusion centers were designed to provide continuous 24/7 watch over maritime traffic, with the ability to track and monitor vessels of interest and gather intelligence.

This movement toward enhanced security also led to the Terrorist Screening Center (TSC), which was established at the joint direction of the attorney general, secretaries of homeland security and state, and the directors of the FBI and CIA. The TSC was created to consolidate the government's ability to screen for known and suspected terrorists. Although the TSC wasn't initially intended to directly apply to port security, government officials came to find it very useful in that regard. Moreover, in July 2003, the US finalized a partnership with several nations to cooperate in detaining and searching ships, aircraft, and vehicles suspected of carrying weapons of mass destruction–related materials as soon as such suspected cargo entered a member country's territory or territorial waters.

All these initiatives came to fruition in 2003, coinciding with the evolving threat seemingly posed by the suspect Paracha father and son and the looming al Qaeda Second Wave. The funding for port security was barely adequate, even as a starting point. Many port officials around the country privately and publicly expressed concern that the distribution of federal grants was grossly insufficient and the process for applying for funding was complicated by federal bureaucracy.

The ports were still not secure. Contraband explosives delivered over the high seas, including the possibility of a dirty bomb or worse, were a tragedy waiting to happen.

CHAPTER 5

MOMENTS OF TRUTH AND TERROR

Majid Khan and Uzair Paracha came from completely different worlds. Yes, they shared a Pakistani heritage, but they had nothing else in common. Although Khan was the one who attended high school in the United States, it was the Pakistan-based Uzair who was regarded as a burger. Things came easy for the rich, well-connected son of Saifullah Paracha. For Khan, it was a different story.

Khan's life was one of poverty and confusion. In 1996, while Farhat Paracha was receiving the best hospital care in New York for her cancer treatment, the Khan family—including a young Majid—illegally entered the United States from Pakistan. The Khans did not attempt to obtain LPR status. Instead, Khan's mother applied for asylum based on a nebulous or contrived fear about ever returning to Pakistan. Two years later, a teenage Khan was granted asylum status, as well. As far as US immigration authorities were concerned, the Khans were Pakistani political refugees.

The family settled in suburban Baltimore, where, by all accounts, Majid's time at Owings Mills High School was unremarkable. Shortly after graduating in 1999, Majid applied for LPR status. It was not granted. He continued to be considered a Pakistani refugee.

Like many Pakistani families, the working-class Khans were close-knit. Majid's father was strict but attentive. His mother was tough but fair. They worked to instill positive values in their children, including the benefits of hard work and responsibility. In fact, the Khans did what many other Pakistani immigrants had done. They became entrepreneurs, ultimately owning a few gas stations in the Baltimore area. The Khan family did not exhibit any dissatisfaction toward the United States. This was their home.

"I learned to speak English from working in that gas station," Khan recalled. "As a teenager, I really wanted to integrate into American culture. My brothers and I even adopted American names. I was 'Bobby' and my brothers were 'Ricky' and 'Sunny.'"

By 2001, Majid seemed to be on track for a positive future in line with his upbringing. He secured a job as a database administrator for Electronic Data Systems (EDS), a computer technology company. Family ties kept him at home near Baltimore despite his job being located over an hour away in Northern Virginia. After his daily, traffic-laden morning commutes, Majid reported to an office near the top floor of a high-rise in the Tysons Corner section of the region, about ten miles west of Washington, DC. He was getting along fine at work.

But something was off. The job was just not fulfilling. He wanted more.

"After graduating from high school, I remember wanting to do something meaningful with my life," Khan later stated. "However, you could say that I struggled with an identity crisis. I doubted whether I was a good person, Muslim, Pakistani, or American and whether I could be all of those things at the same time. I really don't know where I belonged. I felt guilty about my choices in life, like smoking weed on occasion and having girlfriends, and later I started going to the mosque."

Majid became acquainted with an older truck driver from Ohio. His name was Iyman Faris, the man later arrested for targeting bridges on behalf of al Qaeda. One day at Majid's home, Faris regaled him with stories about Faris's time fighting with the Mujahedeen against the Soviets. Faris waxed eloquent on the concept of Jihad, longingly wishing for the day when he could return to the fight against the enemies of Islam. Majid was intrigued. Was Jihad the cause that was missing in his life?

In 2001, Majid continued to contemplate Jihad and started gravitating closer to Islam. He envied the fact that Faris had found his calling—his passion. Majid's parents would never support even the inkling of dalliance with extremism. That was not the future they wanted for their son.

Unfortunately, things started to unravel.

Majid's mother died in April 2001. In the aftermath, he immersed himself more deeply in Islam, increasingly drawn to its most radical teachings. His fixation on extremism and Jihad began to take hold. Then came 9/11. From his office high in Tysons Corner, Majid claimed he could see smoke rising from the Pentagon. The moment intensified his ideological shift—Jihad was no longer abstract. Al Qaeda began to feel like his people. With his connection to Faris and the reach of the internet, Khan soon found direct pathways into al Qaeda's world. As the United States prepared to invade Afghanistan and the nation remained in shock, Majid began to openly sympathize with al Qaeda and the Taliban. He sent an email from his Hotmail account on September 25, 2001, touting a "must read!" interview with Taliban leader Mullah Omar. That interview described Omar's reasons for harboring Usama bin Laden, noting that "America has created the evil that is attacking it."

In a later email, Majid echoed a claim that the media was concealing the "brutality" of the Northern Alliance—America's non-Pashtun, multiethnic allies on the ground in Afghanistan. "It is a very shameful act from those who call them muslims [sic] and they are doing this because USA is backing them," the email stated. "Where are human-rights activities now? Please forward this e-mail to as many people as you can as it will expose the reality."

The emails and internet searches only seemed to cause Majid more agitation. He was not content with being a mere keyboard commando. After all, Iyman Faris didn't just talk. He picked up arms and fought the infidels. Like Faris, Majid wanted to fight. Majid wanted Jihad.

* * *

As Majid Khan drifted toward al Qaeda in the fall of 2001, US society was steeped in unabashed patriotism. American flags were everywhere. New York Mayor Rudy Giuliani positioned himself as "America's Mayor." The mood became an *us* versus *them* mentality. President George W. Bush summed it up when he proclaimed that "either you are with us, or you are with the terrorists." People took that to heart.

On October 7, 2001, the NFL had been back in its routine for a few weeks since the 9/11 attack. But emotions still ran high among the public. Fear. Anger. Camaraderie. Sadness. Hate. A game at Cleveland Browns

Stadium captured all of it. As a sold-out stadium was filling up prior to the game against the visiting San Diego Chargers, two Browns fans stood out. The men were noticeably tall with dark skin and long beards. They each donned white #2 Browns jerseys emblazoned with the name "Couch" on the back for then-quarterback Tim Couch. Large, dark-colored turbans wrapped around their hair were prominently placed on their heads.

The men endured a gauntlet of hate as they strolled through the stadium. "Fuck you, you fucking terrorists!" "Fuck al Qaeda!" "Fuck you!" "Fucking Muslims!" The men did not react. No petty comebacks or defensive statements. No return gestures. The men with the turbans maintained respectful smiles and clearly walked tall and proud. They appeared happy to be at the game.

A few voices of reason could be heard amidst the vitriol. Those declarations coming from small pockets within the throngs of Browns fans echoed the same correction. "They're Sikhs! They're not Muslim!" The back-and-forth went on for a bit. Finally, one of the Sikhs shouted in a singsongy tune, "Here we go Brownies, here we go!" In a deeply ingrained Cleveland tradition, the fans—including those spewing hate—immediately responded with the required refrain. "Woof woof!" Soon, everyone came together to shout "Here we go Brownies, here we go. Woof woof!"

About an hour later, the game was paused and the players remained stationary on the field. The public-address announcer issued a pronouncement to the nearly 68,000 people in attendance. The US military had just invaded Afghanistan. All of Cleveland Browns Stadium cheered with delight.

* * *

In October 2001, while most Americans were engrossed in patriotism, Majid was ready to take a more active role in the fight against his adopted home country. He contacted a human resources official at EDS, his employer, requesting information about the possibility of traveling to Pakistan to get married. EDS lawyers recommended that, considering Majid's asylum status, he not return to Pakistan under any circumstances. He was told that returning to the country from which he had obtained asylum "could be grounds to deny his permanent [application for LPR status]." In other words, if you fled your native country out of fear of death or imprisonment, it raises eyebrows when you go back for a visit.

Majid was undeterred. Where Saifullah Paracha worked within the immigration system to further his goals, Majid chose to flaunt it. On October 16, 2001, Majid applied for a refugee travel document. In his application, Majid fraudulently claimed that he wanted to travel to Dubai to get married, and then to Saudi Arabia for a pilgrimage. Majid also lied to the INS, claiming that he had never obtained a Pakistani passport. He had, in fact, obtained a Pakistani passport in July 2000 from the Pakistan Embassy in Washington, DC.

In December 2001, the INS granted Majid's application, giving him an I-131 refugee travel document that was valid for twelve months, expiring on December 22, 2002. Majid was free to travel anywhere he wished for one year. As far as the US immigration authorities were aware, Majid was going to Dubai to get married and then to Saudi Arabia for a pilgrimage.

Not only did Majid lie to the government, but he also lied to his father. As far as his father knew, Majid was traveling for spiritual enlightenment and to find a bride. His father *was* made aware of Majid's intent to travel to Pakistan, but Majid stressed that his travel to Pakistan was solely for the purpose of arranging a marriage. He even enlisted his sister-in-law for help in arranging a marriage. Majid's father believed this was an acceptable mission.

In January 2002, Majid took a leave of absence from his job at EDS and boarded a plane bound for various third-party countries to hide his plans. But his destination was set. He was flying to Pakistan.

Not everything Majid did before his departure was a complete lie. He really did intend to marry a good Muslim woman. But that was just part of his overall plan to become a soldier for Allah. Majid intended to commence a forty-day spiritual cleansing. He wanted to explore the possibility of moving to Afghanistan to live under Sharia Law. And perhaps most importantly, he wanted to learn the intricacies of Jihad.

Majid made connections before embarking on his travels. He used the internet to arrange meetings with individuals sympathetic to his newfound views. They would meet upon Majid's arrival in Pakistan.

With help from Majid's sister-in-law—and just as he had suggested to his father—a meeting was arranged with a senior Pakistani general to discuss a potential marriage. The general was closely associated with Pervez Musharraf, Pakistan's president. The meeting was scheduled for later in January 2002. So far for Majid, all was going according to plan. Somehow, he had managed to worm his way into the orbit of Pakistan's ruling elite. Of course, Majid's methods were drastically different from those of Saifullah Paracha, a wealthy industrialist with whom Majid was not yet familiar.

Shortly after Majid's arrival in Pakistan, he had what he thought was another stroke of luck. He was able to meet in-person with a Jihadist—Jafar al Tayyar, who previously lived in Florida. Majid didn't know it at the time, but Tayyar was being groomed by KSM to be a sleeper agent in the United States. That meeting, which took place in Majid's rented apartment in Karachi, was a vetting with the men sizing each other up. They watched videos of Usama bin Laden and discussed Islam. Tayyar then introduced Majid to another man.

That conversation was like the ones he had with Tayyar. But then Majid said something that caused the Jihadist's ears to perk up. Majid casually mentioned that he was planning on meeting with the Pakistani general and his family in a few weeks. The Jihadist suddenly became all business: "I have a very important man that I want you to meet."

Soon thereafter, Majid was introduced to a man who went by the name Hafeez. They met on a Karachi street corner. Hafeez, a short, somewhat burly man, instructed Majid to walk with him.

Hafeez was keenly interested in Majid's association with the Pakistani general—the one whose daughter could potentially become Majid's bride. But that was of little concern to Majid. He may have found his in with the Jihadists, with al Qaeda.

Hafeez looked Majid in the eye and gave him a task. He wanted Majid to assess the security surrounding the Pakistani general's home. Majid then was asked to report back directly to Hafeez. Majid agreed.

A few weeks later, Majid traveled to Rawalpindi, Pakistan, where the Pakistani general lived. Majid spent several hours at the general's home, discussing various matters with the general and his wife. It was a pleasant, cordial meeting. After all, Majid could potentially become family. That prospect was looking good.

Majid probably could have spared himself future anguish if he would have abandoned his Jihadist dream then and there to focus on his career and newfound connections. His life would have been drastically different. But that's not what he did. Instead, Majid rushed back to Karachi and immediately contacted Hafeez. They met on another street corner, then took a walk. Hafeez got straight to the point; he was not someone who liked to banter. He asked Majid about the security measures at the Pakistani general's home. Hafeez also asked whether visitors' bags were checked upon arrival.

Majid responded without hesitation. He knew what Hafeez was all about, and he knew why he wanted this information. Majid advised that he did not observe any security measures at the Pakistani general's home. This was his first foray into terrorism.

Soon, Hafeez and Majid started gaming out plans to sneak a suicide bomber into the wedding between Majid and the Pakistani general's daughter. Hafeez noted that President Musharraf himself would likely attend the wedding. Hafeez wanted him dead. In other words, just hours after meeting his potential in-laws, Majid was plotting to bomb his own wedding and kill some of the guests, including the Pakistani president. He actually thought this was a good idea.

Hafeez had mesmerized Majid. But the idea of Majid becoming a valued operative caught Hafeez's imagination, as well. Here was another English-speaking brother with an education and roots in the United States. Jihadists with this type of background were hard to come by.

But was Hafeez letting a few red flags slide?

The first red flag occurred on February 26, 2002. That's when Majid Khan got married. No bombs went off, and President Musharraf did not attend the wedding. Why? Because Majid ended up marrying someone else. The planned arranged marriage between Majid and the Pakistani general's daughter didn't work out. Hafeez's plot was stillborn, thwarted by fate.

Yet Hafeez was undaunted. He decided to let Majid in on a secret: Hafeez was "a leader of the brothers." Majid knew that "the brothers" meant al Qaeda. Then, Hafeez told him something else. His real name was Khalid Sheikh Mohammad.

* * *

Majid Khan had become a pet project for KSM, the architect of the 9/11 attacks. Soon after learning KSM's true identity, Majid was led to believe that he had sinned by his lifestyle in the United States. He was made to feel like a burger. It didn't take much for Majid to be convinced that the only way to cleanse his soul was to become a martyr—to die waging Jihad. After his wedding, Majid notified KSM that he was "ready to complete a job." In other words, Majid was ready to die.

Shortly after the wedding, Majid and his bride traveled to Lahore, Pakistan, for their honeymoon. After only a few days, members of al Qaeda contacted him and ordered him back to Karachi immediately. This was it, Majid thought. He packed his things and followed the order. When he returned to Karachi, KSM filled him in on another plan to assassinate President Musharraf. It was a target of opportunity. KSM was finally going to achieve mission success. Majid's role in the plot: to serve as the suicide bomber.

On March 7, 2002, Majid attended a safe house meeting with several high-ranking al Qaeda operatives. Handlers pulled Majid aside to begin his training. Specifically, Majid was going to learn how to operate a suicide vest. That night, he watched as a young man named Hassan bin Attash constructed the vest to be used in the attack. Hassan looked like he could be no more than twenty years old.

The next morning, Majid was as excited as he had ever been. He was ready for the mission, prepared to die. His handlers escorted him into a room with a video camera. There, Majid recorded a martyrdom video—a form of suicide note justifying his actions. Majid also spoke to his new wife. He told her that he may never return to their apartment. She understood. She knew what Majid had been up to and supported it. Majid's martyrdom would be her honor.

Later that night, KSM, Majid, and other al Qaeda operatives traveled to a mosque where President Musharraf was believed to be praying. Under the cover of darkness, an operative handed Majid a heavy suicide vest, the same one that Hassan bin Attash had constructed the night before. Majid did not hesitate, placing the vest over his shoulders and strapping it on tightly. The vest was outfitted with small ball bearings that would scatter upon detonation. According to Majid, the ball bearings were the "killing machine," the mechanism for inflicting maximum death and destruction. Those ball bearings were going to kill President Musharraf.

KSM hated Musharraf. He couldn't wait for the bomb to go off. And Majid would die a hero.

Majid's task was to kill President Musharraf by detonating the bomb inside the mosque. He waited for the Pakistani president to arrive just outside. As worshippers streamed into the mosque, Majid continued to wait. And wait. The vest was getting heavy. After some time, it became apparent that President Musharraf was not going to show up. The mission to kill the president—with Majid Khan at the center—had once again failed. KSM was visibly upset. He thrust his cell phone into a wall in disgust.

Majid was ordered back to an al Qaeda safe house. There, KSM brainstormed over what to do with Majid now that the Musharraf plot had failed yet again. The conversation quickly focused on Majid's valid US travel documents and the fact that he spoke fluent English and Urdu. KSM also valued Majid's knowledge of computers through his job at EDS in Northern Virginia. But something else sparked KSM's imagination. Majid's family owned several gas stations in the Baltimore area. Perhaps Majid could best be used in a plot to attack the United States.

The idea was simple enough. What if Majid simultaneously exploded gas tanks at multiple gas stations on the East Coast? KSM relished the idea of the chaos such an attack would cause. But with Majid's recent history of unreliability in mind, KSM decided to better integrate his new pet project into al Qaeda's operations and training. The last thing KSM wanted was another inept, untrained operative to cause a calamity.

It was settled. Majid would do two things before heading back to the United States. First, he was ordered to assist KSM and KSM's nephew, a young man named Ali Abdul Aziz Ali—also known as Ammar al Baluchi—on various operational tasks. This included checking al Qaeda email accounts and acting as a courier for messages.

Second, KSM ordered Majid to attend a class on the construction of explosives and timing devices. The eight-hour training was conducted at a Karachi safe house. The teachers were Hassan bin Attash—the man who had constructed the unused suicide vest—and Jafar al Tayyar, the Florida man who was Majid's first real al Qaeda contact. Jafar also had become another KSM pet project.

During the training, Majid was directed to memorize the configuration of wiring and tubing for devices intended to be used as detonators for explosives. He was also told how to connect the device to a watch. After the class, KSM administered a test to see if Majid had retained the information. He must have passed, because KSM revisited the idea of using such an explosives detonator in a future attack on gas station fuel storage tanks in the US. Majid was instructed to research the feasibility of blowing up gas stations and was specifically ordered to research government or otherwise federally associated gas stations as potential targets. For Majid, this was all good. He wanted to gain their trust. This was his life now.

Around this time, in March 2002, KSM and Majid also discussed nuclear devices, uranium, and an odd plot to open a front company to sell poisoned medication to the US. The two also discussed the possibility of opening an import/export company to move explosives by ship into the US. The conversation included talk about using such a business to import nuclear weapons or uranium. KSM was keenly interested in shipping containers. Majid believed someone was clearly piquing KSM's interest in this topic.

Majid opted not to inquire further. He had bigger plans to carry out. Majid didn't know it then, but his direct involvement with al Qaeda would eventually have real-world consequences. People were going to die.

* * *

Half a world away and about a year after KSM and Majid's nuclear conversations, Agent Miller and her FBI colleagues were almost ready. They had been frantically preparing to bring Uzair Paracha into custody. They knew Uzair was living in a room in Brooklyn. They knew about his office building in the Garment District. The FBI even knew about the corner desk where Uzair sat during the workday. The operation still needed to be handled carefully. Uzair couldn't simply be arrested. The facts were much too hazy. Saifullah—the one they really wanted—was still safely untouchable in Karachi.

Certainly, there was an air of guilt (but with no smoking gun) against Uzair. The biggest problem from a legal standpoint was that the FBI did not really have any viable evidence. They had a lot of information about Uzair. But how valuable and how reliable was that?

Enhanced Interrogation Techniques (EIT) had been used to gather information about Uzair. In other words, Majid Khan was tortured by the CIA. Information about Uzair gleaned from Majid was then used to coerce a waterboarded KSM into talking about Uzair. This was hardly admissible testimony or evidence in any US court of law.

The FBI needed Uzair. There was the issue of explosives and the ports. And there was talk of sleeper agents and nuclear proliferation. Uzair was the best chance at connecting the dots and solving those related mysteries.

On March 24, 2003, Agent Miller was preparing her strategy for speaking with Uzair while CIA agents were in the process of boxing KSM in as part of their interrogation. Then, that afternoon, KSM was being waterboarded for failing to provide information on al Qaida operations ongoing in the United States. Essentially, he was being punished. The CIA recounted his punishment as follows:

> On March 24, 2003, KSM underwent his fifteenth . . . waterboarding session due to his "intransigence" in failing to identify suspected Abu Bakr al-Azdi operations in the United States, and for having "lied about poison and biological warfare programs."

KSM was further described as being "composed, stoic, and resigned" during the waterboarding session. That evening, KSM's interrogators received updated reports from Majid's interrogators. Those statements from Majid were gleaned from foreign government officers. By this time, FBI agents—not engaging in EITs—were involved in Majid's questioning, as well. The FBI did not engage in EITs. Majid again referenced Uzair.

After punishing KSM earlier that day, CIA officers called KSM out on not mentioning Uzair or Saifullah. They had the advantage of knowing what Majid was saying; KSM did not. The CIA described their tactic as having KSM "boxed in." "KSM did not volunteer [the explosives plot] information on Paracha," the CIA agents reported. "[KSM] provided this reporting only when confronted with details of his role and other information on the plot, which had been provided by detainee Majid Khan."

When KSM finally discussed his involvement with Saifullah Paracha, he revealed another shared connection—his nephew Ali (a.k.a. Ammar al

Baluchi), a young man who had supported Majid Khan in various operational tasks. Ali, as he became known, worked directly with KSM in facilitating the travel, financing, and training of 9/11 hijackers. He even expressed interest in becoming a last-minute hijacker. According to KSM, however, Saifullah knew Ali by a different name—Mustafa, the man interested in investing 200,000 euros in the Cliftonia real estate project.

After the March 24 statements from KSM, the die was cast against Uzair. Agent Miller decided that Uzair should be brought in as a material witness. In that way, the FBI could temporarily hold him and ask questions without having to make an arrest. As a material witness, it would be up to Uzair whether he wanted to talk. And Agent Miller very much wanted to ensure that Uzair talked. But if she was going to succeed, she needed to be as prepared as possible. She needed to know everything there was to know about Uzair and his father.

As Agent Miller read through the files, she ran across some startling information. It wasn't about Uzair. It was about Saifullah. The FBI had opened an investigation into Saifullah in April 2002, nearly a year earlier than she thought, and this information was very valuable in her case against Uzair. It linked Saifullah and his company, IMG, to some of the most dangerous names in al Qaeda. Uzair was now the company's CEO. That information could support search warrant applications in New York targeting Uzair.

The 2002 information had come from two different raids on al Qaeda safe houses in Pakistan. The first raid occurred in Faisalabad, Pakistan, on March 28, 2002. The CIA and Pakistanis were interested in a man named Hassan Ghul, a courier for Usama bin Laden. During the raid, the CIA gained access to a trove of documents. But the raid was not notable for what materials were found, but who was captured. In this instance, it was Abu Zubaydah—a one-eyed Palestinian who had risen to become a senior al Qaeda leader. Zubaydah was among the most militant of the combatants. He also held the distinction of being the first HVD to be subjected to the EIT program; his responses served as a model for later HVDs.

Zubaydah's capture was viewed as a major milestone in the War on Terror. But buried beneath the headlines and accolades was that trove of seized documents. Each document was categorized and filed away by the CIA. It took them about a month to get down to just a few bits of unexamined paper. The CIA wasn't sure if they were important. Regardless, they passed the data on to the FBI out of an abundance of caution.

One document discussed the idea of setting up a shell company. Another document turned out to be a business card. The name on these documents: Saifullah Paracha. These documents also included three telephone numbers and an address, all linked to the International Merchandise Group. Investigators didn't know it then, but just a few weeks prior to the Abu Zubaydah raid—as it came to be known—KSM had first broached the idea to Majid Khan of opening a front company as part of their discussions about shipping explosives to the United States.

The FBI in April 2002 conducted their due diligence. But during that period, neither Uzair nor Saifullah was in New York. The information was also very scant; it certainly did not raise any significant red flags, particularly less than a year after 9/11 when so much more was going on. That year, the FBI traced Saifullah Paracha's name and company back to New York. Moreover, declassified records later noted that "the FBI interviewed an employer at a New York address and acquired additional information on the business and the Parachas."

The "employer" referenced in those records was likely Saifullah's old friend and longtime New York–based business partner, Charles Stern. As such, Stern likely suspected that something was amiss with Saifullah nearly a year before the FBI would come knocking on his door with a search warrant. Stern did not warn his friend.

Later that year, on September 11, 2002, a raid in Karachi netted another major al Qaeda figure: Ramzi Binalshibh, the Yemeni initially tasked to be the commander of the 9/11 hijackers. Binalshibh's capture was perhaps a bigger deal than Abu Zubaydah's—at least in the public eye—because Binalshibh was an actual 9/11 conspirator who worked directly with KSM to advance the airplane hijacking plot. This was justice being served.

Like the Abu Zubaydah raid, the capture was more significant than the haul of documents. But in both instances, the CIA garnered a lot of useful information. In Binalshibh's case, the CIA discovered a cache of al Qaeda financial documents. Buried in the stacks of paper—there was so much an investigator could have easily missed it—was an email address and phone number, which again led back to that peculiar name: Saifullah Paracha.

The CIA immediately notified the FBI, NSA, and the Department of Treasury that they suspected "Saifullah Paracha was engaged in terrorist financing activities, specifically for al Qaeda." The CIA communication included a detailed report on Saifullah and his company, IMG. Moreover, the FBI's investigation into Iyman Faris, the Ohio truck driver who had enticed Majid Khan into the world of Jihad, revealed that Faris's housemate was coincidentally linked to a company called Paracha Imports.

By the time Majid Khan was captured in early March 2003, Saifullah Paracha clearly had a file within the CIA and FBI databases. But in the pantheon of major terrorist attacks and planned attacks during that time, Saifullah was not a priority. His name was on the back burner.

Then, as more al Qaeda figures were captured—Khan, KSM, and in May 2003, KSM's nephew Ali—Paracha and his son quickly became the highest of priorities. The capture of KSM, Binalshibh, and Ali, combined with the raid evidence, tied Saifullah's name with three of the five men charged with plotting and facilitating the 9/11 attacks.

Moreover, Saifullah was indirectly linked to the other two 9/11 conspirators, if one counts Mustafa al Hawsawi, a Saudi Arabian national who provided travel and financial assistance to the hijackers. He was captured in the same house as KSM. Khallad bin Attash, another Yemeni whose casing of several flights resulted in the sneaking of box cutters aboard passenger jets, was the older brother of Hassan, who trained Majid Khan on the construction of suicide vests.

By March 24, 2003, KSM was finally talking, albeit facilitated by torture. Majid was also continuing to open up to his interrogators. Agent Miller needed to speak with Uzair Paracha in New York. The Paracha case now went well beyond terrorist financing. Shipments of explosives, along with the possibility of weapons of mass destruction, were something far more sinister.

CHAPTER 6

AL QAEDA'S PLOT THICKENS

Majid Khan had returned to Baltimore on March 21, 2002, almost exactly a year before CIA officers would first hear the name Paracha uttered by KSM. As KSM was wont to do, while simply walking the streets of Karachi, he issued an order for Majid to return to the United States. To obfuscate his travels, Majid flew from Karachi to Dubai and Zurich before finally landing at Dulles International Airport near Washington, DC. Once he was back in Baltimore, Majid went to work for his family's gas stations. His days as a database manager for EDS were over. He was now actually working for KSM.

Majid immediately got down to carrying out al Qaeda's business. He made a point to oversee the regular fuel deliveries, which was his primary mission. But Majid didn't stop there. He started to freelance. Not all his freelancing ideas were particularly clever or even useful. There was a time he contacted the US Navy pretending to be interested in enlisting. He even invited a Navy recruiter into his Baltimore home to talk about his potential Navy service. Majid did this to obtain recruitment materials to share with KSM.

A 2012 court document called a Stipulation of Fact described Majid's motives, indicating that he "intended and had reason to believe that the information he was collecting for KSM and other al Qaeda members would be used to injure the United States. [Khan] knew that KSM and al Qaeda were enemies of the United States and [Khan] intended to deliver this information to them as such."

On other occasions, Majid attempted to recruit family and friends to the Jihadist cause. He even assessed a fourteen-year-old boy for recruitment. He wasn't exactly sly about his recruiting efforts. He outright boasted to family and friends that he had been working with the "mujahedeen" while in Pakistan. He bragged about how he had worn a suicide vest and showed family and friends several Usama bin Laden videos he had brought back from Pakistan in his suitcase. Majid believed that if he didn't mention the name al Qaeda, nobody would report him. It was a ridiculous premise, especially less than a year after 9/11, but he was correct in that nobody called the FBI about the conspicuous Jihadist in their midst.

During the summer of 2002, Majid had several opportunities to resume his comfortable life in the US. He was separated from KSM and had family and friends who supported him. The government had no clue about his contacts in Pakistan; in fact, the INS didn't even know Majid had traveled there. Majid could have kissed off the whole al Qaeda endeavor and moved on as a productive member of society. Unfortunately, Majid was still all in with Jihad.

He soon received word that KSM had ordered him back to Pakistan. Undoubtedly, KSM was eager to hear about the vulnerabilities with gas station fuel tanks. KSM also had enough experience with brash young wannabe terrorists that he knew that the impressionable Majid needed to get out of the US as quickly as possible.

At this time, Majid and his father, Ali Khan, were having fierce arguments. His father had often been a voice of reason for the young man, but with the father and son involved in a heated, bitter disagreement, the petulant Majid was more inclined than ever to cast his lot with the enemy and turn back to KSM. In fact, Majid planned on returning to Pakistan permanently. When he started bragging to his family that "the Sheikh" had ordered him back, Majid's father became further enraged and told his son that under no circumstances would he be permitted to return. Ali knew where this could lead his Jihadist son. The detention camps at Guantanamo Bay had just opened. The world was at war. Ali wanted to protect his son from himself.

To this end, Majid's father confiscated Majid's I-131 travel form. Without the form, Majid could not travel abroad.

Resisting the urge to continue fighting with his father, Majid instead pretended to engage in a heart-to-heart. At the end of the conversation, Majid swore that he no longer intended to work for al Qaeda and that he simply wanted to live his life freely—a life of independence with no ties to terrorism.

Wanting to believe his youngest son, Majid's father gave in and returned the travel document, relieved that he had seemingly prevailed with Majid.

On August 11, 2002, Majid returned to Pakistan by way of Zurich. His first order of business was to report back to KSM about what he learned at the gas stations. KSM was satisfied that Majid could become a useful operative, despite the young man's naivety and past penchant for failure. If nothing else, Majid seemed to try his best to follow directions. And KSM couldn't shake the thought that Majid, at least on paper, was a perfect fit to serve al Qaeda as a sleeper agent. He decided to offer the young man more tutelage. Majid was directed to witness security measures employed by his new bosses. A system was in place so that Majid would immediately know when and where to meet Ali Abdul Aziz Ali should the need for Majid's services arise. Majid also was tasked to drive Ali around on a motorcycle through the streets of Karachi.

The motorcycle rides usually involved clandestine al Qaeda meetings Ali needed to attend. During these trips, Ali closed his eyes so that if he was later arrested and interrogated, he would not know where the meetings had taken place. He instructed Majid to "drive as straight as possible and avoid observing landmarks or road signs" so that Majid would also not be able to remember the route that he took. Although this effort at tradecraft was suspect, Ali had a real fear of getting caught. The Abu Zubaydah raid had taken place in March 2002, and in September 2002, Ramzi Binalshibh was captured in another raid, this time in the heart of Karachi.

In September 2002, around the time that Binalshibh was captured, KSM asked to meet Majid in a hotel in the Pakistani border town of Peshawar. There, KSM finally laid out his grand plan for Majid. Their conversation lasted eight hours. Essentially, KSM stated that he needed Majid to serve as an al Qaeda operative within the United States, to become a new model for sleeper agents. KSM explained that Majid had all the intangibles. He was married, spoke fluent English, had a valid US travel document, could maintain a low profile, and could easily assimilate without detection. KSM also explained that the overarching purpose of this new sleeper network was to conduct a terrorist attack inside the United States. Majid readily agreed to the plan. He would return to Baltimore as soon as KSM gave the word.

KSM's plan was methodical, seemingly sound as far as it went. But KSM was unaware that his ideal sleeper agent, who needed to maintain a low profile and assimilate without detection, had openly bragged to family and other people about his affiliation with the "mujahedeen" during his previous trip to the United States.

Majid's recent quarrel with his father further complicated matters. In December 2002, Majid, still the petulant son, allowed his I-131 travel document to expire to spite his father. During that time, Ali Khan had pressed his son to return home. Majid simply used the expiration to convince his father he could never return even if he wanted to. Majid secretly feared that if his family discovered his return, his earlier boasting might come back to haunt him by prompting his family to turn him in to the US authorities. So, Majid was essentially barred from returning to Baltimore.

KSM was furious when he learned that Majid had allowed his travel document to expire. It had only been three months since KSM had confided his sleeper master plan to Majid, who once again had proven himself to be unfit for the assignment. And yet KSM couldn't let go of the idea. He had invested too much time and resources into Majid to cut him loose. And other recruits like Iyman Faris and Jose Padilla hadn't panned out as potential sleepers. Richard Reid, another recruit, had failed to bring down an American Airlines passenger plane in December 2001 using a "shoe bomb." At this point, Majid was still integral to KSM's Second Wave attack plan.

KSM, refusing to give up the evil dream, tasked his nephew Ali with getting Majid's travel documents back in order. Majid, for his part, was sorrowful and apologetic. He renewed his commitment to al Qaeda and vowed to go anywhere to help the organization as soon as he resolved his travel issues.

Under Ali's direction, Majid filled out an application to renew his I-131 refugee document that would again free him to travel. Of course, because Majid was filling out the form in Pakistan, the country he was supposedly seeking refuge from, he had to lie again to the INS. And he couldn't send the form to the INS from Pakistan. If he did, government officials were likely to discover the ruse. By attempting to spite his father, Majid merely created a cascade of problems. Ali was dismayed at being burdened with cleaning up Majid's mess. He hoped to fix the problem as quickly as possible, but there were endless delays.

By late December 2002, Ali realized that he needed additional help to solve Majid's travel issue, and he believed he had the perfect candidate for the job—a person who could readily travel to the US. Ali introduced Majid to a woman named Aafia Siddiqui. Not yet thirty years old, Siddiqui was a Pakistani neuroscientist with degrees from Brandeis University and MIT. She was also an ardent Jihadist. Indeed, Siddiqui had apparently divorced her first husband because he was not militant enough. Six months after that divorce, Siddiqui claimed to have married Ali in a secret ceremony. Despite the secretive nature of the relationship, as part of Ali's courtship, he asked a wealthy Pakistani to contact Siddiqui's family on Ali's behalf as per traditional custom. That reference was Saifullah Paracha.

On December 30, 2002, Siddiqui physically took Majid's I-131 travel form to the US and applied for a PO Box in Gaithersburg, Maryland, opening the box jointly in her name and that of Majid Khan. The application falsely indicated that Siddiqui and Khan were married. That same day, Siddiqui mailed Khan's fraudulent I-131 application for a refugee travel document to the INS. It was later discovered that both Siddiqui's and Majid's fingerprints were on the document.

A few days after sending the document to the INS, Siddiqui returned to Pakistan, delivering the receipts to Majid and Ali. The amount of time and resources required to clean up Majid's mess was remarkable. And even Siddiqui's assistance did not completely solve the problem. The PO Box and postal stamp from Maryland were not enough to ensure that the INS would not dig deeper into Majid's whereabouts. There were other markers that the INS could use to determine whether Majid was indeed living in the United States. These included financial transactions and credit card usage. There was also the matter of retrieving Majid's mail from the PO Box if and when the INS responded. Siddiqui was basically done with Majid after her quick trip to Maryland. She was fiercely headstrong and perhaps mentally ill, but she no doubt saw Majid for what he was, unfit for the sleeper role he was assigned.

Ali understood Siddiqui's reservations about Majid. Although he supported his uncle's vision, Majid was proving to lack the requisite sleeper agent mentality. Ali was devoted to KSM and would follow through with Majid to get the job done.

Fortunately for Majid, Ali knew another person who could help the cause. A Karachi-based businessman named Saifullah Paracha had a son who was a lawful permanent resident of the US. And Ali happened to know that the son, Uzair, was about to leave for New York. Ali noted that the kid was apparently a burger, but that Saifullah wouldn't mind tasking his son with the mission. After all, Saifullah was very eager to please.

* * *

Majid and Uzair came from two different worlds. Majid was a wayward, peevish working-class kid who struggled to find direction in life. As a result, he was frequently pulled in different directions—i.e., Iyman Faris's Jihadist influence, his mother's values of hard work, his father's tough love, and KSM's Jihadist sense of higher purpose. Majid was hardly reliable as an operative on any level.

Conversely, as the revered son of Saifullah Paracha, Uzair had everything handed to him: the best schools, a stable home base, and, most of all, options in life. Uzair and his father saw eye to eye on most things. They shared similar goals. Uzair was not interested in Jihad. He was composed and centered. Instead of being overly emotional, Uzair analytically calculated the resolution to any problems that arose in life. Uzair could always be counted on to competently handle any matter that came his way.

There was one attribute that Uzair shared with Majid, however. They each had an insatiable desire to be wanted—to be needed. For Majid, this explains why he gravitated so closely to KSM's authority. It was the same for Uzair with respect to his father. Both would do anything for these authority figures in their lives.

In late January 2003, Majid Khan and Uzair Paracha first met. The encounter was at a cookout at the Paracha home in Karachi. Ali—then known to Saifullah as Mustafa—informed Saifullah that a young Pakistani man needed some assistance. Saifullah always immediately jumped at the chance to assist whenever Mustafa or Mir needed something. This time was no different. Saifullah was hosting another small event at his home soon, and he invited Mustafa and the young man to attend.

That first meeting was brief. Introductions were made. Ali as Mustafa explained the basic problem for which he needed assistance: Majid lived in Baltimore but was having some issues with the papers necessary for him to return home. Saifullah was no doubt pleased to regale them with stories about how he had gamed the system back in the late 1970s when the government had tried to deport him. Saifullah proudly informed Ali and Majid that Uzair would be happy to assist. The four men agreed to meet again soon.

A week later, in early February 2003, Ali, Majid, Saifullah, and Uzair met at Snoopy's Ice Cream Parlor in Karachi. They essentially used two tables, almost like an adult table and a kids' table at a family gathering. Ali and Saifullah sat at the adult table. Majid and Uzair got to know each other at a separate table. There, they finalized their plans to assist Majid's return to the US.

Majid confided to Uzair that he did not want US immigration officials to learn that he was absent from the United States. Majid explained that he needed assistance obtaining a renewed travel document. As always, Uzair remained cool. He would have no problem helping this guy out. Besides, Uzair was just days away from leaving for a new life in New York. He was the new CEO. Life couldn't be better.

Uzair likely knew that Ali was the guy ready to invest 200,000 euros in the Cliftonia project. This was a big deal. A priority, even. Part of Uzair's job in New York was to promote the Cliftonia property to potential wealthy buyers who traveled back and forth between the United States and Pakistan. Uzair asked what Majid needed him to do.

Majid replied that as soon as Uzair returned to the United States, Uzair should, among other things, deposit money into Majid's bank account and use Majid's credit card. He also directed Uzair to retrieve any immigration papers that may have been mailed to a PO Box in Maryland. Finally, Uzair should use a pay phone to call the INS and pretend to be Majid.

Uzair just smiled and laughed. It all seemed rather silly to him. But if that's what his clients wanted, then Uzair would deliver. Clearly, Uzair knew that his father was involved in some shady dealings. He would later go on to admit that he knew Ali—as Mustafa—was an al Qaeda operative. But as far as Uzair was concerned at this point, Ali and Majid were clients.

Regardless of whatever his father was into, Cliftonia was a legitimate business investment, and it needed to be protected. If the clients needed some silly immigration matter taken care of, then Uzair would take care of it. Business ethics and the potential for legal issues were not a concern. Like his father taught him, it was all about the business.

Majid slipped Uzair a piece of paper with Urdu-language notes scribbled by hand. These were instructions on what Uzair should do when he arrived in the US. The note reiterated much of what Majid said verbally. "Always call from pay phone." "Put some money in my account." "Use it at any gas station." "Good practice of my [signature]." "Mothername Kafiya Khan" and "Fathername Shoulkat Khan." Majid reiterated that it needed to appear that he was not out of the country. Uzair said he understood.

Majid and Uzair concluded their business quickly. Meanwhile, Saifullah and Ali had other business to discuss regarding the Cliftonia project. Saifullah added that he was available to assist with any other matters, if needed. Ali offered up Majid to take Uzair home by motorcycle. As the two young men rode off down the dusty, bustling Karachi road, they were alone for the first time.

The two began to talk. Apparently, Majid had not changed his ways since his most recent travel to Baltimore. He began discussing Jihad. As a businessman is accustomed to do, Uzair indulged Majid with his brash posturing. This seemed to please Majid. He issued a proposal, asking if Uzair would like to officially work for al Qaeda. Uzair politely declined.

Majid's failed effort to recruit Uzair made it clear to the young businessman that Ali and Majid were affiliated with al Qaeda. Uzair realized that his father must also have known about this illicit connection. Uzair was now faced with a choice. He could travel to New York and simply decline to do any more work for these al Qaeda clients. Or he could dig himself deeper into their world. Whatever his motivation may have been, Uzair chose to continue working with the Jihadists. He certainly did not wish to run afoul of his father, and that may have been the deciding factor.

On February 17, 2003, Uzair took a direct flight from Karachi to New York. Shortly after arriving, he found a pay phone as directed. Uzair called the INS to ask some questions. He posed as Majid Khan during the call. Later, Uzair went to his small corner desk at Charles Stern's office in the

Garment District. The desk was bare except for a computer and a telephone. Uzair logged onto a website called "visapro." Uzair then entered the receipt number affixed to Majid's travel document application. Uzair was checking on the status. Majid was still not cleared to travel to the United States.

On several occasions, Majid, becoming increasingly impatient and agitated, called Uzair to check on the holdup. Uzair explained that he did not have some of the documents necessary to fully complete his assignments. Majid failed to provide his bank cards and identification prior to Uzair's departure. Like others who dealt with Majid, Uzair seethed with exasperation. What was he supposed to do?

Majid reported to Ali about the latest setback in obtaining his travel papers. Ali didn't think this issue was insurmountable. He called Saifullah. Within a few hours, everything was arranged. Saifullah would collect the documents and seal them in an envelope. An elderly business associate was ready to travel to New York that very week. Saifullah would simply call in a favor and ask the man to deliver the envelope to Uzair in Manhattan. They agreed that the man would meet Uzair on a street corner in New York near Uzair's office, and that was how the problem would be solved.

The elderly man carried the sealed envelope onto the plane, and though he was reluctant to deliver the envelope—mainly because it was an inconvenience—this Saifullah guy could be pushy and persuasive. In Manhattan, the man met Uzair on a street corner as agreed, and as if he were carrying out a drug deal, he handed the envelope surreptitiously to Uzair. The man never asked what was inside the envelope, and nobody ever told him.

Uzair took the sealed envelope into his office and looked inside. There were a Bank of America credit card and another bank card. There was a student ID for Owings Mills High School. And there were a Maryland driver's license, a key to the PO Box, and a customer receipt. Uzair placed everything back into the envelope. He would deal with it later.

For Uzair, this rather silly job he was doing for Majid Khan was not a priority. He would get to Majid at his convenience. But sometime in early March, Uzair's phone rang. It was his father. A guy named Mir had been captured and was in custody, Saifullah told his son. Mir was known to be KSM, the mastermind of the 9/11 attacks and probably the most wanted man in the world after Usama bin Laden. The young man who needed help with his travel documents was connected to KSM. After speaking with his father, Uzair stuffed Majid's documents into his briefcase. He took the briefcase to his room in Brooklyn and hid them behind his bed. Uzair then went back to his life as if nothing had happened. Whatever was going on back in Pakistan was a world away.

Unfortunately for Uzair, there were actors in far corners of the world that he knew nothing about who were conspiring against him. He didn't know that Khan was in custody. Nor did Uzair know that Khan was talking, or that torture might be involved. As silly and convoluted as Majid's scheme was, the gist of what Khan was telling the authorities sounded much more ominous. Back in Washington, DC, CIA officials disseminated information that broke everything down straight to the point:

> Majid Khan, who was in foreign government custody, provided reporting that Uzair ran the New York branch of his father's Karachi-based import/export business. Uzair was assisting Majid Khan and Ammar al-Baluchi in their efforts to resettle Majid Khan in the United States for terrorism-related purposes. Khan provided a detailed physical description of both Uzair and his father. Ammar al-Baluchi intended to have Uzair use Majid Khan's credit card to create the appearance that Majid Khan was already in the United States. Khan's two meetings with Uzair and his father, and a subsequent phone call with Uzair (following Uzair's return to the United States), all . . . were facilitated by Ammar al-Baluchi.

At this point, Ali (a.k.a. Ammar al-Baluchi) was already one of the most wanted men in the world for his direct role in facilitating the 9/11 attacks. As far as the FBI and CIA were concerned, Uzair was assisting Ali in getting a sleeper agent into the United States. Majid had already discussed his anticipated role in the plot to detonate explosives at gas stations. All of this was in the context of KSM and Saifullah Paracha plotting to smuggle explosives into the US using the import/export business. Uzair, of course, was now the CEO of that business in New York. He had nowhere to run. In fact, Uzair did not consider the idea that he needed to run.

CHAPTER 7

THE WITNESS

At least 10,000 American casualties. That was the goal Usama bin Laden had set for his "Hiroshima." Consider that, by the late 1990s, US investigators were still rattled by a surprise sarin gas attack in Tokyo's subway, in which thousands of people were injured and twelve were murdered. That 1995 attack was conducted by a doomsday cult called Aum Shinrikyo. Al Qaeda wanted something way bigger.

In 2000, then-presidential candidate George W. Bush received a briefing from Ben Bonk, deputy chief of the CIA's Counterterrorism Center. Bonk showed Bush a mock-up suitcase like the one used in the Tokyo sarin attack. But the focus of that conversation wasn't on doomsday cults. It was on radical Islamic terrorists, specifically, al Qaeda.

After the election, President Clinton recalled telling Bush, "I think you will find that by far your biggest threat is bin Laden and the al Qaeda." Bush recalled that conversation differently to the 9/11 Commission. Bush remembered Clinton saying something vague about terrorism, but that Clinton's focus was on North Korea and the Israeli–Palestinian peace process. It appeared that there was a lack of unified focus on al Qaeda during that transitional period.

After the shock of 9/11, experts in various fields openly asked: "Could even worse be coming?" The editors of the *Bulletin of the Atomic Scientists* are the people who run the so-called "Doomsday Clock." Every time the clock inches closer to midnight, it indicates that the world is closer to the precipice of global disaster. In 2002, they moved the clock two minutes closer to midnight and explained, "After the September 11, 2001, terrorist attacks, the United States expresses increasing concerns about nuclear weapons falling into the hands of non-state actors."

To be sure, bin Laden and his deputy, Ayman al-Zawari, met with two senior Pakistani nuclear scientists in the weeks leading up to 9/11. During their Second Wave plotting, investigators learned, KSM and his team had disturbing discussions with another well-connected Pakistani businessman, Saifullah Paracha.

Top nuclear scientists joined American officials in fearing the Second Wave. Matthew Bunn, a professor of energy, foreign policy, and national security at Harvard, described the danger this way: "If the terrorists who attacked on September 11 had a crude nuclear bomb on the plane, it wouldn't have been just the twin towers—the whole lower half of Manhattan could have been turned to rubble and ash, with hundreds of thousands of dead and injured."

With aviation under intense scrutiny in the aftermath of 9/11, a terrorist operation working under the cover of an import/export business was viewed as a potential key requirement in smuggling weapons of mass destruction into the US. Conventional bombs like the one used by domestic terrorist Timothy McVeigh in 1995 could be made within the country using fertilizer and other items. But nuclear and radiological weapons—particularly those secured through the assistance of Pakistani sympathizers—would need to be shipped.

"Any one of those weapons would likely be brought into the US in a ship, perhaps hidden in a container on a freighter," said David Albright, a nuclear proliferation expert at the Institute for Science and International Security in Washington. "The bombs could fit into a large van, and if exploded in downtown Manhattan, might cause tens of thousands to a hundred thousand deaths." Even a "simple" dirty bomb would spread radioactive dust on enormous swaths of the city, "perhaps killing hundreds and requiring a cleanup that could run to billions of dollars. Without a cleanup, the material would cling to surfaces and contaminate the area for decades."

* * *

The raid that netted al Qaeda senior leader Abu Zubaydah occurred in Pakistan on March 28, 2002. After his capture, he was placed in US custody and held for years in the CIA's overseas black site network. He was taken in the same raid as the one that also produced documents introducing the names Saifullah Paracha and IMG to investigators. A few weeks later, business cards and emails led FBI agents to an office in Manhattan's Garment District. There, they interviewed a man who, according to redacted government communications, was referred to only as "an employer."

Exactly a year after the Abu Zubaydah raid, the FBI returned to the same Garment District office, and as the CIA reported, "On March 28, 2003, the FBI would return to the same employer and the same address, leading to the apprehension of Uzair Paracha, who would voluntarily provide significant reporting to the FBI."

Only two people occupied the office at the Garment District address: Uzair Paracha and Charles Stern, Saifullah's longtime partner and dear friend. The office was relatively small and unremarkable. There were some books and standard office equipment, along with cabinets that contained hundreds of files devoted to business paperwork. In essence, it was just two men sitting in front of their computers, occasionally stopping whatever they were doing to make a phone call. The office certainly did not have the look or feel of a clandestine hub for illicit shipments of explosives.

Stern, always wearing his yarmulke, worked at the main desk. This was where FBI agents likely approached him back in April 2002 during the first interview. But it was their second meeting on March 28, 2003, that truly caught Stern by surprise.

Uzair did not have his own office. Instead, Stern allocated a corner table in his office for Uzair's use. The table was mostly bare except for a telephone and a computer. As the FBI soon learned, this was the computer that Uzair used to log on to the visapro.com website to check on Majid Khan's immigration documents.

Uzair had just turned twenty-three when he took over Stern's corner table. He primarily used that small corner of the office to sell Cliftonia apartments to Pakistani nationals living in the US. By all accounts, Uzair was affable and motivated, on the verge of making it as a businessman. But this was the day when everything ended for him. This was the day that he met Agent Miller.

Up until that point, March 2003 had been full of nightmare scenarios suggesting that explosives were being shipped to the US through the country's vulnerable ports system. There was talk about nuclear and biological weapons proliferation, and methods for obtaining them. There was also the business of al Qaeda operatives working to get a sleeper agent into the country, connections to 9/11 conspirators, and, at the center of it all, Saifullah and Uzair Paracha.

For nearly a month, the CIA worked to extract information from captured al Qaeda operatives by virtually any means necessary. Now it was the FBI's turn, Agent Miller's turn. On a warm, partly cloudy Friday—March 28—she entered Stern's office with another FBI agent by her side. The encounter that morning did not take long; pleasant but straight to the point. Miller was working against the clock. She identified herself to Uzair and advised him that he was needed by the FBI to serve as a material witness.

Despite having no clue what that meant, Uzair told Agent Miller that he understood. Some questions needed answers, and the FBI was asking for his help. This was nothing that Uzair couldn't handle. He resolved to go willingly and cooperate.

Uzair shot a quick glance over to Stern, who sat at his desk stone-faced. Agent Miller motioned for Uzair to come with her. He simply nodded. Agent Miller reiterated to Uzair that he was not under arrest, which was technically true, but he was expected to answer some questions over the course of that weekend. No handcuffs were needed.

Uzair departed Stern's prized Garment District office as a free man, albeit a man being escorted out by two armed FBI agents.

* * *

By the time Uzair Paracha was taken into custody, most Americans were cognizant of the terror threat. KSM's capture had been a major news story. The DHS color-coded terror alert system had essentially settled into hues of yellow (elevated) and orange (high). Safe, as in green or blue, was something nobody expected again. In fact, by 2003, the public had largely desensitized to the threats emanating from abroad. The color-coding system had calibrated their anxieties. Sociologists called it "fear fatigue." The deep emotions experienced after the 9/11 attack, all that anger and fear, for many Americans had drifted into something else—uneasy resignation. In April 2003, the Iraq War began, largely based on false intelligence that Saddam Hussein had weapons of mass destruction. Uzair was still in custody that next month when national attention shifted to the invasion of Iraq. And his father was still safely at home in Pakistan.

* * *

Back in Karachi, the elder Paracha was blissfully unaware of what was transpiring in New York. It had been weeks since KSM's disheveled photo was broadcast. After the initial shock had worn off, Saifullah steadily became more comfortable that his connection would not run afoul of US or Pakistani authorities. The reassuring call with Mustafa also put his mind at ease. As far as Saifullah was concerned, Friday, March 28, 2003, was business as usual.

Meanwhile, that morning in America, Agent Miller escorted Uzair out of his New York City office. As a Muslim religious day, in the Paracha household, Friday evenings were devoted to entertaining family, friends, and other associates. Saifullah, of course, enjoyed his perch as the focal point of these weekly events. It was prime time to pontificate and shine in a relaxed, jovial atmosphere. On this Friday, Saifullah missed a call from his business partner back in New York.

Later that night, Saifullah checked his voicemail. Stern's message did not seem out of the ordinary. No panicked words. Just a terse message. Stern asked that Saifullah give him a call as soon as possible. Saifullah figured this was a business call, and whatever business it was, it could wait until Sunday.

The timing of Uzair's FBI encounter further delayed Stern's contact with Saifullah for another reason. Stern was an Orthodox Jew who turned off his phone from sundown on Friday to sundown Saturday. Saifullah knew this, which is why he planned on speaking with Stern on Sunday. During Uzair's first night in FBI custody, Saifullah slept soundly, unaware of his son's plight. To that point, he had never heard the name Special Agent Janelle Miller.

Saifullah was well insulated in Pakistan. Though he didn't know it, the Pakistani government had quietly shielded him from US investigators. Saifullah's name first appeared on US intelligence radar when documents linking him to al Qaeda turned up in the March and September 2002 safe house raids that netted senior figures Zubaydah and Binalshibh, respectively. Declassified CIA documentation confirms that in the months following those raids, US officials made direct overtures to the Pakistani government specifically about Saifullah Paracha. In one instance in December 2002, CIA officials referenced the Paracha documents seized in the raids and made the following then-top-secret overture to their Pakistani counterparts: "Information below leads us to believe that the following individual and phone numbers may have a connection to al-Qa'ida and international terrorism. . . . We request your assistance in investigating this individual to determine if he is involved in terrorist activity."

The Pakistani government failed to act. They never interviewed Saifullah, nor was he investigated. Saifullah maintained his extensive list of connections. In fact, that list continued to grow and his life went on as normal.

Until March 2003, US officials did not provide much, if any, pushback on this matter. There was too much going on. The 9/11 conspirators were methodically being tracked down. Al Qaeda was still plotting terror attacks throughout the world. To keep up, the CIA and FBI had to triage their resources and prioritize their operations. Saifullah was just one of thousands of names being passed around, low on the priority list. And Uzair Paracha hadn't even been a name of interest.

Everything changed later in March 2003 when Majid Khan and KSM began discussing Saifullah and Uzair Paracha in their debriefing sessions. US investigators began connecting their torture-induced revelations with the raid evidence, and suddenly, the Second Wave terror conspiracy became much more real. The FBI urgently pressed to get Pakistan to act on the US requests to investigate Paracha. The Pakistanis did nothing, and Paracha remained untouchable.

Unaware that the FBI was urgently requesting action, Saifullah finally connected with Charles Stern by phone that Sunday. It became very direct and very personal when Stern informed Saifullah that Uzair was in FBI custody.

An unrelenting world was now closing in. Mustafa Paracha, Uzair's younger brother, later recalled this moment, saying, "My father was very, very distraught."

In addition to the sudden anguish, the Parachas were also bewildered. As much as Saifullah liked to claim that he knew about the US legal system from his experience, he was at a loss as to what it meant for his son to be held in custody as a so-called material witness.

"At that time, we had no idea what a material witness was," his wife, Farhat, later explained. "We looked it up on the internet and found that this could mean he has been arrested or that he's simply being questioned—a double-edged sword."

No matter what a material witness was, Saifullah wasn't going to sit idly by. He reached into his pocket and pulled out his Casio device with all his contacts and began working the phones.

One of his first calls was to an old acquaintance, Hamid Gul, the director of the Pakistani intelligence service. It was a logical choice. Gul had a direct line to many US government officials. He could be extremely influential. From the US perspective, Gul's loyalty to the War on Terror cause was questionable. He was long suspected of telling US officials what they wanted to hear while covertly currying favor with the Taliban and al Qaeda.

By all accounts, Gul took Saifullah's call. If Gul knew that the CIA and FBI had contacted Pakistan about Saifullah, he didn't let Saifullah know about it, revealing no more than necessary.

During the call, Saifullah explained the situation Uzair was in, and Gul expressed his sympathy. He told Saifullah that he would investigate and get back to him. For Saifullah, this was momentous. He was relieved and even proud to report to both family and friends that Hamid Gul was looking into the matter at his request.

But in the end, Gul either had no sway or no inclination to get involved with an FBI operation in New York, and the Paracha family simply had no control over what was happening there with Uzair. Saifullah was oblivious to the fact that a number of high-level officials in Washington, DC, were preparing to discuss and debate his own fate at length. The conversations would prove to be unprecedented. Uzair was not enough. The US government now also wanted Saifullah in custody. If Pakistan wasn't going to help, officials needed to come up with some way to apprehend the elder Paracha.

Depending on how things transpired, the end result for Saifullah could become horrifying. Senior US officials were now actually justifying the proposed torture of an American permanent resident. Even in an era when foreign nationals were being subjected to the harsh cruelty of EITs, this was unprecedented. But the explosives and any weapons of mass destruction simply had to be found because the homeland was certainly in grave danger. Official discussions surrounding the extreme measures that would be required to foil this Second Wave attack continued. Meanwhile, Uzair was at the mercy of Special Agent Janelle Miller and the FBI.

* * *

Uzair Paracha and Janelle Miller were both youthful when they first met. Undoubtedly, Uzair's first impression was that he could charm the young woman. After all, Uzair was rich and successful. He was confident and on his way up. He knew his English was impeccable, and being the proud burger that he was, with his carefully sculpted hair and goatee, Uzair was also aware of his exotic good looks.

Most important, Uzair believed he had done nothing wrong. He was a businessman doing what he was trained to do. For Uzair, this thirty-four-year-old female with dark hair, dressed in a typically cliché woman's suit, was just some American functionary overreacting to the 9/11 attacks. Uzair believed he was clever enough to run circles around her, whatever she might have in mind for him.

Agent Miller had known that she wanted to work with the FBI since the 1980s. Like Uzair, Agent Miller had been educated at a top private high school, the Buffalo Academy of the Sacred Heart—a Catholic school in western New York—where she attended a talk given by an FBI recruiter. The recruiter explained the mission and life of an FBI agent, and Miller was immediately drawn to what would become her calling. She later said in an interview, "I was lucky to sort of know what I wanted to do when I was in high school—that I wanted to become an FBI agent."

A star softball player, young Janelle Miller had a reputation for being studious and bright, but also incredibly tough. She suffered no fools, tolerated zero bullshit. But instead of acting out in the face of adversity or conflict, one of her greatest attributes was the ability to maintain her composure. She realized that adversaries could be disarmed with her quick smile. Those who underestimated her did so at their peril.

After high school, Miller decided to attend SUNY Brockport, where she earned a softball scholarship. Perhaps it is a metaphor for her career choice, but Miller continues to hold the school record for the most sacrifice bunts and fly balls in one softball game. At Brockport, she studied criminology to pave the way toward her goal of joining the FBI. Miller later earned a master's degree from Southern Illinois University.

After college, Miller believed that she was not quite ready to join the FBI. She needed more experience and more qualifications; she still felt like a blue-collar girl from Tonawanda, New York. For her, nothing was simply handed to her. She had to scrape and hustle for everything that came her way.

Janelle Miller and Uzair Paracha were nothing alike.

Although Miller believed she was not yet ready for the FBI, she knew where her career trajectory would lead. As such, she took a job as a police officer in Baltimore—Majid Khan's adoptive hometown. Miller threw herself into her work. Finally, in 1996, Miller fulfilled her youthful dream and became an FBI agent.

Her first assignment was in the FBI's Phoenix field office. In addition to the typical rigors of the job, Agent Miller was faced with the realities of sexism—from alleged criminals, sources, and from her colleagues.

"It is a male-dominated agency and law enforcement is by nature," she later said, vowing to serve as a role model for future female agents. "It's important that we try to recruit more female agents and minorities in the FBI because we want to represent the communities that we serve. And it's not all, obviously, male."

From the start, Agent Miller thrived in the FBI. Her work ethic was infectious. As in her youth, she carried a sense of calm determination into everything she did. She was always well prepared and an excellent interviewer. Through a mix of dogged preparedness, firmness, and an edge of humor, Agent Miller quickly became highly regarded for her ability to establish rapport with a variety of criminal suspects. Even tough suspects were broken after sitting in a room with her. FBI senior officials clearly took notice of her drive and street smarts.

After five years, Agent Miller was transferred to New York City. She arrived just three months before 9/11 and soon became embedded with the Joint Terrorism Task Force (JTTF). This was the unit tasked with the seemingly impossible mission of stopping the next terror attack—the front lines in the War on Terror. That is how Agent Miller came to be in Pakistan when that call came regarding Saifullah Paracha. And her assignment to the JTTF was how she came face-to-face with Saifullah's son, Uzair. Court documents and author interviews with Agent Miller and other FBI personnel provided insight into their interactions.

Agent Miller and an FBI colleague escorted Uzair to a hotel room. It was a comfortable setting for what was expected to be a weekend full of questioning. They sat Uzair down in a chair in front of a table and asked if he needed anything. Uzair flashed a smile at the young woman sitting across from him. He indicated that he was ready to cooperate. Pizza was served. Uzair leaned back in his chair. He was relaxed yet animated, even boastful. The atmosphere during the first day or so of questioning was just as Agent Miller intended.

At first, Uzair confirmed what was already known. He was indeed a Pakistani citizen with lawful permanent resident status in the US. He had just arrived in mid-February 2003 and was staying with relatives in Brooklyn. He was working in the Garment District, and his company had a branch in Karachi. On this last point, the burger in him was at full tilt. Uzair believed that Agent Miller was very impressed with his business acumen. She nodded at his answers and did not ask him anything particularly difficult. Uzair became even more comfortable. He figured he was going to charge through the interview unscathed and go home.

Uzair was in complete businessman mode, just as he had watched his father do so many times before. No matter the question, Uzair had an answer for everything. Agent Miller appeared to be buying it. Here was Uzair, fast-talking and the smartest person in the room, or so he thought.

During the conversation, Agent Miller asked Uzair about Majid Khan. With a wave of his hand, Uzair dismissed the question. That guy was just a business contact of his father, Uzair told her. What about Mustafa (a.k.a. Ali Abdul Aziz Ali or Ammar al-Baluchi), Agent Miller asked. Uzair replied that he, too, was just another business contact of his father. In other words, according to Uzair, there was nothing to see here.

For the rest of that first day of questioning, Uzair skirted around his association with Khan and Mustafa. Agent Miller chose not to press him too much. Uzair even expressed some sympathy for the FBI having to investigate this matter, though somewhat condescending with his attitude.

Agent Miller kept asking questions into the night. Uzair continued to evade artfully. He wasn't sure when it happened, but at some point, after midnight, Uzair began to realize that Agent Miller had been slowly turning the screws on him, probing with her questions, which were getting much tougher. The atmosphere had changed. Uzair's cavalier answers earlier in the day were starting to come back at him. Agent Miller relentlessly pointed out his inconsistencies. Bleary-eyed and utterly exhausted, Uzair realized with some desperation that he had been outplayed and was trapped in a corner. He attempted to regroup, but it was too late.

Agent Miller's focus was on an unexpected topic. It wasn't directly related to Khan or Mustafa. Instead, she asked a lot of questions about money. The 200,000 euros his company had received. At first, Uzair dismissed the money as payment in exchange for help in obtaining US documents. In any event, Uzair told Agent Miller that it was his father who had arranged that deal. He repeatedly insisted that Saifullah was responsible for securing that investment from his contacts. Uzair was just helping his father with the business. Under pressure, Uzair disclosed what initially seemed like a trivial detail: Saifullah may have known that Khan and Mustafa were affiliated with al Qaeda. If Uzair thought this would get the FBI off his back, by pinning the al Qaeda aspect on his father who was safely in Pakistan, he was wrong. Agent Miller pounced.

Uzair was suddenly in deep and no longer the confident, alpha male. Nor was he that pompous burger. He was in over his head.

Soon, the truth started coming out. Uzair told Agent Miller that Khan and Mustafa wanted to invest the 200,000 euros in the Cliftonia project. Uzair also revealed that Saifullah advised him not to ask any questions about the money because Khan and Mustafa were supporters of Usama bin Laden. After further pressing questions from Agent Miller, Uzair admitted that, despite his claims made earlier in the day, the money did in fact belong to al Qaeda. And there it was: the first direct admission of a link between the Parachas, father and son, and al Qaeda.

At this point, Uzair still held out some desperate hope that he could find a way out. He began to further throw his father under the bus. He informed

Agent Miller that Saifullah's connection to al Qaeda led all the way up to Usama bin Laden. According to Uzair, his father "admired" bin Laden and described him as "a very humble guy." Uzair then suggested that al Qaeda was using Saifullah to keep the large amount of funds liquid to be retrieved by al Qaeda operatives on short notice. Uzair attempted to justify his own actions with respect to Khan by telling Agent Miller that if he did not assist Khan, then the money would not be invested in Cliftonia. This was Uzair's businessman defense, and Agent Miller didn't buy it.

An increasingly dejected Uzair once again discussed the meeting at Snoopy's Ice Cream Parlor in Karachi, the one where Khan provided written instructions about how to pose as Khan to make it appear that he was in the US. Uzair confirmed that the PO Box in Maryland was held jointly by Khan and a woman. According to Uzair, Khan described the woman as a "good sister" who was helping them out. Uzair added that he was tasked with closing the PO Box on the premise that he (posing as Khan) and the woman were no longer seeing each other. That woman turned out to be Aafia Siddiqui.

When Agent Miller applied further pressure, Uzair not only linked Saifullah to al Qaeda but also admitted that he himself understood Khan and Mustafa were al Qaeda operatives. For the FBI, that admission by Uzair would be crucial. If Uzair knew he was working with al Qaeda operatives, then he could be charged with federal crimes. But if Uzair was for the most part unaware that Khan and Mustafa were al Qaeda, then Uzair was likely to be set free with no more issues.

By Saturday morning, Uzair was in serious trouble. He began discussing obvious al Qaeda tradecraft. Apparently, Khan did not want to know any personal information about Uzair so that Khan could not reveal it if he were ever arrested and interrogated. But if Uzair's knowledge about the al Qaeda links was tenuous before, it wasn't anymore after he recounted his motorcycle conversation with Khan. Uzair confirmed that Khan told him that al Qaeda needed "brothers" like Uzair, and that different people provided different levels of assistance to the organization. Uzair added that he believed that Khan was recruiting him to al Qaeda. So, once again, Khan's boasting and freelancing came back to harm the al Qaeda cause. This time Khan took away any plausible deniability Uzair Paracha could have had.

Quite simply, Uzair knew he was assisting al Qaeda operatives. And that was indeed a federal crime.

Agent Miller wrote the following: "Because he was aware that [Khan] and [Mustafa] were associated with al Qaeda, Paracha knew that, by performing the tasks that [Khan] had asked of him, Paracha would be acting on behalf of al Qaeda."

During the weekend, Agent Miller also convinced Uzair to consent to a search of his Brooklyn home. His thoughts returned to the call earlier that month with his father after KSM was first captured, and how Saifullah had advised his son not to throw Khan's documents in the trash. Within a few minutes in the house, the FBI found the documents that Uzair had tried to hide.

Among other items, they found the Maryland driver's license with Khan's photograph. They found Khan's Owings Mills High School ID. The Bank of America card with the name Majid Khan embossed on it. Even Khan's Social Security card was there. And, of course, the FBI now was in possession of the PO Box information, the I-131 travel documents, and the notes written in Khan's handwriting issuing instructions for Uzair to follow.

This was particularly significant. Khan was believed to be an al Qaeda sleeper agent attempting to get into the country. Khan's necessary documents were behind Uzair's bed, complete with Khan's photo. Now the FBI had hard, tangible evidence against Uzair. The real danger still lay with whatever Saifullah had been up to. But the FBI now had a federal case against his son.

A grand jury was convened. An indictment was issued. And Agent Miller signed the arrest warrant.

Uzair Paracha was charged with conspiracy and multiple counts of providing material support for terrorism.

CHAPTER 8

AMERICAN TORTURE

"Dynamite." That was the term used by a senior CIA official in a partially declassified email sent to CIA senior lawyers on May 6, 2003. The bulk of the email was a plea from the CIA Counterterrorism Center (CTC) Chief of Operations regarding Saifullah Paracha, advocating for torture with this grammatically incorrect message: "we MUST have paracha arrested without delay and transferred to cia custody for interrogation using enhanced measures. i understand that paracha's us person status makes this difficult, but this is dynamite and we have to move forward with alacrity. what do you need to do that?"

The gravity of what the CTC Chief was seeking is difficult to understate. The CTC head is one of the highest and most influential positions in the CIA. With the writing style of a middle schooler, the CTC head was openly advocating to torture a US person. "Enhanced measures," as the email described them, were employed during the interrogations of KSM, Abu Zubaydah, Majid Khan, and Ramzi Binalshibh, among others. And the measures had been used before on other foreign nationals with no known active US immigration status. But Saifullah Paracha was different.

Saifullah was a lawful permanent resident of the United States. He owned a home in New York and paid taxes. The constitutional ramifications alone were mind-boggling, not to mention the slippery slope regarding CIA authorities in matters relating to torture. If a lawful permanent resident could be tortured by the CIA, then where would it stop?

Jose Padilla, the US citizen dubbed the "dirty bomber," as well as two other US citizens accused of being affiliated with al Qaeda, Yasser Hamdi and Ali Saleh al-Marri, had already been placed in military custody at a Navy brig in Charleston, South Carolina. And this military detention of US civilians was already causing alarm in some circles. But torture? The debate had been raging since March 2003 when KSM and Majid Khan began discussing the Second Wave plots. Now with Uzair's arrest and other fast-breaking developments pertaining to KSM's nephew Ali, government officials could no longer demur on this most unsavory subject.

Many in the CIA leadership chain supported using EITs on Saifullah, assuming the CIA could get their hands on him. The problem for them wasn't morality or effectiveness. The CIA impediment came down to the more mundane reality of lawyers blocking the way.

CIA lawyers, however, were extremely uneasy about the use of EITs on Saifullah. In fact, the lawyers questioned whether the CIA could hold him in custody for any significant period at all. Legal counsel certainly understood the scenario. By this time, the word was out on Saifullah and his connections within al Qaeda. More disconcerting was the mounting evidence that Saifullah was involved in the shipment of explosives through US ports under the cover of his business. The lawyers understood all of this. But the issue was unprecedented. It apparently required further research to attain legal authorization.

Another issue that gave the lawyers trepidation was Saifullah's US immigration status itself. Government records clearly confirmed that Saifullah was a lawful permanent resident. But there was some question regarding whether Saifullah was technically a US citizen. CIA officials pored through records. The last thing they wanted was to torture an actual citizen in an overseas black site. That could be a disaster on many levels, possibly enough to destroy the EIT program itself.

The LPR status was certainly enough to label Saifullah as a US person, a term of art that confers some rights afforded to US citizens abroad. CIA lawyers were extremely diplomatic, but they gently pushed back, articulating their concerns. CIA leadership, for their part, continued to press their lawyers to come up with something that would give them a go-ahead. The situation was dire, and hence the term, dynamite, was apropos. There had to be some sort of legal loophole that the CIA could exploit.

As the debate went back and forth, CIA leadership raised the stakes. They took the issue to the Department of Defense with the goal of obtaining an official determination declaring that Saifullah Paracha be designated "an enemy combatant." The CIA's request was highly unusual. It raised eyebrows within the intelligence community, the FBI, and the Pentagon. Even White House lawyers were brought in. If the CIA was hoping to make a government-wide case for detaining and torturing Saifullah, the issue was now front and center.

Typically, terror suspects were designated as enemy combatants after they were captured—not before. Evidence was then presented to make that important distinction. As enemy combatants, suspects were generally subject to detention for an indefinite period pursuant to the 2001 Authorization for Use of Military Force (AUMF) that was finalized shortly after the 9/11 attacks. Detention was exactly what the CIA wanted. The FBI was more agnostic about it. All the FBI knew was that Saifullah needed to be captured.

With Saifullah's case now reaching the highest levels of government, officials began consolidating the facts. The narrative remained ominous, casting Paracha as a dangerous combatant. The debate echoed back to November 2001, when the CIA had first received its expanded detention authority. At the time, James Pavitt, the CIA Deputy Director of Operations, participated in a classified briefing to a Senate committee on the anticipated boundaries for the nascent EIT program, stating, "You're not going to engage in torture. But, that said, how do I deal with somebody I know may know right now that there is a nuclear weapon somewhere in the United States that is going to be detonated tomorrow, and I've got the guy who I know built it and hid it? I don't know the answer to that."

It was undeniable that Saifullah was directly connected to KSM and Ali. Not only were KSM and Ali responsible for the 9/11 attacks, but government investigators were confident this duo was actively plotting the Second Wave attacks. Majid Khan was believed to be playing a significant role, and Khan, of course, was also directly connected to Saifullah. Moreover, Saifullah had the means to assist KSM and Ali in shipping explosives into US ports. In correlation with Pavitt's doomsday scenario, Saifullah was said to have "recommended to an al Qaida operative that nuclear weapons should be used against US troops and suggested where these weapons might be obtained."

The danger was imminent and very real. And Uzair Paracha had recently told the FBI that Saifullah had traveled to Afghanistan to meet personally with Usama bin Laden. Pentagon leadership had seen enough. Paul Wolfowitz, the deputy secretary of defense, signed off on a memorandum. Saifullah Paracha was now designated an enemy combatant. Back in Pakistan, Saifullah had no idea that he had become a wanted man by the United States. He wasn't on the Top Ten Most Wanted List. His photo was not posted on the internet or in post offices across the country. Instead, Saifullah was listed in a secret memo where he was the only name. Saifullah Paracha was now officially labeled an enemy of the United States.

The legal disagreements over torture continued throughout the spring and into the summer of 2003. But one thing was clear. Saifullah Paracha needed to be captured, and it had to happen as soon as possible. He needed to talk.

A different debate began taking shape. It involved the FBI, CIA, and the military. The White House also provided input. The question: How exactly do we get this guy?

* * *

Pakistan continued to ignore US requests for information regarding Saifullah Paracha and failed to intervene in any way with Uzair, who by late April 2003 had been sitting in a New York jail cell for a month waiting for a court date. When it came to the Paracha family, Pakistan officials were ambivalent. The Pakistan Inter-Services Intelligence agency (ISI), which was headed by Saifullah's acquaintance Hamid Gul, had a lead on some other terrorist activity. The result of that lead would have a profound impact on Saifullah's case, including adding additional fuel to the debates raging back in Washington, DC, regarding torture and efforts to capture him.

In April 2003, Pakistani authorities began receiving reports from covert sources regarding attempts by al Qaeda operatives to procure explosives. In many ways, the Pakistani response was akin to old-fashioned police work. Apparently, explosives and weapons were set to be transported in a pickup truck to a specific location in Karachi. The Pakistanis planned to intercede.

Ultimately, their covert sources were correct. A pickup truck was right where they said it would be.

On April 29, 2003, Pakistani officials stopped the pickup truck and looked inside. They discovered explosives, detonators, and ammunition. The driver pleaded ignorance and immediately told the Pakistani authorities where the cargo was supposed to be delivered. That information led the Pakistanis to a house in Karachi. Two people inside that house were particularly notable: Khallad bin Attash and Ali Abdul Aziz Ali. The Pakistanis had captured two of the 9/11 conspirators.

Ali had not even been escorted from the house when he started talking to Pakistani authorities. He told them that the explosives were intended to be used in an attack on the US Consulate in Karachi. Later, Ali added that the plot involved the use of a motorcycle. A bomb strapped to the motorcycle would be used to breach the perimeter wall of the consulate. Al Qaeda operatives would then send a vehicle filled with explosives through the newly created breach in the perimeter wall to directly target the building and kill as many people as possible.

CIA interrogators in early May 2003 described Ali as "chatty," or at least more talkative than his colleague, Khallad bin Attash, who had been captured at the same time. A CIA document characterized Ali's involvement in the US Consulate plotting this way: "[Ali] acknowledged plans to attack US Consulate officials at the airport, the Consul General's Residence and the Consulate itself."

Ali and Khallad's capture wasn't publicly heralded like KSM's. There were no breaking news interruptions. No photos distributed to every media outlet in the world depicting disheveled terrorist masterminds. Publicly, the news was just another day in the War on Terror. Saifullah Paracha did not know that Mustafa, like Mir before him, had been captured.

* * *

Ali Abdul Aziz Ali and Khallad bin Attash had evidently become partners in crime. Despite their differences, the two bonded over their lifelong familial relations with terrorists. For Ali, his uncle, of course, was KSM, mastermind of the 9/11 attacks. And his cousin was Ramzi Yousef, the mastermind of the 1993 World Trade Center bombing. Meanwhile, Khallad was essentially al Qaeda royalty. His father was a prominent member of Usama bin Laden's inner circle. Most of his brothers fought in Afghanistan against the Soviets and/or the Northern Alliance. Khallad himself lost his leg during a 1997 skirmish. Terrorism was in their blood. Ali and Khallad had the bona fides to prove it.

Khallad and Ali differed in how they approached the family business. Khallad was more bluntly in-your-face about his militancy. He could be personable, even a little goofy at times. Yet on a dime he could turn darkly horrifying. Khallad was very vocal about the fact that he had no qualms about killing—be it men, women, or children. He even seemed to enjoy it. A lawyer with extensive access to the 9/11 conspirators described Khallad like this: "KSM has feelings and is capable of empathy; I never saw that with Khallad. Khallad is the true psychopath of the group."

Ali, on the other hand, was more cerebral. This is probably not a big surprise. Ali's uncle, KSM, was an engineer by trade and had a propensity for blending into his environments. Ali was more interested in computers. He had received various certifications in the computer field. Ali also eschewed traditional religious garb like Khallad, instead favoring a more professional appearance. Ali's professional demeanor made him the perfect choice to ingratiate himself within the business community. Wealthy elitists such as Saifullah Paracha would likely find such an overtly militant fanatic like Khallad to be unseemly. But Ali was different. Ali was someone who Saifullah could work with.

Despite their differences, common cause makes strange bedfellows. Khallad and Ali bonded over their desire to hurt the West. Beginning in 1999, they got their chance.

Khallad was one of the first operatives to be informed about the 9/11 plot, becoming involved about a year earlier than Ali. In early 1999, Usama bin Laden personally directed Khallad to obtain a US visa so that he could travel to the US and obtain pilot training for what Khallad referred to as the "Planes Operation." Bin Laden clearly trusted Khallad enough to make him the first choice to be a hijacker, and Khallad was eager to oblige.

Khallad's attempt to use an alias to obtain a US visa failed—the application was denied. Undeterred, in September 1999, Khallad administered a forty-five-day course in hand-to-hand combat training at an al Qaeda camp in Logar, Afghanistan, with the specific purpose of identifying trainees qualified for the "Planes Operation." At the conclusion of the course, Khallad selected Khalid al Mihdhar and Nawaf al Hazmi. They would be the first hijackers selected to travel to the United States.

In November 1999, Khallad took Hazmi and Mihdhar to Kandahar, Afghanistan, where they moved into a house shared by KSM. There, they studied books, flight simulators, flight timetables, and CDs regarding aviation. KSM, who had been educated in the US, taught them some English phrases such as "Get down," "Don't move," "Stay in your seat," and "If anyone moves, I'll kill you."

By late December 1999, KSM believed that Hazmi and Mihdhar were ready. But first, some additional surveillance needed to be done that the flight simulators and other research did not cover. As the twentieth century became the twenty-first, Khallad was flying all over Southeast Asia at KSM's direction. He traveled to Malaysia, Thailand, and Hong Kong, keeping notes along the way. Khallad's cover story was that he was traveling to purchase a new prosthetic leg. He was really researching vulnerabilities in the airline industry. By the end of the trip, he found one.

Upon his return to Karachi, Khallad prepared a written report about what he had found. He also briefed KSM and Abu Hafs, al Qaeda's military commander. Khallad's surveillance reported a simple but effective vulnerability in the airline system: Razor knives could be snuck onto every flight.

During the same time frame, as previously described, a group of friends studying in Hamburg, Germany, had made their way to an al Qaeda training camp in Kandahar, Afghanistan. Among them were Ramzi Binalshibh and three other men (Mohamed Atta, Marwan al Shehhi, and Ziad Jarrah) who would later go on to receive flight training in the United States.

After submitting his report about the razor knives and facilitating the first two hijackers' entry into the United States, Khallad moved on to other al Qaeda business. His task with the "Planes Operation" was essentially complete. Khallad then began working full-time on something called the "Boats Operation." Like the name implies, Khallad, along with a man named Abd al-Nashiri, focused their efforts on attacking targets in the sea. The results of their work included the deadly attacks against the USS *Cole* and the Belgian tanker MV *Limburg*.

With Khallad mostly out of the Planes Operation, new blood was needed. Hijackers were being selected. They needed to be funded for their travel to the United States. KSM needed someone workmanlike, someone good with finances and computers. He needed a cerebral operative. KSM didn't have to look far. His nephew Ali was more than willing to help.

In early 2000, would-be pilot hijacker Marwan al Shehhi traveled to Dubai to meet with Ali. KSM ordered them to use the internet to purchase a video entitled "CityBird." The video depicted cockpit operations on a Boeing 767-300. Ali and Shehhi also purchased a flight simulator for the Boeing 747.

A few months later, in April 2000, KSM gave Ali more than $100,000 to be utilized for what was described as "operational purposes." That same month, Nawaf al Hazmi, who was selected to be a hijacker by Khallad, spoke with Ali over the telephone. Hazmi was already in the United States. He asked for money. On April 16, 2000, Ali transferred about $5,000 to Hazmi. On several more occasions, Ali incrementally transferred large amounts of money to bank accounts used by hijackers such as Shehhi and Mohammad Atta. On August 29, 2000, Ali sent $20,000 to Shehhi and Atta's joint SunTrust Bank account. In September 2000, another transfer totaled more than $70,000. Ali had become an integral part of the "Planes Operation." The money he provided to the hijackers became their lifeblood.

Khallad, for his part, made something of a cameo in the "Planes Operation" in December 2000. The fourth and final pilot hijacker had been identified. Already a pilot in Saudi Arabia, Hani Hanjour needed to connect with the other hijackers who, at that time, were attending flight training in the United States. Khallad gave Hanjour an email address he could use to contact Nawaf al Hazmi, one of the two hijackers that Khallad initially trained and selected for the job.

On December 5, 2000, Ali helped Hanjour open a Citibank account and deposited $3,000. Ali also reserved Hanjour's plane ticket to the United States so that Hanjour could join the other hijackers. A few days later, Hanjour sent a message to Ali letting him know that he arrived in San Diego safely. From this point, Ali began shuttling back and forth between Dubai and Karachi.

Once 2001 came around, KSM was fully engaged in shepherding the "Planes Operation" to fruition. At the same time, he was cultivating his relationship with Saifullah Paracha. The "Planes Operation" was clearly the priority; but KSM was already thinking about what would be a second wave of attacks. He realized that his operational abilities would be much more difficult after the initial attack took place. As such, he needed to have the relationships and infrastructure in place and ready to go. Saifullah was well connected and eager to please. He could provide expertise and cover within Pakistan as the heat turned up.

In 2001, it was mostly KSM who dealt with Saifullah. The two met in Saifullah's Karachi office on numerous occasions throughout the year. As Saifullah continued to prove his worth, KSM already had it planned out that he would turn over the care and feeding of Saifullah to Ali once the "Planes Operation" concluded. In the meantime, Ali was needed to take care of the hijackers.

Indeed, Ali continued to transfer money to the hijacker bank accounts. As more of the newly selected hijackers—those known as "muscle hijackers"—traveled to Dubai on their way to the United States, Ali and an associate, Mustafa al Hawsawi, were there to assist in the purchase of food, clothing, lodging, rental cars, traveler's checks, and other travel arrangements. Hawsawi would later be captured in the same 2003 raid that netted KSM.

Sometime in June 2001, Ali began to question his role in the "Planes Operation." He wasn't having second thoughts. On the contrary, he wanted to do more. He had watched as all these men shuttled through Dubai on their way to martyrdom. Ali wanted that for himself.

On June 26, 2001, Ali flew from Dubai to Karachi to meet with his uncle. Ali told him that he was willing to do anything to help the mission, including being a martyr. KSM indicated that he understood. He told his young nephew to apply for a US visa. If Ali wanted to be a hijacker, then so be it. KSM would not stand in his way.

In late August 2001, Ramzi Binalshibh sent KSM a message. The message stated that Mohamed Atta, the hijacker commander in the United States, had chosen September 11, 2001, as the date of the operation. KSM immediately traveled to Afghanistan. He reported the chosen date to Usama bin Laden, who began preparing al Qaeda members and their families in Afghanistan in anticipation of a US military response. KSM then returned to Karachi.

Hawsawi, Ali's logistical compatriot, busied himself in Dubai collecting funds that went unused by the hijackers. Ali, meanwhile, had applied for a visa to travel to the United States. In his application, he listed September 4, 2001, as his travel date. He was supposed to stay in the US for one week. The visa application was denied. Martyrdom denied.

On September 10, 2001, Ali took a plane from Dubai to Karachi. Hawsawi left early the next morning after handling some last-minute financial matters involving the hijackers. The "Planes Operation" has since been referred to by government officials and terrorists alike as an example of a "spectacular attack" due to its scope and extensive death toll.

After the attack, KSM recorded numerous news stories for future use in propaganda films. During the same period, KSM and several associates traipsed back and forth to the office of Universal Broadcasting in Karachi. This was one of the businesses owned by Saifullah Paracha.

Once Saifullah and Uzair's names surfaced in connection with several 9/11 plotters, it led to an obvious question. Did the Parachas—Saifullah, in particular—have any prior knowledge about the "Planes Operation"?

The timeline certainly made this scenario possible. Uzair told the FBI that his father met Usama bin Laden in 2000. In 2001, KSM was doing business with Saifullah at his Karachi office. Moreover, the relationship continued through 2002 and 2003 with Ali taking a lead role. As more information was gathered in April and May 2003, it only raised more concerns about Saifullah. Ali's capture served as a tipping point.

* * *

In May 2003, Ali Abdul Aziz Ali was in custody. Majid Khan and KSM were in a CIA black site. Uzair Paracha was in limbo at the Metropolitan Correctional Center in New York still awaiting a court date. But Saifullah Paracha remained free.

Ali's capture was a major boon for the CIA. There was no question that Ali played a significant role in the 9/11 attacks. But post-9/11 intelligence also indicated that Ali continued to be a major player in KSM's Second Wave attack planning, linked to Majid Khan, and therefore directly involved in sleeper-cell plotting designed to target gas stations in the US. Moreover, Khan, KSM, and Uzair Paracha linked Ali to Saifullah Paracha, the import/

exporter with ties to New York. To investigators, this meant that Ali may have been involved in plans to ship al Qaeda explosives through the ports with New York as a possible destination. How far had that planning progressed?

When Ali was finally captured, along with Khallad bin Attash, the CIA realized that KSM was holding back information. This resistance caused serious frustration, especially since CIA officers were subjecting KSM to EITs. CIA officials worried that additional attack plans had gone undetected. KSM never informed CIA officers about the active plot to attack the US Consulate in Karachi. There was also the open question about whether Saifullah Paracha had facilitated shipments of explosives or weapons of mass destruction. Until Ali's April 29, 2003, capture by the Pakistanis, the CIA had been stymied in their efforts to get a lead on him.

The CIA officers counted themselves lucky, as suggested in this May 20, 2003, communication: "[W]e consider KSM's long-standing omission of [this] information to be a serious concern, especially as this omission may well have cost American lives had Pakistani authorities not been diligent in following up on unrelated criminal leads that led to the capture of Ammar, bin Attash, and other probable operatives involved in the attack plans."

Based on Ali's history and intimate knowledge of KSM's operations, he was a prime candidate for EITs. The CIA pressed Pakistani officials to hand him over for interrogation, even though Ali was already speaking rather openly to his original captors. Indeed, Ali's most important assistance to the CIA was the fact that his statements could be used to confront KSM. Weaponizing Ali's additional al Qaeda insight was a similar tactic used on KSM with Majid Khan's statements regarding the Parachas. To a lesser extent, it was a tactic that Agent Miller used on Uzair Paracha as she questioned him in that New York hotel room.

A CIA Deputy Chief wrote in an email that KSM was "obstructing our ability to acquire good information," noting that he "misidentifie[s] photos when he knows we are fishing. . . . [We] remain concerned that KSM's progression towards full debriefing status is not yet apparent where it counts most, in relation to threats to US interests, especially inside CONUS (Continental United States)." A major benefit of having Ali in custody turned out to be that the CIA would not have to do as much fishing. Instead, they could use Ali's statements to manipulate KSM and force him to speak more truthfully.

This strategy bore some fruit, as one CIA officer noted in June 2003: "KSM's pattern of behavior over the past three months, trying to control his environment, lying and then admitting things only when pressed that others have been caught and have likely admitted the plot, is a cause for concern. . . . [W]hat KSM's doing is fairly typical of other detainees . . . KSM, Khallad [bin Attash], and others are doing what makes sense in their situation - pretend cooperation."

Despite Ali's obvious usefulness, the CIA couldn't get out of its own way in the early days of his detention. During that time, a Pakistani security officer had developed a useful relationship with Ali. No torture techniques were used, and Ali was talking. CIA officers watched the early interviews via a video feed. A CIA communication noted the following: "The foreign government officer who had developed rapport with Ammar al-Baluchi was conducting all the questioning and obtaining intelligence from Ammar al-Baluchi on the plotting against US interests in Pakistan, as well as other matters."

Ignoring the Pakistani officer's success, CIA officers pressed their counterparts to allow the CIA to participate in the interrogations based on the threat to US interests. A few days later, Ali was rendered to the CIA and subjected to EITs. By all accounts, replacing Ali's comfort zone in Pakistan with harsh methods conducted by Americans caused him to shut down and hold his cards much closer to his vest. Government reports suggest that Ali disclosed little more under EITs than he did during his earlier interrogations with the Pakistani officer.

The CIA had urgent questions about "US interests" that, in their view, justified taking custody of Ali. Chief among them were inquiries into Saifullah Paracha's ties to al Qaeda and the Second Wave plot.

By May 2003, Saifullah was a touchy subject in relation to the Pakistanis. For months, the US government had attempted to get Pakistan to investigate him because his corporate information had been seized in those two separate raids on al Qaeda safe houses. Even with the new information provided by Khan and KSM, as well as Uzair Paracha's arrest in New York, Pakistan proved to be unable or unwilling to act. The CIA believed that the Pakistani interrogator would not dig deep enough into the subject. They needed Saifullah to be a priority.

On May 2, 2003, the Pakistani interrogator specifically asked Ali about Saifullah Paracha. The CIA did not deem that discussion to be enough. The questioning was relatively limited. But Ali did confirm that he knew Saifullah, referencing Saifullah's links to media equipment and shipping. The details were not very specific, and the Pakistani interrogator did not press the matter further. The CIA needed more. Had the Pakistani interrogator delved deeper into Ali's relationship with Saifullah, the CIA's treatment and custody over Ali would have been far less brutal.

Neither the CIA nor the FBI had any further certainty on whether explosives were on their way toward US ports. Majid Khan provided tangential evidence of an overall plot—but Khan appeared to be more of a back-end recipient of any explosives that would make their way through the US port system. In addition, Uzair Paracha confirmed to the FBI that Saifullah was directly connected to Usama bin Laden and knew he was working with al Qaeda operatives. Meanwhile, KSM discussed a plot involving Saifullah Paracha and the shipment of explosives only when confronted with details provided by Khan. The CIA believed Ali might prove to be the key in solving the Paracha mystery. Unfortunately for them, the gambit only created more questions and ambiguity.

Ali was subjected to EITs immediately upon being rendered to CIA custody. A few days later, on May 20, 2003, the CIA stopped the torture. Once that happened, Ali gave a surprising statement that rippled throughout the intelligence community: "Ammar al-Baluchi denied that he and Sayf al-Rahman Paracha agreed to smuggle explosives into the United States. Ammar al-Baluchi stated he only asked Sayf al-Rahman Paracha questions and made inquiries about how explosives shipping could be done. Ammar al-Baluchi maintained that he did not take any action based on the discussion."

Upon further questioning, Ali stated that Saifullah was "unwittingly being used," adding that Ali was using his relationship with Saifullah as part of the Majid Khan plot to attack the US. Mainly, Saifullah had knowledge about establishing a business in Pakistan. Saifullah also had a business in New York that he seemed open to using to assist. In short, Saifullah was kind of a dupe.

Ali's statements about Saifullah ended up adding to the confusion. They also contradicted statements made by KSM. In some ways, Ali contradicted himself. Who was lying, if anyone?

Despite Ali's claim that Saifullah was "unwittingly being used," Ali also confirmed that Saifullah "probably knew [Ali's] al Qaeda affiliation." That point was hammered home by Ali's revelation that Saifullah continued to meet with Ali after KSM was so publicly captured. If nothing else, Saifullah was clearly working with al Qaeda.

The previous month, KSM also attempted to downplay Saifullah's role in al Qaeda operations. Like Ali, KSM depicted Saifullah as a wannabe terrorist who could be easily manipulated. KSM did confirm—under torture coercion—that Saifullah had agreed to use his business as a cover to smuggle explosives. To make matters even more perplexing, the CIA noted the following in March 2003: "KSM claimed that Ammar al-Baluchi and Majid Khan approached Sayf al-Rahman Paracha with a plan to use Sayf al-Rahman Paracha's textile business to smuggle explosives into the United States. KSM stated that Paracha agreed to this plan and was arranging the details with Ammar al-Baluchi and Majid Khan at the time of his (KSM's) capture."

Saifullah's culpability, not to mention the status of any explosives traversing the sea-lanes, was now as clear as mud. Some in the US government couldn't reconcile the fact that a successful, wealthy industrialist would be so deferential to a group of on-the-run terrorists. Others started to wonder if Saifullah Paracha—that self-proclaimed titan of industry and achiever of the American Dream—really was kind of a sucker.

One Paracha skeptic—a senior CIA counterterrorism official—put it this way in a grammatically incorrect email at the time: "Again, another ksm op worthy of the lamentable knuckleheads . . . why 'smuggle' in explosives when you can get them here? neither fertilizer for bombs or regular explosives are that hard to come by. ramzi yousef came to conus with a suitcase and hundred bucks and got everything he needed right here. this may be true, but it just seems damn odd to me."

Others, however, rationalized that Ali and KSM were doing what seasoned terrorists do—bending the truth where it counted. They noted that detainees would often give up certain information that was already known by US officials but would withhold facts pertaining to operational matters still in the pipeline. Certainly, the Paracha matter could be construed as operational. One example pertained to a burgeoning plot to attack

Heathrow Airport in London. A June 2003 CIA communication stated: "KSM, Ammar, and Khallad bin Attash remain loathe to reveal details of the Heathrow plot . . . and [they] so far clung to such information . . . deflected questions."

Despite the assertions and lack of clarity, one thing was certain. KSM, Ali, Khan, and Uzair, to a degree, all confirmed the efforts to use the Parachas to fraudulently facilitate Khan's return to the US. There also was something there regarding shipping and explosives. KSM and Ali both mentioned it in some capacity. Even the senior CIA skeptic acknowledged that the plot to ship explosives "may be true."

The matter was simply too urgent to ignore. Too dangerous. Four people were now in custody with some information about the plot, including men accused of conspiring to carry out the 9/11 attacks. Saifullah Paracha was still out there. Senior government officials believed now, more than ever, that he held the key to the entire matter. The brainstorming in Washington, DC, over Saifullah's fate continued unabated.

* * *

In Karachi, Saifullah never stopped working the phones. It had been more than two months since Uzair had been arrested in New York. The other children were distraught and Farhat couldn't stop fidgeting over her son's plight. She rationalized that Uzair's detention was rooted in what she deemed to be post-9/11 US paranoia about Asians, particularly Muslims.

"I was horrified," Farhat later stated. "Since September 11th, 2001, I believe Americans have become very paranoid and doubtful of Muslims of Asian appearance, particularly Pakistanis. Since my son had his schooling in Pakistan and then went to the States on business, we thought it was due to his obviously Asian appearance and paranoia on the part of individuals that led to his detention. We did not expect it to last more than a few days.

"He has been linked to al Qaeda and is accused of agreeing to assist Al-Qaeda associates get into the US. There have been many other charges framed against him, some of which seem so ridiculous, that they seem funny, in a very tragic way."

As the days went by and Saifullah's efforts to find help for Uzair consistently came up short, Farhat's optimism faded. The high they felt after

Pakistan intelligence chief Hamid Gul agreed to look into the matter had dissipated under the cruel reality of the situation. Uzair may end up behind bars for an indeterminate period. Farhat felt helpless. So did Saifullah.

"My husband was such a strong person, but Uzair's abduction broke him," Farhat later said. "The first time I saw [Saifullah] cry was then. He felt so helpless to be unable to help his son."

It was suggested that Saifullah personally travel to New York to see if he could do anything, but the notion was quickly dropped. The risk was too great that Saifullah could get pulled into whatever mess Uzair had gotten himself into. Uzair's loss was bad enough. If Saifullah were to be detained, the family businesses would suffer, and their lifestyle would be diminished. Saifullah felt it best to remain safely in Pakistan where he could continue to make calls and work without any problems.

Saifullah was adamant that the businesses were a priority. His office was large—10,000 square feet on the eighth floor of a Karachi tower. He had two female receptionists and an elderly office manager. A security guard was employed, as well. On the front wall of his office, two flags were crossed—one Pakistani and one American. From that office, Saifullah managed several businesses. This included his still active role in IMG and its New York affiliate, Chenco. He was chairman of the board, and there were stockholders.

He also had his burgeoning media company, Universal Broadcasting. Other endeavors under his control included something called Abson Industries, which primarily made cement bags. The Council of Welfare Organizations—his charity group—did business at the office. And, of course, his recent priority was the Cliftonia Real Estate Developers group. Saifullah had invested huge sums of money in the Cliftonia apartment project. Uzair was his partner in that enterprise. With Uzair in FBI custody, it was on Saifullah to sell apartment units. Saifullah made a choice. The business must go on.

CHAPTER 9

SETTING A TRAP

Senior officials in Washington, DC, fretted over the fact that Saifullah Paracha remained free. As of June 2003, all their efforts to get at him had failed. Pakistan was refusing to take custody, and a prospective raid into Saifullah's gated community in Karachi was deemed off-limits by policymakers. US leadership reasoned that a unilateral operation into such a wealthy neighborhood would cause an excessive amount of friction in an already tenuous US/Pakistan relationship. Saifullah was just too well connected and too entrenched within respected Pakistani society for such a raid.

But with KSM, Khan, Ali, and Uzair all in detention, Saifullah's continued freedom was increasingly untenable. Frustrated FBI and CIA officers lamented the fact that if Saifullah remained in Pakistan, he was safe from American justice, a dangerous threat still at large.

CIA officers reported that "KSM, whom detention site personnel described as 'boxed in' by the new reporting, then stated that Uzair's father, Sayf al-Rahman Paracha, had agreed to smuggle explosives into the United States."

There was some hope that Saifullah would rush to New York to assist Uzair. That certainly would make things easy and clean. But by the summer of 2003, it was obvious that Saifullah was not going to just walk into US custody. He was staying put. Officials would have to come up with something else.

In many ways, the limitations over how to capture Saifullah helped resolve the ongoing debate about what to do with him once he was in custody. Senior CIA leaders were still advocating to detain him. The prospect of EITs was still on the table. In July 2003, the CIA made one last pitch:

> Simply put, detainee information has *saved countless American lives* inside the US and abroad. We believe there is no doubt al-Qa'ida would have succeeded in launching additional attacks in the US and that the information obtained from these detainees *through the use of enhanced measures* was *key to unlocking this information.* It is our assessment that if CIA loses the ability to interrogate and use enhanced measures in a responsible way, we will not be able to effectively prosecute this war.

No dice. As a plan to capture Saifullah slowly took shape, it became evident to all parties that the CIA would need to take a back seat. Paracha was too prominent. He also had American status. Sure, the CIA would be involved in Saifullah's capture, but the proposed plan itself was so nuanced that it needed to be orchestrated by the FBI. There was no other way.

The FBI was generally opposed to the CIA's use of EITs. Senior FBI officials and agents alike viewed torture techniques as inappropriate and ineffective. One only needs to look at Agent Miller's methodical takedown of Uzair Paracha in New York as an example of a professional, clean interrogation. Perhaps another example is that of the "chatty" rapport established between Ali and his Pakistani interrogator immediately after Ali's capture.

The CIA was forced to make a difficult choice. The CIA could abandon the only shot the US government *writ large* may have in capturing Saifullah—essentially, take their ball and go home—or the CIA could allow the FBI to drive the train on Saifullah's capture, understanding that the CIA wouldn't have custody. The CIA relented. Once the operation to capture Saifullah was complete, the CIA agreed to relinquish control of this prized detainee to the military. For the CIA, this was a hard pill to swallow. But it also was necessary.

The plan required capturing Saifullah outside of Pakistan. Any operations within Pakistan—a sovereign, noncombatant nation—were out of bounds. After several months, the FBI and CIA watched and waited for any indication that Saifullah would travel abroad. It didn't have to be travel to the United States. It just had to be somewhere—anywhere other than Pakistan.

The FBI needed to lure Saifullah out of Karachi. But with what?*

Instead of being constrained by Saifullah's professional standing, the FBI sought to use it against him. They realized that the one thing that could lure a successful international businessman out of the country was the prospect of more business. Saifullah's demise would be his desire for more wealth.

Although Saifullah was not aware of how wanted he really was, the Uzair situation likely keyed him into the idea that he was much safer in Pakistan than anywhere else. Any business endeavor requiring his presence outside of the country would have to be major, something huge. Essentially, it would need to be the kind of offer that he couldn't refuse.

The FBI found the answer at Kmart.

In building their profile of Saifullah, the FBI noted that he had been specifically intrigued by the idea of obtaining business contracts to ship clothing sold by Kmart. That yearning to work with Kmart dated back to the 1980s. The trick was to make Saifullah believe that—if he left Pakistan—he would finally have his shot with the then-retail giant.

Many of the actual details surrounding the Kmart ruse cannot be published. The general, unclassified logistics of the plan can be described. Charles Stern, Saifullah's New York–based business partner, would get wind of a major business opportunity with Kmart. Stern would relay to Saifullah that buyers for Kmart were prepared to meet in early July 2003. The meeting was expected to take place in Bangkok, Thailand. Stern would be there, as well. Once Saifullah arrived in Bangkok, the plan generally entailed some CIA involvement with his capture and initial detention until the military could ultimately take Saifullah into custody. To avoid any international outcry, Saifullah's detention would be kept quiet for as long as possible.

Senior officials understood the brazenness of the FBI's plan. Logistics alone were a nightmare. There were FBI, CIA, and military requirements.

* Internal documents and author interviews with government officials from multiple agencies detailed their thinking.

Pakistan was still a factor. If the Pakistanis got wind of Saifullah's travel plans, they could shut it down by preventing his departure. Then there was the introduction of Thailand into the plan. Saifullah would need to be captured there before being rendered to the military.

Other factors came into play as well. Saifullah was considered a US person. At a minimum, he was a lawful permanent resident, if not a full-fledged citizen. Lawyers pored through case law, policies, and regulations. Was such a plan even legal? The plan required Saifullah to be detained by the CIA for at least a short period of time. Then he would be handed off to the military. At least Jose Padilla was detained at a Navy brig inside the United States. Under the FBI's plan, Saifullah would be captured and shipped off to Afghanistan. Ultimately, the FBI lawyers agreed that the proposed plan was legally sufficient—with one caveat. Saifullah would need to be treated with kid gloves. Harsh treatment was officially ruled out.

Saifullah was nearly fifty-six years old and in questionable health, anyway. The physical capture in Thailand would be conducted as gently as possible.

But gentle is a relative term. Saifullah wasn't a small man. He was somewhat obese. The plan essentially required that Saifullah be physically accosted. A certain amount of violence was expected. In fact, it would be unavoidable.

Beyond the logistical issues, it was far from a sure thing that Saifullah would leave the safety of Pakistan in the first place. The betting odds were that Saifullah would refuse to travel. If that were to happen, the FBI's idea would be dead in the water. Officials openly expressed serious doubts that the plan would work. There was just so much else that could go wrong.

To make matters even more complicated, there also was the Stern factor. The plan hinged on Stern selling Saifullah on the Kmart meeting, with the FBI pulling the strings. Stern could quite easily prove to be a flop. After all, he had watched the FBI escort Uzair out of his Garment District office. Stern could theoretically advise his longtime friend not to travel.

The FBI's plan to capture Saifullah Paracha was a Hail Mary, but it was the best idea they could devise. The Bureau proposed the idea to their relevant interagency partners—the CIA, Department of Defense, and the

White House. Despite the skepticism, all agreed to give the plan a shot. At this point, the US had nothing to lose.

* * *

Charles Stern called Saifullah on Saturday, July 5, 2003, speaking quickly and excitedly, even violating the Jewish Sabbath to make the call. He was slightly manic.

For Saifullah, the news Stern conveyed was too good to be true.

Stern was staying at the Shangri-La Hotel in Bangkok, a five-star luxury resort known for hosting high-level diplomatic and business events. He was in Thailand on a work trip when he had a chance meeting with some buyers from Kmart. They wanted to make inroads into the Pakistani textile market. Stern, of course, informed the buyers that his partner specialized in textile imports and exports involving Pakistan. Stern reiterated to Saifullah that the Kmart buyers were major players in the industry and such a deal did not come along often. These men were already in Bangkok on other business and wanted to fit in a meeting with Saifullah and Stern. This could be a very big deal.

Saifullah was caught off guard, and he told Stern to calm down. It was a lot to process with the overseas travel, the preparation required, and logistics. Saifullah wanted to think things through. To him, something just did not feel right at first. He wanted to go into this with a clear head.

But Stern was adamant. He told Saifullah that the meeting was scheduled for the morning of Monday, July 7. He added that Saifullah's presence was required to close the deal.

As the call continued, Saifullah became increasingly agitated. Wasn't Stern perfectly capable of handling the business meeting? He was Saifullah's partner, after all. He'd managed many similar meetings on his own with no problem. In fact, Stern was quite adept at negotiating agreements that focused on the Pakistan market. IMG itself was for years devoted to imports/exports between the US and Pakistan. Saifullah continued to question why the buyers insisted on Saifullah personally traveling to Bangkok to meet with them.

Stern repeatedly brushed those concerns aside. All he knew was that Saifullah needed to be there. The buyers were ready to make a deal and wanted to meet with him personally.

Saifullah had never really seen this side of Stern. He took a deep breath and told him he would make the travel arrangements, which he did by calling his travel agent and arranging for an airline ticket to Bangkok scheduled for that night.

Then came a hiccup. Saifullah was informed that his airline ticket was refused. A visa was required, and it couldn't be prepared in time.

Normally, Saifullah would be up in arms. He would call one of his many contacts to get his visa expedited. But in this instance, Saifullah was rather relieved. Although he should have been exhilarated at the prospect of finally gaining a Kmart contract, something just didn't seem right about the situation. Saifullah couldn't identify exactly why he was so blasé on the matter. His gut indicated that something was off. But that was now moot. His travel request had been declined.

After receiving word that his airline ticket was rejected, Saifullah called Stern at his Bangkok hotel to break the bad news. In a reversal of their usual work styles, Stern was up in arms. He told Saifullah that the deal was too important to lose out on. Stern would stay in Bangkok and convince the buyers to wait for him if need be. Stern then told Saifullah to stand by. He was handwriting a letter on Shangri-La Hotel letterhead. When he got off the phone, Stern faxed the letter to the Thai Consulate in Karachi.

Saifullah never saw the letter. All he knew was that a travel visa had been miraculously approved in what seemed like record time. He'd gone from receiving an outright refusal to process his visa to a visa approval for travel that same day. In just a few hours, Saifullah was booked for Thai Airways Flight TG502 departing later that night out of Karachi and destined to arrive in Thailand. He was assigned seat number 62F.

Saifullah's apprehension continued. Farhat sensed that her husband was "quite perturbed at Charles's insistence." But being the sort of alpha male that he was, Saifullah believed that it was his obligation to attend the meeting. As he said many times before, the business must go on.

It was settled. Stern had arranged for a car service to pick Saifullah up at the Bangkok airport. The driver would take him to the Shangri-La Hotel. The meeting with the Kmart buyers would take place on Monday morning.

Saifullah should have been excited, but as he packed his bag, he began to have second thoughts about the trip.

* * *

Saifullah was driven by limousine to the Karachi airport, accompanied by his wife, Farhat, and their son, Mustafa. The boy was fourteen at the time, and he could tell that his mother did not want Saifullah to travel. They were just going through the motions because that is what Saifullah did. He wasn't particularly driven by emotions. But his father was always a businessman first and foremost. The trip was set up, and everything had been arranged for the meeting in Bangkok. It would be rude for Saifullah to back out now.

"I think he had the idea that something was about to go wrong, but he didn't really have an idea what," Mustafa later recounted, adding that he also had a "weird, impending feeling of doom."

Mustafa, who was into video games, felt like he needed to say something as his father was preparing to depart. He quietly asked Saifullah to bring him back a computer graphics card from Bangkok. Saifullah offered his son an indulgent smile and said he would.

Standing in the walkway outside the airport terminal, as Saifullah kissed Farhat goodbye, they exchanged quizzical looks. It was almost as if they were both overcome by sadness for a moment but didn't know why. Saifullah attempted to lighten the mood by flashing his goofy grin. It didn't work. Farhat feigned a smile and turned around to leave, with Mustafa in tow.

Alone now, Saifullah made his way through the Karachi airport, procuring his ticket and checking a bag inside the terminal. His next stop was at the Pakistani immigration desk. There, the Pakistani Federal Investigation Agency (FIA) was tasked with permitting or denying travel abroad. The FIA maintained what was known as an Exit Control List (ECL), which barred certain people from traveling outside of Pakistan. The thought crossed Saifullah's mind that he might be on that list.

At the FIA station, Saifullah waited as the officer checked his passport and looked him up and down. The officer appeared perplexed. He checked his computer screen and took another look at Saifullah. Then he checked the screen again. The process seemed to be taking longer than normal. Saifullah stood there waiting for the verdict. Finally, with a wave of the officer's hand, Saifullah was allowed to proceed to the Thai Airways gate, where he waited for the plane to begin boarding.

Saifullah's apprehension had not subsided. He considered turning around and going home, imagining what he would say to Stern to explain why he had declined to attend the meeting. But backing out wasn't something Saifullah was used to doing. His failure to make the trip at the last minute would be viewed as poor form and could even jeopardize the Kmart deal. Saifullah needed to do something to keep his mind occupied while he waited to board the plane. He sat down, pulled out his cell phone from his pocket, and called his eldest daughter, Muneeza. They chatted for a while. Their conversation continued as passengers began boarding the plane. Saifullah did not leave his seat in the waiting area. He remained on the phone, talking and joking with Muneeza.

Eventually, the gate attendant announced that it was Saifullah's turn to board the aircraft, but Saifullah remained in his seat. He was still on the phone and in no hurry to get on that plane. He continued to talk to his daughter. After another long minute had passed, Saifullah looked up and realized that he was nearly alone in the waiting area.

All the Thai Airways Flight TG502 passengers had boarded the plane except one.

CHAPTER 10

RENDITION AND DARKNESS

The buzz at Bagram's military detention zone was at fever pitch. Army soldiers were told that the HVD—the much-anticipated big fish—might be arriving in the next few days. But it was hardly a done deal, with some placing the odds at 50/50. Regardless of the uncertainty, the soldiers were ordered to prepare the detention facility for the arrival.

Agent Ruby, the investigator for the DOD Criminal Investigative Task Force (CITF), was now openly lobbying her supervisors to let her have a crack at the HVD, should he actually arrive at Bagram. It was no secret that Agent Ruby felt she was ready for more substantial interviews than mere foot soldiers or innocent Afghans caught up in the military dragnet.

In early July, the CITF leadership at Bagram had relented to some degree. They told Agent Ruby that they had no objection to her participation in any interviews regarding the potential HVD. At the same time, her CITF supervisors attempted to tamp down her expectations. As a preliminary matter, she was reminded that the HVD might never make it to Bagram. Officials in Washington, DC, might change their minds and hand him over to the CIA, after all. Things changed all the time in Afghanistan. The CIA pulling a fast one to take control at the last minute? Not unheard of. In fact, some in leadership believed that to be the most likely outcome.

Or it could be that the US government might simply fail to capture the HVD. For CITF, many of the particulars surrounding the FBI's Kmart gambit were vague. What they did know was that the entire operation hinged on whether the HVD would leave Pakistan. By early July 2003, no one seemed to know what he would do.

Regardless, preparation was key for any investigator. CITF leadership provided Agent Ruby with everything they knew about the potential detainee. His name was Saifullah Paracha, a Pakistani national who held some sort of US person status as a lawful permanent resident. The Department of Defense had undertaken the unusual process of designating Paracha as an enemy combatant prior to capture. Paracha was accused of plotting with senior al Qaeda operatives to ship explosives, possibly nuclear weapons, into the United States under the cover of his import/export business.

Agent Ruby couldn't wait to get at Paracha. Of the hundreds of detainees who passed through Bagram during her time there, none were so brazenly involved in a plotted attack within the US itself. This was big-time. It was what Agent Ruby had been training for her entire career. Perhaps for her entire life. She was extremely confident that she could get Paracha to talk and would go to bed knowing that she had saved lives.

Of course, the Fourth of July is an American holiday, but at Bagram, the work never stopped. There were countless detainees to care for. Interviews needed to be conducted. Combat missions were in full force. New detainees were streaming in. Certainly, there were some Independence Day gatherings on the base for service members and contractors to attend. Some special meals featuring hot dogs and hamburgers, and it was movie night. But other than those small reminders of home, the mission continued unabated.

Agent Ruby received a short briefing on that day. CITF supervisors told her that Paracha was expected to arrive at Bagram sometime during the upcoming week. But again, they reminded her that all of this was contingent on Paracha leaving Pakistan. Agent Ruby also learned that some other people were set to arrive at Bagram. They were involved in the Paracha case. Some of these individuals would most likely participate in Paracha's interviews if he showed up. Agent Ruby understood this was a major case. To her, it would be fun to have some other agents in the room. She could work with anyone. Most of Agent Ruby's previous detainee interviews were conducted with another CITF agent in the room, and they had always gone well. CITF supervisors advised Agent Ruby to meet with her fellow interviewers once they arrived, if indeed it all panned out with the detainee.

The next day, Agent Ruby's colleagues arrived at Bagram. Agent Ruby sought to meet them several times. They were always someplace else when she got there. A few times, the door to a conference room or office was closed, indicating that a briefing was going on. That evening, Agent Ruby became increasingly agitated. It didn't make sense that these people were going out of their way not to meet one of the agents expected to be engaged in the interview. This was a priority case, after all.

Agent Ruby confronted her CITF leadership, asking them what the deal was. They just shrugged their shoulders. They did inform her, however, that the two other interviewers were holed up in an office. One was an FBI agent. The other was a representative from the ubiquitous "Other Governmental Agency (OGA)"—which usually meant CIA. Frustrated, Agent Ruby dashed out and rushed to that office.

When she got there, the door was closed. She loudly rapped on the door three times. A woman's voice responded from the inside. "Come in," the woman called out, pleasantly enough but with a firm tone.

Agent Ruby opened the door and entered the small room. Papers and documents were strewn over a table. A computer with access to the classified networks was on. Several phones were scattered on a desk.

At the table were two people, a man and a woman. The man smiled and offered a polite wave. The woman was all business. She nodded at Agent Ruby and offered a crisp, "Hello."

Agent Ruby introduced herself and informed the duo that CITF had tasked her with interviewing Paracha when he arrived. The man and woman shot each other a quick look. This was expected, the woman said, shrugging her shoulders with subtle resignation but otherwise continuing to maintain a polite demeanor.

The man introduced himself as "Bob." As he stated it, his role was to essentially be a "potted plant." In other words, Bob intended on being in the room with Paracha but was not planning on asking many questions. The woman introduced herself as Janelle Miller. She was an FBI agent and had been working this case for some time. Agent Miller and Bob made it abundantly clear that the FBI agent was taking the lead during the interview. Agent Ruby bristled at this supposition and bluntly stated that she was well prepared and preferred not to be just a second "potted plant." Bob and Agent Miller gazed back at Agent Ruby as they listened to her speak. Their expressions betrayed some surprise at Agent Ruby's aggressive attitude, but they just nodded and said they understood.

Agent Miller remained noncommittal regarding Agent Ruby's specific role. Instead, she advised Agent Ruby that there were some complications that might make the entire conversation moot. Essentially, neither the FBI nor the CIA could confirm whether Paracha had even boarded the plane to Bangkok. Agent Miller, Agent Ruby, and Bob were in the dark, and it could be several hours before they would know for sure.

Meanwhile, as the sun was setting over Bagram, an Army Specialist (SPC) attended a briefing with his commander and a few noncommissioned officers (NCOs). An Army SPC is what's known as a lower-enlisted soldier who holds the pay grade of E-4. The SPC rank is one step above Private First Class and within the same pay grade as a corporal. An SPC is one step below that of a buck sergeant.

SPC Smith was told to pack a small bag.* He might be going on a quick trip. The commander didn't tell him where he was going. In fact, the commander didn't provide much detail at all. Instead, the specialist was informed that, for the foreseeable future, he needed to be on call. His commander and NCOs should be able to always reach him. The soldier would inform his NCOs whenever he went to sleep, ate chow, or attended a social event. He was to alert them about all his movements.

SPC Smith didn't ask any questions. Instead, he just nodded and said he would follow the orders. The conversation took less than five minutes. But as of the evening of July 5, 2003, SPC Smith knew that, at any moment, he could be ordered to board a military aircraft and fly to an unknown destination. SPC Smith would then ultimately escort a singular detainee onto the aircraft.

The commander added that he did not believe the mission would take place. In fact, based on the information that he had received, the need for SPC Smith to travel was looking extremely unlikely. But, the commander added, he wanted to get SPC Smith up to speed anyway, just in case.

* * *

* SPC "Smith" and other military personnel described his role to the author in interviews several years later.

Darkness. Completely and totally black. He couldn't hear anything, either. Not a sound. His limbs were not working. He wasn't even sure if he was standing or sitting. And his shoulder hurt. He was in pain. He tried to speak, but he couldn't tell if any sounds were coming out of his mouth when his lips moved. It was complete and utter disorientation.

Just minutes earlier, Saifullah had disembarked from the plane. He retrieved his bag and spotted his driver, who was waiting for him. It was just as Stern had said. The driver stood inside the airport displaying a placard that said, "S. Paracha."*

Now that Saifullah was on the ground in Bangkok, he was starting to feel better about things. His anxiety all but vanished. He began preparing his game face for the big Kmart meeting, even allowing himself to anticipate all the benefits and accolades that would be coming his way if he could close the deal. He was looking forward to his next stop, which would be the luxurious Shangri-La Hotel.

Then something happened. Saifullah recalled walking in a parking garage. Masked men suddenly appeared. Someone placed a bag or a hood over his head. He felt his body slam onto the ground. Or was it the trunk of a car? Saifullah tried to struggle but he was overpowered. He could barely move. Saifullah sensed that the masked men were struggling to lift him. He was, after all, a heavyset man.

The masked assailants finally managed to toss Saifullah into some kind of vehicle. Maybe a van or station wagon? Someone probably landed on top of him, pinning him to the floor. Saifullah screeched in pain.

"My shoulder! My shoulder!" he screamed. His mouth was quickly muzzled.

As far as Saifullah could tell, the masked men never spoke, just a few grunts as they attempted to take him to the ground. He lost his sense of time. He was aware that the vehicle was now moving. But where were they taking him?

The hood made it difficult to breathe. He realized that he was huffing and puffing. He feared that he would have a heart attack. Did these masked

---

* This account of Saifullah's time in Thailand is based on author interviews with government officials, Saifullah's attorneys, internal documentation, court records, and Saifullah's statements to the FBI.

men know that he had medical conditions? His shoulder continued to hurt. Saifullah tried again to speak out, but he couldn't get anybody's attention. Nobody was going to help him.

Saifullah tried to calm himself down. He forced his mind to be analytical. As he later recalled, his first thoughts were the following: "This is an American operation. I'll be all right." Somehow, his theory that the Americans were behind his kidnapping put him slightly more at ease than the thought of being taken by Pakistanis, who in 2003 were notorious for brutality. The CIA's EIT program was not yet public knowledge.

A lawyer by the name of Gaillard Hunt, who later represented Saifullah on a habeas corpus petition filed in 2004, summed up his client's attitude: "He definitely was abused, at the first encounter there in Thailand. But his policy all along was 'I'm completely innocent, I'll talk to anybody. No need to use thumbscrews.'"

In the darkness, Saifullah began piecing together the events of the last few days. He now realized that the Kmart deal was too good to be true. If Saifullah could move his legs, he would kick himself for not trusting his instincts. He never should have boarded that plane.

His mind eventually drifted back to his theory that this was an American operation. In Saifullah's eyes, he was a New Yorker. He was tough. He could handle anything the Americans had in store for him. Besides, America was based on the rule of law. He told himself he would be okay. The matter would be resolved and Saifullah would return to his family. Like Uzair's situation, this was all just one big misunderstanding. Saifullah just needed to put on his businessman hat and make a deal. It was no different than negotiating with Kmart. Saifullah would work it out and be home soon. With any luck, he would even be able to negotiate Uzair's return. Perhaps there would be a silver lining.

As the vehicle bounced along toward its mysterious destination, Saifullah continued to fret about his family, knowing they would be worried sick. Hopefully, he would be able to send them a message. But first, Saifullah needed to figure out where he was going.

At some point, Saifullah sensed that the vehicle had stopped. He could feel his breath on the bag or hood that covered his head. His legs and hands were cuffed behind his back. The masked men had essentially hog-tied him.

He was moved to what he described as an "unknown place," put in a chair, still cuffed. His eyes and ears remained covered. He waited and waited for someone to provide instructions. Or to at least identify themselves. But while in this unknown place, no one spoke to him. He was trapped alone with his thoughts.

The brief interactions were swift and impersonal. Someone provided liquid nourishment, possibly a dietary supplement like Ensure. There were no bathroom breaks—only a bucket. Someone might have briefly looked at his shoulder. He wasn't sure. It was sore but the pain had subsided. And that was the extent of Saifullah's interactions with anything outside of his own mind and that solitary chair in this unknown place. Saifullah spent hours, or it might have been days as far as he could tell, just feeling himself breathe.

As he sat there, he began to stew. At a certain point, he was downright angry. Didn't these people know who he was? Saifullah resented being treated like some animal. He was a sophisticated man. A respected philanthropist. Why couldn't these people simply talk to him like a human being? Saifullah was open to that. They could cut a deal.

A year later, Saifullah described his anger as follows:

> I reached Bangkok International Airport . . . and at the airport I was illegally and immorally arrested—back hand/leg cuffed, black big mask on my head up to neck, was thrown on floor of station wagon facing down. I am heart patient / diabetic / high blood pressure / skin disorder, gout; it could have been fatal, there was no human consideration at all. From the airport I was taken to unknown place for few days and kept eyes covered, ears cover, handcuffed, leg cuffed. . . . Am I being considered human being or animal, or is USA my God?

Saifullah and his lawyer suspected that the "unknown place" was "most likely a black site in Thailand operated by US intelligence agencies." But stuck to that chair, Saifullah had lost all sense of time. All he could do was stare into the blackness.

After much time had passed—he didn't know if it was day or night—Saifullah sensed some activity around him. Then someone stood him on his feet. They were moving him, guiding him as he shuffled his feet. That's all he could do considering the shackles on his ankles.

Saifullah hoped that he was finally going to get his chance to speak to somebody. Anybody. His eyes and ears were still covered, and someone was leading him, almost like a dog.

Saifullah soon sensed that he was outside. His invisible leader forced Saifullah to stop. He stood still for what seemed like several minutes. He wondered if anyone could see him.

Then Saifullah was again on the move. He shuffled some more. He was forced to stop again. Then more shuffling. He was now making his way up a ramp of some sort. The floor felt like it was vibrating. At the top, he was again forced to shuffle and felt his thighs brush against some hard objects.

Someone gently pushed his head down. Saifullah went to his knees. He was then placed onto a floor. It was still vibrating. He couldn't tell how long he had been there when the vibrations suddenly intensified. For the first time in days, Saifullah recognized something familiar about his surroundings. The movement and feel of the floor were unmistakable. Saifullah knew he was in an airplane.

* * *

SPC Smith's mission was kind of boring. It caused him to miss a prearranged phone call home with his fiancée. But whatever, he thought. It was only a day out of his routine.

His commander had asked him to be on call. If the word came, SPC Smith was expected to drop everything and board a military aircraft. From there, he would sign a document confirming the transfer of a detainee into military custody. This is exactly what occurred.

Once the plane landed, SPC Smith stepped onto the tarmac. A detainee—hooded and cuffed—shuffled toward him. Some other men not in uniform were moving him along. One man simply pushed a clipboard into SPC Smith's face. SPC Smith didn't think much about it—he didn't even read the paper. He simply removed a pen from his pocket and signed at the bottom. SPC Smith then guided the detainee toward a ramp and up into the aircraft. Per instructions, SPC Smith positioned the detainee on the floor.

One of the men from the tarmac briefly joined SPC Smith on the plane. The man carried a bag. Inside the bag was the detainee's "pocket litter," as well as corresponding inventory slips documenting each item. The detainee had Pakistani documentation that identified him as Saifullah Paracha. He also had a New York driver's license from the 1980s for some reason. In addition, there was a checkbook from a Pakistani bank. Curiously, the name on the check was not Saifullah Paracha. It was Sharafuddin Shamim. There was one other notable item in his pocket litter. A Casio electronic planner. After dropping off the bag containing the pocket litter, the man quickly departed.

The plane's engines never stopped running. SPC Smith didn't even see the pilots step out of the cockpit. They were probably on the ground for less than thirty minutes.

With the detainee safely secured on the floor, SPC Smith could relax while the aircraft returned to Bagram. He noticed that the detainee was a big guy. Not tall and muscular; more like kind of a fat dude. And maybe old, too. SPC Smith just looked down at the detainee and shrugged his shoulders.

After eating a candy bar while slouched in a seat perched above the detainee, washing it down with a bottle of water, SPC Smith dozed off at some point. When he came to, the plane was getting ready to land. The detainee's chest was still rising and falling—so he was still alive. Overall, the trip to take custody of detainee Paracha was a pleasant getaway for SPC Smith.

When the plane landed, several young soldiers were on hand to greet the new arrivals. Saifullah was quickly whisked away into a detainee induction room. SPC Smith then hooted and hollered with some of his friends as they discussed the day's events. They watched as the detainee was stripped naked for his medical examination. At that point, SPC Smith and some of his friends grimaced. They had no desire to see a naked old man.

Someone yanked the hood off Saifullah's head. The detainee was wide-eyed as he took in his new surroundings. He had a thousand-yard stare as a young female soldier took photographs of his naked body. These pictures were to document the detainee's physical condition. A doctor asked the detainee about any medical issues. The detainee complained about some shoulder pain. He then listed off several prescriptions and medical conditions. He just kept going on and on about it. All of this was in English, which was different from the normal guys who filtered through Bagram. The Urdu interpreter silently stood there and never had to say a word. The doctor promised the detainee that he would work to get the prescriptions as soon as possible. The detainee was then taken away.

SPC Smith continued to hang around, joking with his friends. They made plans for dinner at the chow hall later that evening. After that, SPC Smith thought he might try to give his fiancée a call.

* * *

July 6, 2003. Farhat's worst fears began early that day. She had dropped Saifullah off at the Karachi airport the night before. Their oldest daughter, Muneeza, reported that Saifullah had called her right before boarding the aircraft. They at least could confirm that Saifullah made it onto the plane. Something must have happened after that because she hadn't heard from her husband, and everywhere Farhat turned, she received no answers.

The phone eventually rang, and it was Charles Stern. Of course, this immediately caused concern. Saifullah should have been with him. Why on earth would Stern be calling?

The alarm intensified once Stern began speaking and asked, "Why didn't Saif come to Bangkok?"

Farhat shook with emotion. Obviously, Saifullah *had* gone to Bangkok. She barked into the phone, demanding that Stern explain.

"The car that I sent to pick him up from the Bangkok airport returned empty," Stern replied. In other words, Saifullah never made it to the Shangri-La Hotel. He was nowhere to be found.

Farhat was in a full-blown panic. Her husband was missing. He might even be dead.

Had Saif suffered a heart attack during the journey? As his wife for many years, Farhat was acutely aware of her husband's medical conditions. Although he had never had a heart attack, Saifullah was diabetic and had high blood pressure. Farhat believed that Saifullah might be in a foreign hospital somewhere. She was desperate to find him.

After listening to Stern for another minute, Farhat slammed the phone down. Stern was useless. According to Farhat, Stern was devoid of emotion during the call. He also demonstrated no initiative whatsoever in helping Farhat locate her husband. She was already extremely angry that he essentially "coerced" Saifullah into traveling. But she'd deal with Stern's nonsense later. Her primary concern was determining whether her husband was even alive.

Farhat's first call was to the police in Karachi. They expressed confusion as to why she would be calling them. The police refused to register a complaint regarding a missing person. Farhat then began calling virtually all relevant Pakistani offices that she could think of to find out where her husband had been taken, likely a hospital somewhere, she told herself.

The Pakistani authorities were completely unhelpful. They had no information to provide. Farhat was incensed. Saifullah would never be treated this poorly if he were making these calls. Yet, Farhat was getting the complete runaround. It was like the Pakistani authorities were going out of their way to frustrate her efforts.

In addition to the Pakistanis, Farhat also attempted to contact Thai authorities, beginning at the Thai Consulate in Karachi. She wasn't asking for the moon, she thought. Farhat just wanted to know where her husband was. The Thai authorities were equally unhelpful. The airline confirmed that Thai Airways Flight TG502 had landed on time without any issues or delays. The airline refused to confirm whether Saifullah was even on the flight. The confusion and distress were overwhelming.

After getting nowhere with both the Pakistani and Thai authorities, Farhat was at a loss and struggled to maintain her composure. She couldn't comprehend what was happening. Airline passengers simply don't just vanish into thin air. She kept glancing over at the front door of their Karachi home, expecting Saifullah to waltz in with some type of crazy excuse. But that wasn't like him.

"To not inform us of his whereabouts of his own accord was extremely unusual for him," she later recalled during a press interview. Farhat knew something was very wrong. She'd had a sense of foreboding even before Saifullah departed that night.

Farhat went over things in her head for the thousandth time. Stern pressured Saifullah into traveling to Bangkok. Farhat and Mustafa dropped Saifullah off at the Karachi airport. According to Muneeza, Saifullah made it to the gate and must have boarded the plane. But nobody could confirm for sure whether he made it onto the flight. Now Stern says that Saifullah never used the car that was dispatched for him at the Bangkok airport, nor did Saifullah arrive at the Shangri-La Hotel via some other means.

As Farhat slowly took stock of the situation, she began to suspect that maybe it wasn't a coincidence after all that the authorities were failing to act. Her mind turned to Uzair. Her son had been rotting away in a New York jail ever since late March 2003, when she learned through a heart-wrenching phone call that her son was accused of assisting al Qaeda operatives. Could Saifullah's sudden disappearance be related?

Farhat resolved to continue making inquiries. But first, she had to tell the children, not an easy task. Farhat's words to her children were firm and clear. She was not going to give up and was most certainly not going to take the Pakistani and Thai authorities' intransigence lying down. Instead, she would do what Saifullah always did, fight like hell. In another press interview, Farhat recounted her efforts to locate Saifullah:

> We tried to locate him through Thai Airways and whatever other resources we had, but to no avail. Finally, when no trace of my husband was found for three days, a letter was sent to the Thai Airways on July 8th in which a request for providing the flight record was made. But the local manager of the airline declined to receive the letter. Subsequently a registered letter was sent to the airline. In reply, the airline confirmed that Mr. Paracha had indeed left by the TG flight. During this period, I also wrote letters to the President, the Interior Ministry, the Foreign Ministry and the Pakistani embassy in Bangkok, but no reply was received. I filed a petition in the Sind High Court on July 25th to find out the whereabouts of my husband, in which the government of Pakistan, Thai consulate, Thai Airways and Pakistani intelligence agencies were parties. This was done because I was frustrated at the silence from all quarters.

Farhat's persistence would later be rewarded with answers, some more harrowing than she or her family could bear.

CHAPTER 11

THE INTERVIEWER, A NOTETAKER, AND A STORY

In 2003, the FBI's relationship with the Department of Defense's Criminal Investigative Task Force (CITF) was still being defined. Tasked in 2002 with essentially being the military's law enforcement arm, the CITF had the responsibility of gathering evidence for the nascent military commission war crimes trials. These trials were expected to take place at the detention facility at Guantanamo Bay, which received its first detainees in January 2002.* Once the CIA transferred custody of detainees to the military, the CITF by design gained a seat at the table regarding any law enforcement actions.

In practice, the FBI typically took the lead.

The relationship between the FBI and CITF was highly uncertain when Saifullah Paracha first arrived at Bagram Air Base. At the time, there was no procedural mechanism for information sharing with respect to law enforcement functions. A Memorandum of Understanding (MOU) between the FBI and CITF designed to fix this relationship would not be signed until late 2004. And that MOU was believed to be necessary, in part, because of the CITF experience in the Paracha matter.

Agent Ruby Caine, the Army sergeant assigned to CITF, had received bits and pieces of information about Saifullah, but mostly to do with Saifullah's potential arrival at Bagram rather than the particulars of his case. She

* Former CIA captives such as KSM, Ali Abdul Aziz Ali, and Majid Khan would not be transferred to Guantanamo Bay until 2006.

knew about Saifullah largely through generalities gleaned from informal dissemination of information. Meanwhile, the FBI's Janelle Miller and Bob from the CIA could practically recite Saifullah's entire life from memory. In addition, every bit of data on Saifullah was contained in the thousands of documents at their disposal. Agent Ruby had to rely on raw information and data that was hastily transcribed by hand onto loose pieces of paper. She didn't even know about Uzair's arrest.

Agent Ruby was not happy—underused and disrespected. When in the room with Agent Miller and Bob, her body language betrayed her muted aggravation at being abused in this way.

The truth was that the CITF's role wasn't factored in when the FBI was drawing up plans to capture Saifullah. The reason was that the FBI did not really view Saifullah as a typical war criminal. He wasn't believed to be the stone-cold killer like KSM and the other 9/11 plotters. Paracha also did not fit the more traditional war criminal *modus operandi* of detainees such as the Afghan, Obaidullah, who was accused of storing bomb-making materials on behalf of al Qaeda and the Taliban. Instead, Saifullah was viewed more in the prism of traditional law enforcement along with his son, Uzair, albeit through a much more serious lens. In that respect, Saifullah was essentially looked upon as a shifty New York businessman and lawful permanent resident who had cast his lot with al Qaeda. The FBI went into the case as if it were a traditional law enforcement matter and not necessarily a military issue.

On July 5, 2003, Saifullah had ended the call with his daughter at the Karachi airport and boarded his flight for Thailand. Until that moment, the FBI had serious doubts that they would ever be able to get a hold of the elder Paracha as much as the FBI wanted to get him into their custody. The race to capture Saifullah became a completely interagency affair. This meant that the FBI was forced to work directly with the CIA, and vice versa, and the military also eventually played a role.

During that interagency process, the CIA continued to hold out hopes that they would gain exclusive custody of Saifullah. Torture was on the table based on the seriousness of the matter. The CIA's efforts led to Saifullah being declared by the Department of Defense an enemy combatant. That designation caused Saifullah to fall into the military paradigm. Although it was ultimately the FBI that orchestrated the plot to lure Saifullah out of Pakistan, the die was cast. Saifullah was not going to end up in federal court. Instead, he would belong to the military.

Agent Ruby remained largely in the dark. All she knew was that this detainee was transferred into military custody, which meant he was in her pond. Sure, he was more like a white-collar war criminal, but he was a war criminal, nonetheless. Therefore, Agent Ruby reasoned that CITF agents should be the ones to take their crack at Saifullah, even—as she realized after meeting Agent Miller and Bob—it became clear how unprepared she was to take the lead.

As all three agents prepared to meet Saifullah for the first time, Agent Ruby readied several questions she was determined to ask the detainee. But in each instance, Agent Miller shot her down. The FBI agent wasn't being malicious or petty at all. She just believed that this specific detainee interview required significant rapport building. They needed to build trust with Saifullah rather than peppering him with accusatory questions, which would be counterproductive in the long run. The interview needed to be subtle, prolonged.

Agent Miller's vision for the interview was to be guided by much the same strategy that she had pursued with Uzair. Allow the detainee to talk, even pontificate. And when the time is right, let the detainee proverbially hang himself with his own noose. Bob appeared to be 100 percent on board with Agent Miller's strategy, and his deference to the FBI irked Agent Ruby to no end.

As the moment to meet Saifullah approached, Agent Ruby threw her hands in the air, protesting fiercely to the others, "I'm not just a notetaker! I want to play a real role."

Agent Miller sighed as Bob looked on without expression. Although nobody recalls the exact language that Agent Miller used, she essentially issued the following demand to the upstart CITF agent: You can sit in on the interview; you can take notes during the interview; you will keep your mouth shut during the interview.

Agent Miller maintained her firm, businesslike demeanor. If it wasn't clear before, then it was now. She was in charge.

* * *

Agent Miller had been warned. Bagram handled detainees differently than the Bureau did. She could expect to be surprised—shocked even—by the treatment of Saifullah Paracha she would witness. And while she certainly expected that Paracha would be somewhat haggard, particularly considering how he was captured and rendered to military custody, when she finally met him for the first time, she was quite taken aback.*

Earlier, FBI agents who operated in Afghanistan had informed Agent Miller that it was common to find detainees hooded or blindfolded. One agent reported that soldiers had placed green sandbags over people's heads. Ostensibly, the hoods were used for military safety and security purposes. The military didn't want detainees observing their surroundings. This was much different than how typical criminal suspects or convicts in FBI hands were treated. Uzair Paracha wasn't even handcuffed when he was first escorted out of Charles Stern's Manhattan office.

Agent Miller was now ready to meet Saifullah. She had been preparing for this moment since his name resurfaced in connection to Majid Khan and KSM back in March. And while Uzair's effort to assist Khan entering the US had been thwarted, Saifullah was much more aligned to senior al Qaeda leaders. Most importantly, Saifullah was key to learning about the plot to smuggle explosives—possibly even a nuclear device or chemical and biological agents—into the US through the port system. Many within the intelligence community still believed that weapons of mass destruction might be on their way, or at least in an advanced stage of shipment. Time was of the essence. The responsibility fell to Agent Miller to dissect the plot and determine exactly how far it had progressed. Countless lives could be in danger. It all hinged on getting Saifullah to talk—the old-fashioned way. Torture was not permitted, not that Agent Miller wanted that option anyway.

The key component of Agent Miller's interrogation technique would be to develop a rapport with Saifullah. She decided to greet him in his cell and personally escort him to a meeting room.

So, she asked to be guided to Saifullah's cell by a uniformed military NCO. She was dismayed by what she saw when the cell door opened.

---

* Court records, internal documentation, and author interviews detail Saifullah Paracha's interactions at Bagram.

She later recounted that Paracha was "in his cell . . . sitting on the ground, blindfolded with ear coverings on." She said he was shackled and silent. The room was cold. His only real human contact in days had been when he was stripped naked during his medical exam and photographed by the female soldier. Otherwise, Saifullah's treatment was defined by prolonged sensory deprivation. For a man who craved the limelight and demanded respect, this was deeply humiliating.

Agent Miller asked her soldier escort why Saifullah was being subjected to sensory deprivation. The soldier had no real answer; perhaps it was for some undefined safety reason. The soldier also conjectured that the treatment may have been designed to make the detainee more cooperative during his interrogations. It remained unknown who ordered Saifullah to continue being deprived of sensory stimuli. It certainly wasn't Agent Miller, who bristled at how this detainee had been tormented in this way.

The NCO advised Agent Miller that Saifullah would have to continue wearing the blindfold, ear coverings, and shackles during his transport to the meeting room. It was standard operating procedure, the soldier noted. Agent Miller cringed. This was not how she wanted to start her interview. But she couldn't run the risk of defying the military at this point. She followed along as the soldier guided Saifullah out of his cell. The sound of chains on his hand and leg shackles clanked with his every movement.

Eventually, the group made it to the designated meeting room. Military guards were waiting at the door. The windowless room itself was small and bare except for a table and chairs. Metal loops were secured to the floor. The military guards assisted in seating Saifullah at one of the chairs. A guard then attached the shackles to the loops on the floor. Agent Miller shook her head. She wanted to say something about the shackles, but she decided to wait so Saifullah could hear her objections and feel like she was looking out for him.

Agents Miller and Ruby, and Bob, stood toward the back of the room. Each carried a small notebook and pen. After Saifullah was seated and shackled to the floor, a guard carefully removed the ear coverings. Saifullah could now hear the choreographed movements of the guards as they prepared the room. After the ear coverings, a guard removed Saifullah's blindfold. He squinted at the fluorescent lights. The room wasn't particularly bright, but it was the first light he had seen since his medical evaluation.

After his eyes adjusted, Saifullah began assessing the room. That's when Agent Miller first spoke—not to Saifullah, but to the guards.

"Let's remove his shackles," she firmly stated.

The guards looked at each other quizzically.

"Ma'am . . ." one guard started to say, clearly objecting to Agent Miller's request.

The FBI agent wasn't having any of it. She interrupted the guard, stating that it was her interview and she preferred that "Mr. Paracha" be unshackled.

The guards were clearly unsure of how to proceed. Finally, Agent Miller proposed a compromise. Mr. Paracha could remain shackled to the floor, but his hands needed to be free.

The military guards reluctantly agreed as Saifullah quietly watched. Within seconds, Saifullah's hands were free from restraint for the first time since he was violently thrown into that vehicle in Bangkok. Agent Miller then motioned for the guards to leave the room and told them to close the door. There were only four people left in the meeting room: Saifullah, Agent Miller, Agent Ruby, and Bob. Saifullah was only making eye contact with one of his interviewers. That was Agent Miller. He already knew that she was in charge.

Agent Miller pleasantly introduced herself. Saifullah appeared pleased when she extended her hand. He gladly shook it. "Saifullah Paracha," he announced loudly, looking Agent Miller directly in the eye and holding his head up high. He also straightened his posture. Saifullah was transitioning into business mode. He had been looking forward to this opportunity since he was captured.

"It's nice to meet you," Agent Miller responded. She then introduced Agent Ruby and Bob. Everyone shook Saifullah's hand. The interviewers then sat down in their chairs, which were located across the table from Saifullah. Agent Miller sat in the middle, directly across from her subject. Agent Ruby was to her left and Bob sat to her right.

The FBI agent asked if Saifullah would like an Urdu translator. Saifullah scoffed. He explained that he was a lawful permanent resident of the United States and then immediately began rattling off his résumé. "I studied physics in Karachi in college and graduated with honors. I then got admission at the New York Institute of Technology in New York City and was funded by one organization in Pakistan, a youth organization. I studied as a computer systems analyst. I worked in the US for a few years. I pursued business opportunities there. I had offices in Washington, San Francisco, and New York."

Agent Miller nodded, smiled. Saifullah wanted to feel important. She was going to let him speak, even air some of his grievances. He was not happy with how he had been treated. He declared that his treatment was unjustified and unwarranted.

"It was ugly and unprofessional how I was picked up," Saifullah responded angrily, staring intently into Agent Miller's eyes as he leaned his face closer. "I was abruptly and roughly seized when I arrived in Bangkok. I didn't have to be arrested in that manner."

Agent Miller nodded. She indicated that she would have preferred a different approach. She informed Saifullah that she had met his son, Uzair, and spoken to him on numerous occasions.

Saifullah waved his hand. He was animated. "I know the ambassador of Pakistan," Saifullah interjected, speaking loudly and with authority. "I lived there in Pakistan since '86, and I wrote to her when my son was detained in New York. I wrote to her a detailed letter asking to discuss my family's involvement in these affairs. I have called many times to the embassy to clarify myself. They haven't done anything from there."

Saifullah then suggested that the matter could easily be cleared up if he just had the opportunity to follow up with the ambassador. He could even make the call from Bagram. The FBI could listen in for all he cared. Saifullah reminded Agent Miller that he was a well-known businessman and philanthropist in Pakistan.

"You'll need to talk to us first," Agent Miller replied coolly.

"I offer myself voluntarily for anybody," Saifullah stated. "Anywhere. Anytime."

The conversation then moved on to a lively discussion about religion and terrorism. Saifullah stated that he had always been against terrorism. His life's mission, he said, was devoted to bridging the gap between Islam and Christianity. To that end, Saifullah said that he had written numerous letters to US government officials on the subject. It turned out that he was a prolific letter writer. In typical Saifullah fashion, he forcefully stated that not only was he not a terrorist, but that he could have stopped the 9/11 attacks if only powerful Americans would have paid attention to his wisdom.

Saifullah intently discussed how, back in May 2001, he wrote a five-page letter to President George W. Bush and his father, George H. W. Bush. The letter suggested that the Taliban could help the US tackle "communism, terrorism and controlling drugs," if only sanctions would be lifted.

Saifullah told the agents how, after the 9/11 attacks, he wrote additional letters to George W. Bush, urging him to pursue peace in Afghanistan. "People's lives would not have been lost if they paid attention," Saifullah insisted, repeating himself. "Why did no one pay attention to [my first] letter? 9/11 would not have had to happen."

Agent Miller continued to let Saifullah speak. It was good for him to get this out after the circumstances of his capture. After a while, Saifullah offered an unusual proposal, saying in a measured tone, "Please, according to the Bible and Koran, if wisdom were applied, the situation would be different. I am a student of the Koran and of history. I offer my services. I can help to control terrorism, and I need no reward for that. By the law of the Lord Almighty, I have written many papers on Afghanistan and terrorism and will give them to you. You will be pleased to receive them. I am just giving you a brief background. This could be handled more effectively; we could stop terrorism, and terrorism would die itself."

Agent Miller indulged Saifullah, then reiterated that her priority was to learn more about his links to certain al Qaeda operatives. To that end, she wanted Saifullah to answer some questions. Agent Miller firmly conveyed that she needed to hear his answers before anything else could happen.

Saifullah was happy to talk and announced confidently, "I have nothing to hide."

And so it happened that Saifullah was finally able to tell his side of the whole story, which he would retell a number of times while he remained in custody during the years ahead . . .

* * *

It wasn't every day that someone captured Saifullah's attention and imagination. But back in 2000 in Afghanistan, he found himself awestruck. A man was speaking to a group of about fifteen people from Saifullah's philanthropic delegation, who had traveled from Pakistan to extend their charity work to poor Afghans. The speaker was profoundly articulate, almost otherworldly with his ability to cast a spell over his audience, and he had an excellent grasp of the Quran. But more importantly to Saifullah, he was rich, powerful, and influential. Saifullah had to meet him.

One of Saifullah's traits was vociferousness. Saifullah could exude money and power whenever he chose. During this event, with such a charismatic keynote speaker, Saifullah sold himself as a very important person. He hoped that his standing as a wealthy Pakistani entrepreneur would catch the man's fancy.

It did. And the speaker was Usama bin Laden, referred to by his initials, UBL, in various FBI and court documents.

Saifullah recounted for Agent Miller in that initial interview how his first meeting with bin Laden was facilitated. "After the presentation, a gentleman approached me and praised my efforts. He asked me questions about my background and told me his name was Maulana Mahar. He invited me to meet Usama bin Laden. UBL had a very controversial personality. He had close alliance with [the] US during [the] USSR invasion in 1978 into Afghanistan. UBL was very popular and respected among most [of the] Muslim community. He was known throughout the world while the western countries portrayed him as a devil. He was from a very rich and influential Saudi family. His father was [a] close friend [of] the Saudi King."

In his discourse while being questioned by Agent Miller, Saifullah added that bin Laden was not the militant fanatic that the West had made him out to be. "When I met Usama, he delivered [read] the Qur'an [presumably to the audience in the hall], and said he was a prophet. He said nice things, very impressive. He said nothing hateful or negative about the West or any other nation."

When asked by Agent Miller why he would seek a private audience with Usama bin Laden, Saifullah scoffed at the question, suggesting that it was a privilege to meet with such a person. "I was a chairman of Universal Broadcasting in Karachi, which was a television recording studio. I saw an opportunity and requested him to record a TV program in English and gave him my card. He said he would think about it and someone would contact me."

With a straight and earnest face while being questioned by the FBI agent at the table in the interview room, Saifullah said that he had envisioned a television program where he would get bin Laden to discuss efforts to bridge the divide between the West and Islam. Saifullah evidently chose to ignore the fact that, just a few years earlier, bin Laden had declared war against the United States and advocated for the murder of civilians and soldiers alike. As far back as August 1996, bin Laden issued a public "Declaration of Jihad Against the Americans," in which he called for the murder of US military personnel serving in the Arabian Peninsula. Then, in May 1998, bin Laden issued a public statement entitled "The Nuclear Bomb of Islam" under the banner of the "International Islamic Front for Fighting Jews and Crusaders." In that statement, bin Laden flatly stated that "it is the duty of the Muslims to prepare as much force as possible to terrorize the enemies of God."

When Agent Miller confronted Saifullah with those facts, Saifullah didn't think all of that was indicative of bin Laden's true feelings. In fact, Saifullah freely admitted to Agent Miller that he had heard bin Laden speak during a similarly styled Afghanistan trip in 1999 that concluded with a brief meet-and-greet. That trip was no big deal either, he said. Saifullah explained how bin Laden was a kind of folk hero in Pakistan. And if anyone could get to the truth and root of the issue—like the conflict between Islamic nations and the West—it was Saifullah, or so he claimed.

"I wanted to make a program on a common personality between Christian[ity], Judaism, and Islam," Saifullah told Agent Miller matter-of-factly. "The program was designed to try and reduce the gap between the international communities and the Muslim community as much as we can. There are many similarities between the Koran and the Bible, and we wanted to produce those types of programs; ones that describe what the Koran says about Abraham, Mary, Moses and Jesus."

Saifullah explained his private bin Laden meeting in 2000 with gusto. He seemed to be bragging about his ability to connect with such a famous figure. During his discussions with Agent Miller, while Bob and Agent Ruby mostly looked on quietly, Saifullah often incorporated facts about his own businesses that sounded like a sales pitch. He frequently boasted how "Universal Broadcasting has the best equipment." Saifullah came across to Agent Miller and the others in the room as pompous and condescending.

Saifullah also defended his travel to Afghanistan, arguing that it had nothing to do with terrorism. Saifullah insisted that his 1999 and 2000 meetings with Usama bin Laden were solely to, as he put it, "extend our charity work to poor Afghans."

Leaning back in his chair, Saifullah argued that he'd been invited to Afghanistan as part of a delegation of wealthy businessmen. He'd proposed several ideas, including one involving the creation of a bicycle factory. He explained, "I felt extremely [sym]pathetic towards Afghans, therefore, I prepared a small booklet on Afghanistan and requested Pakistan to make investment in basic cottage industries and in farming to create jobs rather than donation. That report was published in the newspaper. Pakistan Rice Exporters Association requested me to lead a delegation of about 90 businessmen and others to Afghanistan. In Kandahar, before the Taliban's Governor and Ministers, I made a humble presentation to the delegations to teach Afghans 'to catch fish rather than feed them fish.'"

As he went on, Saifullah boasted to Agent Miller, Bob, and Agent Ruby about his wealth. He boasted about his philanthropy. He boasted about his connections. Also, it was evident while he was being interviewed by Agent Miller that Saifullah was seeking to bolster his credibility as a secular businessman with honorable, peaceful intentions. Saifullah repeatedly insisted that he was the direct opposite of a hardcore Jihadist.

At one point during the interview, he said, "My organization [Counsel of Welfare Organizations] is a conservative organization formed many years ago; we don't receive or give any money. Being or having lived in the West, I know [how to use] the system to organize things. I wanted to organize education, health and justice, to work them more effectively. I wanted to tell people how to put these on track and be more effective. In order to tell people these things are workable, and we were about 30 people; [all] of them are businessmen and have their own resources. We don't ask people to contribute to this charity work. We ask them for their experience in charity work. We have the soundest schools in poor areas, and we help give them a good secular education. Pakistan and Afghanistan are known for Islamic schools called madrasas. We are emphasizing secular education, because you need a formal education to get a livelihood. . . . I also helped the largest hospital in Karachi—300 beds—that was in bad shape. They had no good toilets, and I helped with my own personal [re]sources."

If Agent Miller's strategy was to let Saifullah get comfortable, it certainly worked, and it didn't take long. The man spoke with pride and without any hint of guilt or remorse. As Saifullah repeatedly told Agent Miller and the others in the room, "I have nothing to hide."

His story about traveling to Afghanistan and meeting Usama bin Laden sounded far-fetched, especially with how things would later turn out. Agent Miller began pressing Saifullah on some outstanding questions. How could Saifullah not know that Usama bin Laden was the leader of al Qaeda, particularly with his declarations of war against the United States and his known involvement in terrorism even before 9/11?

Saifullah simply doubled down. He replied dryly, with a note of petulance, "I never saw any definition of al Qaeda. The time I heard this was from President Bush who said, 'al Qaeda.' I went to Afghanistan not to meet Usama, but people took me to help Afghan people with education."

And even as he denied ever hearing of bin Laden's role with al Qaeda—despite being such a sophisticated, well-connected businessman—Saifullah provided Agent Miller with even more fantastical and self-serving statements. He even suggested that he was on the verge of convincing the Taliban—an organization well known for its exclusion and subjugation of females—that it should fund schools for girls. "I was the one who convinced the Taliban government to have a [girls'] school. I said we would put up the money and give you credit for that. Someone else scheduled to meet Usama took me along with him. I don't have any contact. I was made to meet him, and that's it."

At this stage, it was difficult to tell if Saifullah was lying or just delusional. Agent Miller believed he was indeed deluded in some respects. But it was also obvious that he was leaving some key elements out of his story, such as exactly what he and bin Laden discussed. It just seemed ludicrous that bin Laden would even consider participating in such a peacemaking television program. It also sounded preposterous that Saifullah would even propose such an outlandish idea in the first place.

Then again, Agent Miller couldn't help but recall that KSM and Ali Abdul Aziz Ali referred to Saifullah as something of a dupe.

Saifullah seemed to sense Agent Miller's skepticism, which was shared by her two silent cohorts. After some further discussion led by the agent's probing questions, Saifullah finally acknowledged that perhaps he "was duped by the trustees [of his charitable organization] to visit Afghanistan," after all. Regardless, Saifullah was sticking to his story. He was just a businessman who wanted to produce a television show.

* * *

He never had anything to do with explosives, or any other weapon, for that matter. Saifullah also denied any real affiliation with al Qaeda. His background and personal history proved his innocence. "I have a white American Jew in New York who has been my partner for years," he said, adding that after the 9/11 attacks, he immediately called Charles Stern to make sure he was safe and to offer his condolences before then sending condolences to the US Consulate in Karachi. He also reminded his interviewers that he wrote several letters to George W. Bush urging him to pursue peace in Afghanistan. He suggested that the FBI go and find those letters, as they would prove that the man before them was not a terrorist.

Every time Agent Miller delved into the more sensitive topic of shipping explosives, Saifullah adamantly denied any knowledge. At times he couldn't even deign to respond to such questions, giving the impression that they did not apply to him. He was even more indignant when it came to matters pertaining to nuclear weapons proliferation. "Is a nuclear weapon something I could buy off the shelf?" he asked, with an arrogant smirk. "Can you buy it from [British Prime Minister] Tony Blair? Is that something to say to anybody?"

He alternated between peevish denials and typically self-serving platitudes. He piously declared, "I believe in the Koran, that killing one innocent person is equal to killing all humanity. I believe . . . that and practice that."

Agent Miller had fully expected that Saifullah would initially deny any knowledge regarding the explosives or nuclear weapons. She decided to move the conversation along to other topics before coming back to the primary reason for Saifullah's detention at Bagram—the al Qaeda plot to ship explosives and/or WMDs through the ports. While she used restraint in that regard, she raised the question of how it was that after meeting bin Laden in Afghanistan, Saifullah began working with Khalid Sheikh Mohammad, the man he knew as Mir, who had orchestrated the 9/11 attacks.

Though the association required an answer, Saifullah was evasive, saying, "One day the receptionist called me to say a gentleman who has my card from Afghanistan wants to see me. Our security guard brought him to my office. . . . He introduced himself as 'Mir.' Mir is a very large tribe in Sind, Pakistan. This man was from Nawanshahr, an agriculturist. He presented my business card and told me he received a message to see me about recording TV programs from Afghanistan. He also told me he helps in media related matters. He had a lot of knowledge of media, cameras, production and editing."

Saifullah told Agent Miller that Mir arrived in his office about six months after Saifullah had offered his business card to bin Laden. That meant Saifullah and KSM as Mir became acquainted sometime in the spring of 2001, several months before the 9/11 attacks. In other words, while Saifullah and Mir were getting to know each other, Mir was managing perhaps the most elaborate terrorist plot in modern history. The fact that Mir took time away from his "Planes Operation" to develop an association with Saifullah raised eyebrows among the interview team and increased their shared suspicion of their detainee.

But Saifullah insisted that his interactions with Mir were strictly business and benign. He stated, "Mir was dressed in casual Western dress, spoke Urdu Pakistani and English clearly, was clean shaven and showed no signs of extremist personality."

Saifullah also suggested to Agent Miller that Jihad wasn't just limited to terrorism. From Saifullah's perspective, Jihad also meant money. He figured Mir shared the same mindset. "After USSR invaded Afghanistan, a holy war [was] declared against infidel communists by Muslims worldwide and Jihad became fashionable and lucrative to raise money." Saifullah lectured Agent Miller and the others in the room, saying, "Politicians, government officials and religious leaders were exploiting young Muslims. A large percentage of young male Pakistanis are still glorified for Jihad and they are everywhere, soliciting cash and kind. It is impossible to avoid them if you are living in Pakistan."

Saifullah went deeper into Mir's expressed desire to work with Universal Broadcasting. "I showed Mir our studio, editing room and clips of our religious interviews and current affair programs," Saifullah recalled. "I proposed to make a small recording studio anywhere in Afghanistan, soundproof and proper lighting arrangements. Universal Broadcasting will pay. They can select and buy all recording equipment. [Mir] observed our staff in the IMG office, as our staff was busy and he asked about it. I explained to him and gave him our brochure. It gave brief details of our buying houses. We shook hands. He saw the US and Pakistan flags, and I told him about my partner, Charles Stern. He did not show any concern and said he was also in the United States [during college]."

Saifullah was blasé about the extent of his continued relationship with Mir. "We met on and off [about] media," he said at one point. But as Agent Miller's line of questioning became more intrusive, and as other FBI agents behind the scenes gathered additional information for Agent Miller to use, it became clear to the investigators that more was going on than just a standard business relationship. It was particularly obvious because of the timing, since Saifullah and Mir's interactions were intensifying just prior to 9/11.

The FBI learned that Mir was a frequent visitor to Saifullah's Karachi office. Apparently, Mir often traveled long distances by car during the night to get there, something Saifullah acknowledged to Agent Miller. Moreover, Mir didn't always come alone. Witnesses described a completely different office dynamic and vibe whenever Mir or his associates were present. There were secretive meetings where the blinds were closed, and private rooms for Mir and his men to work. Even Saifullah was reportedly acting differently. Whenever Mir needed something, Saifullah was a lapdog ready and eager to help. Eventually, Saifullah designated an area of the office to be off limits to anyone other than Mir and his men. Saifullah told his staff that the area was under construction. The whole operation was strange. It was obvious to witnesses that something suspicious was going on. But they couldn't say what it was.

Witnesses close to the situation also reportedly resented Mir and his associates. For instance, one individual who had known Saifullah for many years described how Saifullah turned cold toward his longtime colleagues when Mir was around. Saifullah appeared to be keeping secrets. "Mir was a bad influence on Saif," the longtime colleague had recalled.

Based on the evidence, including the descriptions and timing of Mir's visits, Agent Miller and her fellow FBI agents behind the scenes had developed theories on what Mir—a.k.a. Khalid Sheikh Mohammad—was doing with Universal Broadcasting. One prevailing theory that Agent Miller entertained revolved around al Qaeda propaganda videos. KSM was the head of al Qaeda's "Media Committee." Experts noted that the quality of certain videos began improving, as evidenced by a particularly well-produced propaganda video that was released in 2001 pertaining to the USS *Cole* bombing. The video quality might have been accomplished by Saifullah's equipment.

In any case, Agent Miller could see that the association was a far cry from the "on and off" meetings that Saifullah described. Under further questioning, Saifullah also was forced to admit that he assisted Mir in other ways beyond simply the media company. Of course, Saifullah played down each of these tasks, describing them as normal activities. Describing one such task, Saifullah stated: "[Mir] wanted me to show him the area [where] I live, so I took him around. He said he doesn't live in Karachi, but [comes] from far away, from other cities in the interior of Pakistan." Another undertaking with Mir was described by Saifullah as a simple business favor: "[Mir] requested my help to open an account at a bank [where] I do [my] banking."

As that interview session continued, it became clear that many of these tasks were far from typical business dealings. In addition, as the earlier small tasks were accomplished (i.e., driving Mir around the area), Saifullah was increasingly asked to perform more important services, including one that involved fraudulent bank accounts and a bag containing half a million dollars in cash.

To Miller and her fellow agents at the FBI who had experience with gangs, terror groups, and the mob, Saifullah's relationship with Mir—and later with Mustafa a.k.a. Ali—was indicative of someone being manipulated and groomed. In some ways, Saifullah's gradually increasing responsibilities were like KSM's development of Majid Khan. And the fact that it was bin Laden himself who dispatched KSM to work with Saifullah made this supposition even more compelling.

But Saifullah simply dismissed all his dealings with Mir as a natural, mundane part of the job for someone in his position. He pointed out that Mir's passport and identification displayed the Mir alias. "I have a copy of his identification in my office in Pakistan," Saifullah said. After he acknowledged that he helped Mir open the bank account, he also admitted that the account was opened under another fictitious name: "Sharafuddin Shamim." Notably, when the CIA captured Saifullah and collected his "pocket litter," one of the items in his possession was a checkbook under the name Sharafuddin Shamim. Moreover, a co-signer for the fake Shamim account was a woman, and her name happened to be Farhat Paracha.

Again outmaneuvered and put on the defensive by Agent Miller, Saifullah could only insist that this was simply how business was conducted in Pakistan. "Mir put maybe $15,000 to $20,000 in the account," Saifullah said. "So I said it would be wise to make an investment with that, and get some return on it."

Now, Miller and her fellow investigators came to believe that Saifullah had been providing crucial financial assistance to KSM in the days leading up to the 9/11 attack. Agent Miller couldn't prove that Saifullah had actual knowledge about the Planes Operation, but it was increasingly clear that he was playing the role of useful idiot. Miller didn't buy Saifullah's contention that he didn't know that Mir, and Usama bin Laden for that matter, were terrorist operatives.

Saifullah stuck to this story even when confronted with the fact that he continued to perform tasks for Mir after the 9/11 attacks—when *everyone* knew that bin Laden was the leader of al Qaeda. The financial relationship exposed the true nature of Saifullah's involvement. Sometime in 2002, Mir had asked Saifullah to take possession of a bag that contained $500,000 in cash. Mir's instructions were simple: hold onto the money until Mir asked for it back. To Agent Miller, the purpose of Mir's tasking in this case was obvious. This was al Qaeda money that KSM wanted to keep liquid, quickly and safely accessed as necessary, particularly in the post-9/11 environment when the heat would be ratcheted up on al Qaeda. Any savvy businessman would have known this. But apparently not Saifullah, who had an answer for this transaction as well.

"[Mir] was negotiating to make me a part of one of the programs or shows that is popular in Pakistan TV," Saifullah said. "I have had experience in the States, and I needed seeding money, and [Mir] invested $500,000 in that business. There is a gentleman named Jabbar who has the rights, and he wanted to sell me the rights, but the plan fell through, so I could not be a partner. I did not go through with the proposal, so I returned the money. I kept it for six months."

Saifullah argued that $500,000 was "chump change" for the rights to a television show. He followed that up with more boasting. "The bank—it was a prime bank in Karachi—was willing to give me a credit line of $3 million. I was primarily dealing with Jabbar, and he has an office in New Jersey."

To Agent Miller, it was quite a staggering cover story with a touch of half-truths mixed in. It was true that Saifullah deposited the $500,000 into a bank account. The deposit went into the recently acquired account held under his fictitious name, Sharafuddin Shamim. Bank records also confirmed that about six months later, around the fall of 2002, the money was withdrawn from the account. In that respect, Saifullah was telling the truth. But under questioning, Saifullah's story about how he returned the money was more akin to a drug deal than a legitimate transaction.

By late 2002, Mir had introduced Saifullah to Mustafa, who would later turn out to be Ali Abdul Aziz Ali, one of the 9/11 plotters and KSM's nephew. It was Saifullah's understanding that Mustafa was to be Mir's representative while Mir tended to other matters elsewhere. One day, Mustafa informed Saifullah that Mir needed him to return the $500,000. Shortly after receiving that command, Saifullah boarded a domestic flight. Among his carry-on luggage was the bag containing $500,000 in cash. Saifullah then traveled literally across the country of Pakistan about 700 miles to the capital, Islamabad.

In Islamabad, Saifullah received a phone call on his cell phone. It was Mustafa, who directed Saifullah by phone to a designated location. Mustafa asked Saifullah if he saw a man nearby. Saifullah said he did. Mustafa asked Saifullah to lift his arm up and down. Saifullah did as he was told. He was then approached by a man who also had a cell phone and walked over to him. Mustafa instructed Saifullah to hand the bag to the man. Once the handoff was complete, Saifullah turned around and returned to Karachi. He claimed he never spoke to the man to whom he gave the bag of money.

The business with the $500,000 indicated to Agent Miller that KSM trusted Saifullah. This trust was likely bolstered by Saifullah's prompt compliance with the directive to return the money. It also demonstrated Saifullah's willingness to work with KSM, even when the benefits to Saifullah were not at all clear. To Agent Miller at this point in the interview, irrespective of Saifullah's culpability pertaining to explosives and shipping, he was obviously assisting terrorist operatives in their financial dealings.

Agent Miller confronted Saifullah on this issue. She asked why he was so eager to assist Mir and Mustafa, who were clearly associated with bin Laden. Once again, Saifullah had a ready answer to this perceived paradox. Saifullah's justification was the same exact one used by his son Uzair when confronted with his own willingness to assist in Majid Khan's immigration matter: The answer was his Cliftonia real estate venture, in which Saifullah was heavily invested. He and Uzair staked a large amount of time, money, and reputation on turning a shabby piece of seaside Karachi property into luxury housing. Mustafa was promising to become a major investor with the sum of 220,000 euros. Saifullah couldn't afford to lose that investment.

Saifullah recalled, "This is a large, 300-room apartment building in Pakistan, but it turned into a slum. The residents weren't interested in it. The mayor of Karachi is a very close friend. One day, he visited me and we went to that area. I negotiated with the people to get 80 percent of the share, and I helped with the financing because financing was a problem for them. I reached a silent agreement with them, and they would get occupants, recover the money and reinvest it. It took a while, but they offered me 70 apartments with a million-dollar investment on my part and recovery for the investment."

Continuing his story, Saifullah said, "Because my son had been to the US, we advertised it heavily in the Pakistani community in the US, and we had a good response and there were about 45 potential buyers negotiating for them in New York."

Left unsaid was the fact that Uzair was arrested by Agent Miller while negotiating with the potential buyers in New York. According to Saifullah, the Cliftonia project became a major focus during his meetings with Mustafa. They not only discussed financing, but also specific details of the project, down to the doors. The 220,000 euros was indeed a significant investment, and Saifullah justified his relationship with Mustafa as a legitimate business alliance.

Agent Miller speculated that Ali, playing the part of Mustafa, may have had ulterior motives for investing in Cliftonia. FBI agents had analyzed the Cliftonia schematics, and they also dug into al Qaeda's incessant hunt for safe houses for their operatives. Ali and KSM were heavily involved in such matters, as evidenced by KSM's request that Saifullah show him around Karachi during their early meetings.

Agent Miller's working theory was that Ali and KSM were interested in using Cliftonia as an al Qaeda safe house. The idea had merit. The promised lavish surroundings of Cliftonia would potentially render such clandestine housing hidden in plain sight. Moreover, the first-floor units of the complex would be situated such that occupants could come and go without being seen by guards or cameras. For Agent Miller, it remained an open question on whether Saifullah had knowledge of Ali's plans. But in the end, the official FBI position was that there was already enough evidence to justify Saifullah's detention as an enemy combatant. Saifullah, meanwhile, continued to confidently justify everything he did. He was still treating his interrogation as a business meeting.

The matter with Majid Khan was no different for Saifullah—just another misunderstanding in what he described as an unfortunate string of misunderstandings. Saifullah was simply helping the kid out as a favor for one of his investors, Mustafa. Saifullah repeated yet again that he had nothing to hide. "Mustafa met me in the area of Karachi [where] I live. He introduced us both, my son and I, to a man that used to live in Baltimore named Majid Khan. We were sitting and eating at a table, and he mentioned he had an immigration problem, and he wanted to keep his bank account active. My son was working on the website for the apartments in the US, and he asked my son to help, and I said of course he can help while he was there [in the US]."

Saifullah began to shake his head in disbelief. "Those documents were recovered by my son, and they say he is a terrorist. I don't know."

Agent Miller sketched out a brief flowchart and showed it to Saifullah. It highlighted Usama bin Laden at the top, with an arrow pointing down to KSM, then to Ali, then to Majid Khan. She told Saifullah it was extremely obvious that KSM, Ali, and Khan were all directly linked to bin Laden; consequently, they were part of al Qaeda. Agent Miller starkly questioned how Saifullah could sit there and deny that he suspected they were terrorist operatives.

Now perhaps for the first time during his long, initial interrogation, Saifullah began to waffle with his answers.

* * *

While Saifullah Paracha was secretly being interrogated, Americans back home found themselves in a profoundly more confusing world. It was July 2003. The swift Iraq War invasion was slowly devolving into insurgency. The 101st Airborne Division was in the mountainous Mosul region hunting Uday and Qusay, the sons of Iraqi dictator Saddam Hussein. A bombing targeting the United Nations Human Rights Commission in Jalalabad, Afghanistan, reminded people that the "other war" was still going on. Back home, the Dixie Chicks country music group had become persona non grata for criticizing President Bush's decisions. Patriotic acts such as Toby Keith, Alan Jackson, and Lee Greenwood were feted with airplay. A "witch doctor" named Bernard Williams was found guilty in federal court for sickening airplane passengers when ammonia and other hazardous materials disguised as cat litter leaked into the plane. On July 8, the first interim report from the 9/11 Commission was published.

"We must look backward in order to look forward," the report noted. "The contemporary history of the country passed a watershed on 9/11. We must do the job we are required to do by law so that we may understand how we came to this turning point in the way we think about our security and to understand the choices that lie ahead."

The amount of news was overwhelming. Enter the ticker. It is now commonplace for most cable news channels to incorporate a news ticker at the bottom of the screen. That was not the case prior to 9/11. But with so much news happening at once, the newsreaders could not keep up. The ticker remained necessary in 2003 to keep viewers informed in what had become a twenty-four-hour news cycle.

* * *

The meetings with Saifullah became increasingly intense. He was questioned by Agent Miller, with Bob and Agent Ruby in the background, for hours on end every day for well over a week. When he wasn't answering questions, Saifullah sat in his tiny, cold cell at Bagram.

During his interviews, the same questions continued to come up, and each time, Saifullah gave similarly evasive answers. But unlike in their early days together, Agent Miller wasn't letting little slips of the tongue or discrepancies slide. Now she was relentlessly demanding answers. She had bank records and other documents on hand, as well. Meanwhile, Bob mostly sat there. He stepped in to ask Saifullah to clarify something. But otherwise, he merely watched. Agent Ruby also barely said a word, looking impatient and anxious. Saifullah paid her and Bob little attention. Agent Miller was the one who mattered.

During another interview, on July 17, 2003, things became particularly tense. Agent Miller accused Saifullah of lying to her about his knowledge of Ali and KSM's affiliation. She had stopped referring to them as Mustafa and Mir. They were now Ammar (Ali's common alias) and KSM.

Saifullah attempted to reiterate that he was unaware that these men were al Qaeda operatives. Agent Miller told Saifullah to stop wasting everybody's time. The FBI had all the evidence they needed. Saifullah pleaded with her; he was telling the truth, he said. Agent Miller then slammed a piece of paper onto the table. It was Saifullah's email pertaining to the establishment of fictitious shell companies used for shipping merchandise that was seized in the 2002 Abu Zubaydah raid. She demanded an explanation.

Saifullah admitted for the first time that there had been some discussions with KSM regarding the establishment of shell companies. Agent Miller demanded that Saifullah tell her more. He said, "I saw an advertisement in *Newsweek* about offshore banking, and I gave a copy of this advertisement to KSM." That response elicited Agent Miller's fury, her harshest words in over a week. She laid into Saifullah, asking how stupid he thought she was. She reminded him that he was in a very precarious position. If he ever wanted to get out of Bagram and see the light of day, then Saifullah had better shape up and start telling the truth. Or he could expect to be locked up with no future in sight.

Saifullah began to falter, acknowledging that he probably knew that Ali, KSM, and Majid Khan were somehow affiliated with al Qaeda. Agent Miller would not let up. She pressed Saifullah with questions about the explosives and possible WMDs. He tried to deny knowing anything about any of that, but Agent Miller kept up the attack.

A declassified dispatch from Bob to CIA Headquarters captured Saifullah's next admission: "Saifullah Paracha stated that Ammar al-Baluchi had asked if he knew a forwarding agent who could ship garments and 'materials' to Europe, which Saifullah Paracha inferred were either explosives or chemicals."

After all those months of speculation and recent weeks of denials, Saifullah finally confirmed that he had discussed explosives with al Qaeda operatives in relation to potential terrorist attacks. This admission would lead to further information about the Second Wave plot. Saifullah had begun to crack. He rubbed his eyes with shaky hands. His voice became quieter, almost solemn. It appeared that he had resigned himself to finally telling the truth. His condescending demeanor was gone. He was no longer pontificating or bragging. He had been broken.

Agent Miller went in for the kill.

She ordered Saifullah to tell her about his conversations with KSM and Ali regarding the explosives, whatever they were. Saifullah nodded slowly. He closed his eyes and took a deep breath as if he were about to confess his deepest, darkest sins. The truth was about to come out. Agent Miller held her breath as she stared authoritatively into Saifullah's eyes, compelling him to proceed. The answers to those dire questions were about to be revealed.

"We need to take a break!" a shrill female voice suddenly barked.

Agent Miller froze. Her eyes widened and her jaw dropped. She turned her head to the left and saw Agent Ruby glaring at her.

"We need to take a break," Ruby repeated, her boot tapping on the floor, her voice impatient, even disdainful.

Agent Miller stared at Agent Ruby in disbelief. Bob remained frozen in his chair, stone-faced.

"I need to pee," Agent Ruby announced.

Afraid to speak because she was not sure what would come out of her mouth, Agent Miller could only nod slowly. She then looked across the table at Saifullah. He blinked a few times and began scanning the room. Saifullah's hands were no longer shaking. He leaned back in his chair and appeared much more relaxed. He exhaled deeply. The spell had been broken, and Saifullah's face melted into an expression of relief.

Agent Miller knew what that meant, that Saifullah was not going to tell the truth about the nature of the explosives and his involvement in the Second Wave. All that time and energy over the past week, to say nothing of these last four months, had been invested specifically to get Saifullah to this point where he could be broken down to talk. This was one bell that could not be unrung.

Decades later, Agent Miller still counted Agent Ruby's interruption as one of the most shocking and unfortunate experiences in her entire FBI career. But in the shorter term, she could only continue to ask that most agonizing question for which she still had no answer: Was this pathetic man at the center of a plot to smuggle explosives and weapons of mass destruction into America?

CHAPTER 12

A BOMB AND A MISSING MAN

Saifullah Paracha had been missing for nearly three weeks. His son Uzair was in an American jail. The rest of the Paracha family was in agony. It appeared that the entire world, which had previously been so good to them, had suddenly turned its back on the family in the harshest of ways. Everything had gone awry, and nobody was helping.

Saifullah had disappeared seemingly without a trace. Farhat contacted everyone she could think of, but the Pakistani and Thai authorities had gone silent. Even Charles Stern appeared to have turned on the family, and Farhat began to suspect that Stern might have played a role in Saifullah's vanishing.

By July 25, 2003, Farhat was running out of options. She later recalled Stern's hostility regarding Saifullah and IMG financial matters. "Charles had sent me hate mails when I did not even know where my husband was and this added to my distrust about him. Can you imagine the mental agony we experienced as a family when this happened and there was no response from anyone? . . . Muneeza is at college, Mustafa and Zahra are at school. They are no longer carefree children, but have become suspicious and worried."

Desperate for answers, Farhat soon sought assistance from an attorney. She found a lawyer by the name of Nisar Mujahid, who specialized in business matters, as well as preemptive legal challenges. Mujahid had previously provided legal services for Saifullah for some of his business ventures.

Mujahid informed his client that he would put pressure on the Pakistani government to provide information about Saifullah and his whereabouts. After Farhat provided background details, Mujahid told Farhat that he shared his suspicions that Saifullah was a victim of what he termed "enforced disappearance." Saifullah was likely in American custody, he explained, and he also believed that the Pakistani authorities had assisted in Saifullah's having gone missing.

But Mujahid was not done. He had known the Paracha family for years, and to him Saifullah and Uzair were the furthest thing from extreme Jihadists. Mujahid believed there were other, more sinister factors at play. His initial theory was that Uzair and Saifullah were framed, and that the culprit was the partner, Stern. Mujahid had seen this type of behavior before during his long career as a business attorney in Pakistan. His initial impression was that Stern needed to get the Paracha family out of the way to advance his own business interests.

Farhat tried to make sense of this theory: "I had met [Charles's] wife many times when she visited Pakistan. There was no animosity between us at all. But Charles did owe Saif a lot of money, which came to hundreds of thousands of dollars. He also [owed] money to other companies in Pakistan. Charles and Saif had been partners for a long time and though this partnership was bumpy at times, it was never too bad."

Mujahid's suspicions seemed far-fetched, but as Farhat recalled recent events involving Uzair and now Saifullah, she began to think that perhaps Stern was involved, after all. She revisited Stern's manic pleas designed to "coerce Saif"—as she put it—out of Pakistan. And, of course, there was Stern's miraculous success in procuring for Saifullah a Thai visa almost immediately upon request. And now, with Saifullah missing without a trace, Stern was already harassing Farhat about money. Yes, she thought, Stern must be involved.

Farhat asked Mujahid what they needed to do. Stern would be dealt with, he replied, but the priority had to be locating Saifullah. The good news was that Saifullah was probably alive. The bad news, of course, was that Saifullah might be subjected to harsh treatment in custody—even torture. Mujahid promised Farhat that he would immediately press the Pakistani government for answers and redress.

That same day, Mujahid filed a habeas corpus petition in the Sindh High Court in Karachi on behalf of Farhat Paracha. The goal of the petition was to demand that the Pakistani and Thai governments disclose what had happened to Saifullah Paracha. The basis of their case was simple: Saifullah, like his son Uzair, might have been taken into custody over alleged links with al Qaeda.

In early August 2003, the Pakistani court began to hold hearings regarding the unknown plight of Saifullah. At this point, Farhat was still in the dark about her husband's disappearance and couldn't even tell her children whether their father was alive or dead. In fact, Farhat had no validation that Mujahid's theory about Saifullah's enforced disappearance was accurate.

During the initial hearing, Saifullah's fate remained a mystery. Mujahid elicited information from the Pakistani government that, albeit circumstantial, began to validate his theory. Additional light was shed on Pakistan's actual role and knowledge of Saifullah's disappearance. In fact, it seemed that Pakistan may have played a direct role, after all.

A Pakistani government lawyer revealed in the hearing that Saifullah was on the Exit Control List (ECL). That list is maintained by the Pakistani Federal Investigation Agency (FIA), which is tasked with permitting or denying travel abroad. Unbeknownst to Saifullah, he had been barred from leaving Pakistan. Saifullah was permitted to proceed to his flight destined for Thailand. A lawyer for the Pakistani government stated in court that Saifullah had been *accidentally* cleared by FIA immigration staff at Karachi airport. The lawyer added that the computers in the terminal were not working at the time, which played a role in granting permission for Saifullah to leave the country. Subsequent litigation in Pakistan revealed that other passengers on the same flight had observed that all the computers appeared to be working that day.

Mujahid, and later Amnesty International, speculated that Pakistan refused to permit Saifullah's arrest in Karachi because of his privileged status. They also speculated that Saifullah's arrest in Pakistan could have led to local protests. Based on Saifullah's "accidental" departure from the country, it is now believed that Pakistan at some point acquiesced to US demands so long as any action took place elsewhere. If the Pakistani government was indeed in cahoots with the FBI or CIA in assisting with Saifullah's exit out of Pakistan, that has never been revealed publicly, nor has such collusion been confirmed through declassified documents.

During the habeas corpus hearing, which coincidentally took place on the same day and in the same court where men convicted of murdering *Wall Street Journal* reporter Daniel Pearl filed their own appeals, Mujahid began putting everything together for the court on behalf of Farhat. He argued that Saifullah was promptly issued a Thai visa that had been hastily facilitated by his partner, Stern. Considering the FIA's "accidental" clearance for Saifullah's departure, and Stern's phone call indicating that Saifullah had not taken a car ride to the Shangri-La Hotel, Mujahid suggested that Saifullah "must have been whisked off in the course of embarkation or of disembarkation." In other words, Saifullah was taken by some unknown entity either at the Karachi airport or as soon as he exited the airplane in Bangkok.

The primary questions regarding Saifullah's fate remained unanswered.

On August 5, 2003, Farhat finally learned about Saifullah's current status, but not from legal proceedings. She learned about it from an NBC News report broadcast in the United States. The two-minute newscast was ostensibly focused on newfound vulnerabilities associated with the US port system that could be exploited by terrorists. As the camera panned across a view of New York Harbor, reporter Lisa Myers stated that al Qaeda terrorists were plotting to smuggle a yet unspecified variety of explosives through the port. In what was termed an exclusive report, Myers went on to mention Saifullah Paracha with regard to the arrest of his son Uzair, linking the two of them to KSM. Other news outlets soon followed up on the story and these two alleged al Qaeda plotters.

To Farhat and her children, the NBC News report would have just been another galling insult, except that it confirmed that the elder Paracha was also in custody and therefore still alive. The report also noted that Saifullah was being held in Pakistan. An NBC News reporter soon contacted Farhat for comment. She said that neither her husband nor her son was a terrorist. At the same time, Uzair's lawyer, Anthony Ricco, a veteran New York criminal defense attorney, stated publicly that Uzair had been manipulated into participating in the events that led to his arrest. Nevertheless, as far as the media was concerned, Uzair Paracha's arrest validated the premise that al Qaeda had targeted the ports through which to smuggle all kinds of explosives and possible weapons of mass destruction—including nuclear, chemical, and biological.

With the NBC News confirmation, Farhat and her lawyer again pressed the Pakistani government for answers, determined to find out if Saifullah was well and how he was being treated. Farhat demanded to know what he was being charged with, and when he could come home. Yet the Pakistani government refused to provide answers.

On August 23, 2003—more than six weeks after Saifullah disappeared—Farhat received her first official confirmation of his whereabouts. But even in this instance, the news did not come from the government. Instead, it was from the International Committee of the Red Cross (ICRC). She learned that Saifullah was not in Pakistan as had been reported in the news. He was at the Bagram Air Base in Afghanistan in the custody of the US government.

* * *

The first exclusive NBC News reporting on Uzair and Saifullah Paracha was extremely provocative, highlighting the terrorist plot against New York Harbor. The port security story was not the lead on that evening's news coverage, however. The broadcast opened with the story of another al Qaeda operation at a Marriott Hotel in Jakarta, Indonesia, that was responsible for dozens of casualties. Investigators soon realized that one of the operatives involved in that attack was already in CIA custody, namely Majid Khan. Money handled by Khan to fund the murder was indirectly connected to Saifullah Paracha.

The attack plan had originated in January 2002, when KSM had sent another al Qaeda operative, Mohammed Jabarah, to meet with the leader of Jemaah Islamiyah, an extremist group in Thailand. The leader of that group, Encep Nurjaman, who went by the alias Hambali, announced in the meeting that he planned to have his group conduct small bombings against soft targets such as bars, cafés, and nightclubs frequented by Westerners. Hambali boldly threatened to carry out such attacks in Thailand, Malaysia, Singapore, the Philippines, and Indonesia. Hambali revealed to Jabarah that he already had one ton of explosives in Indonesia ready to go.

KSM's operative, Jabarah, returned to Pakistan to report to KSM. Later that year, in September 2002, KSM met with Majid Khan in a hotel in the

Pakistani border town of Peshawar. This was where KSM laid out his grand plan for Majid to become an al Qaeda operative within the United States. But during the hotel meeting, KSM told Majid that he would be required to perform other tasks in the meantime. One of those tasks involved travel to Thailand to meet with Hambali.

KSM explained that he wanted Majid to deliver money in Thailand and ordered him to obtain a Thai travel visa and then take his new wife with him to Thailand as cover. The funds were initially to be delivered from Pakistan to a middleman in Thailand through the hawala system, an untraceable, unofficial black-market method of financial transactions in some parts of the world. Once Majid arrived in Thailand, he was tasked with retrieving the funds. KSM's goal was clear. He wanted the money to be transferred without detection and for Majid to avoid physically carrying such a large amount of cash out of Pakistan.

Majid was ecstatic to be playing this new role, viewing this assignment as his first major test assigned by KSM since his return from Baltimore that summer. Majid was certainly aware of his previous failures, including KSM's disappointment in his effort to assassinate the Pakistani president. Majid was determined not to let KSM down this time. A court document later described Majid's thinking as follows:

> Although neither Ali nor KSM told [Khan] what the money was intended for, [Khan] believed that the money was being used for al Qaeda operational purposes (or terrorist attacks). This was consistent with [Khan's] plans: he volunteered to assist al Qaeda in this way, and would have delivered the money even had he been specifically informed that it was for a terrorist operation that was intended to kill people.

KSM gave Majid $50,000 of al Qaeda funds. A short time later, KSM's nephew Ali called Saifullah requesting that Saifullah return the $500,000 in cash that KSM had provided sometime in 2002. During her interviews with Saifullah a few months prior to the attack, Agent Miller theorized that KSM needed the $500,000 to be liquid—or readily available—if needed for al Qaeda operations. Her theory appeared correct. Uzair had also alluded to something similar during his initial meeting with Agent Miller. It is likely that KSM needed to replenish his coffers after dispensing $50,000 for Majid's Thailand operation. As a man of his word, Saifullah quickly returned the money.

By December 24, 2002, Majid and Ali had already enlisted the assistance of Aafia Siddiqui—the militant Jihadist educated in the United States. Siddiqui, along with separate aid from Uzair and Saifullah Paracha, was to help with Majid's most recent failure regarding the expiration of his US travel status. While Ali worked with Siddiqui to solve Majid's immigration problem, Majid was set to travel to Thailand with his wife to assist in Hambali's operation. The couple would stay at the Sofitel Hotel in Bangkok from December 24, 2002, through December 29, 2002.

Upon Majid's arrival in Bangkok, he contacted Ali regarding the money delivery. They used coded email messages and even had code names. On December 26, Majid sent a coded email message to Ali confirming that the $50,000 was successfully delivered.

Upon his return to Karachi, Majid's next priority was getting everything in order for his anticipated return to the US. KSM was still determined to use him as a sleeper agent. After Aafia Siddiqui's initial attempts in Maryland, Majid would soon become acquainted with Uzair and Saifullah Paracha as part of his efforts to resolve the immigration problem. The results of Majid's financial delivery to Thailand remained to be seen.

After Majid had handed the last installment of the $50,000 to his contact back in Thailand, the money was quickly secreted away. A man named Zubair took the funds to a Bangkok apartment for safekeeping. He shared the apartment with another one of Hambali's lieutenants called Lillie. In January 2003, another al Qaeda courier gave Zubair an additional $49,000. That money was added to the pile already hidden in the Bangkok apartment. The next month around the time that Uzair was traveling to New York, Zubair and Lillie took the $99,000 in cash and exchanged those funds for various currencies. Some of the money was then transferred to operatives in Indonesia. Hambali made it clear to Zubair and Lillie that the money was being used to fund an upcoming operation.

By June 2003, KSM, Ali, and Majid Khan were all in CIA custody. Each of these men was subjected to the CIA's EITs. Investigators were expending a significant amount of time and energy to determine Saifullah's role in al Qaeda's plotting, including whether weapons of mass destruction were on the way to the US. At the same time, Hambali's plot in Southeast Asia continued to progress. He was still issuing orders about how the funds, including the $50,000 delivered by Majid Khan, would be dispensed. Meanwhile, Noordin Mat Top, the chief bombmaker for the group, began using the money for his operation. By July 2003, Noordin and two others, Mohammed Ikhwan, a.k.a. Ismail, and Dr. bin Hussein Azahari, traveled to Jakarta, Indonesia, where they rented a small house with a garage. In that garage, the trio constructed a truck bomb.

Noordin and Azahari took a few field trips into the city. They were looking for targets. Ultimately, they settled on the JW Marriott Hotel. They chose this hotel for one reason. There were many Americans who were staying there.

On August 5, 2003, as NBC News was preparing to broadcast its major exclusive involving KSM and Saifullah Paracha's involvement in the al Qaeda plot, a man named Asmar Latin Sani stopped in a Jakarta mosque to pray. When he finished his prayers, he got into a truck and followed a motorcycle through the bustling streets of Jakarta. Ismail and Azahari, two of the three men who had used Majid's $50,000 to finance their bomb plot, were on the motorcycle. The motorcycle led Sani's truck near the JW Marriott Hotel, turning left on the street near the hotel. Ismail and Azahari paused to ensure that Sani's truck had properly turned into the Marriott's driveway. The truck turned toward the hotel as expected.

Sani stopped the truck just outside the front entrance of the Marriott. He then detonated the bomb that was hidden in the back. The blast killed eleven people—ten Indonesians and one Dutchman—and wounded eighty-one others. Sani's severed head was later discovered in the wreckage.

About a week after the Marriott attack, Hambali was captured and rendered to CIA custody. His key lieutenants, Zubair and Lillie, soon joined him. CIA records confirm that KSM and Majid Khan had been actively discussing this deadly stratagem with Southeast Asian operatives as early as March 2003. Investigators were unable to stop the attack. A declassified CIA briefing slide prepared for Josh Bolten, President George W. Bush's chief of staff, recounted the main points:

> During KSM's interrogation we acquired information that led to the capture of Hambali in August 2003 and to the partial dismantling of the Jemaah Islamiyah leadership in SE Asia. KSM first told us about Majid Khan's role in delivering $50,000 to Hambali operatives for an attack KSM believed was imminent. We then confronted Khan with KSM's admission and [signals intelligence] confirming the money transfer and Khan's travel to Bangkok. Khan admitted he delivered the money to an operative named "Zubair," whom we subsequently identified and captured. Zubair's capture led to the identification and subsequent capture of an operative named Lillie who was providing forged passports to Hambali. Lillie identified the house in Bangkok where Hambali was hiding.

After the Marriott bombing, things started looking worse for Majid. He was now directly culpable for murder. Things also didn't bode well for Saifullah. By August 2003, his family had learned only that he had been captured by the US government. Saifullah was already directly connected to bin Laden and several of the 9/11 plotters. Now he was directly linked to one of the facilitators of the Jakarta Marriott bombing as well. With his interrogations at an impasse, Saifullah's situation was about to get much more precarious.

The Marriott attack was definitive proof that KSM's involvement in deadly al Qaeda operations had not stopped with his capture. Were KSM's efforts to obtain nuclear weapons or to smuggle explosives into US ports ongoing as well? Paracha had the answers, and he wasn't talking. After Agent Ruby's poorly timed interruption of Agent Miller's rapidly developing interrogation of him, Saifullah reverted to his denials regarding explosives and WMDs. He also denied providing any real advice to Ali and KSM on the subject.

Government officials couldn't help but wonder if the plot to smuggle explosives into US ports was essentially another Marriott scenario. Were they missing something? Until the matter was resolved, one thing was obvious. Saifullah would remain in US custody.

* * *

Beginning in late 2003, Farhat—at home in Karachi—had a recurring dream. Her husband had returned. Saifullah had dark circles under his eyes and was not talking much. Then Uzair—very well-groomed in a light beige suit—would run upstairs, smiling as if nothing had happened to him. Farhat later recalled, "I was prodding [Saifullah] to give me hurried advice on how to run the family business, since I felt in the dream that he was to go back [into detention]."

In early August 2003, a judge in New York denied Uzair's request for bail. Although this did not come as a surprise for Farhat, it was still jarring to be told that her son would remain behind bars. While things for Saifullah were incredibly complicated, Farhat was now convinced that Uzair had been framed.

With the help of the Red Cross (ICRC) beginning in late August 2003, information began trickling in and Farhat learned that Saifullah was at Bagram Air Base near Kabul, Afghanistan, and he had been assigned a number—B626. The ICRC also referred to her husband with a number of its own—ABZ 016091. Farhat's proud, dignified, and accomplished husband was being reduced to a cruelly bureaucratic system of alphanumeric codes.

She later lamented, "I could not imagine how the American agencies could take a Pakistani citizen who has no criminal record whatsoever, has been a taxpayer, and has through his business brought in valuable foreign exchange. I cannot believe that this was possible without the knowledge of our government. . . . How he got there is still a mystery. . . .

"I had started doubting whatever information I was getting. I was not sure if what the ICRC was saying was true. If it was true, even then I was uneasy because of all the negative accounts that had been circulating about the treatment of detainees there."

In early September, the ICRC passed along a handwritten letter from Saifullah to his family. The note was short, apparently written in haste. Farhat later described the letter as "hurried scribblings at the back of International Committee of the Red Cross pages." But at least it was Saifullah's handwriting, and it suggested that he was indeed alive.

Saifullah's first correspondence indicated that he was reasonably comfortable at Bagram. He noted that the heating arrangements in the cold

Kabul weather were adequate. The food was good. He was given medicines, a Koran, and some other reading material. The Americans generally treated him with respect.

Several more letters arrived at irregular intervals—delivery being an excruciatingly slow process—some coming two at a time. Despite Saifullah's relatively positive notes, Farhat remained suspicious. Too much had already happened to accept things at face value.

She later said, "I don't know if he writes under duress as there is nothing much in those letters except that he is ok. ICRC messages have to be of non-discriminatory nature as stated on the letter sheets given by them. So, we have to accept whatever he has written."

It would be nearly six years before Farhat would hear Saifullah's voice. Until then, she was writing at least two letters a week, only a portion of them apparently making it into Saifullah's hands.

Meanwhile, Uzair was also sending letters and being allotted one fifteen-minute phone call each month by New York jail officials. Those calls boosted Farhat's spirits, but only briefly.

"Uzair is also a very positive person," she said of her son. "He tries to make the best of what he has. He is in very good health. He is provided books (from an approved list) by relatives through Amazon.com. Sometimes he seems depressed and he stops writing to everyone. Since he is a young man, full of energy, his life in limbo demoralizes him. We feel that he tries to raise our spirits by cracking jokes and trying to appear strong and in control. He says [the staff] have a pretty good attitude towards him. There are times when he has a problem with cellmates because they keep on changing and so does his cell."

And what about Farhat's three children in Pakistan? They had begun lashing out in uncharacteristic ways shortly after Saifullah's disposition became known. Farhat said at the time, "All three kids have been hurt beyond expression. They feel insecure and this has affected their performance in school and also their relationship with their friends. They have become more aloof and do not possess the carefree attitude they previously had. They have become more suspicious of everybody and say that America is no longer the land of the free and they would not care about ever going there again."

In addition to caring for the children at home, Farhat was now faced with the task of running the business interests that Stern did not manage. The problem was that Saifullah had so many businesses, it was difficult to prioritize. He was such a hands-on executive that Farhat was starting at a disadvantage trying to step in for him. Farhat resented the Pakistan and US governments for her situation, and her ire toward Charles Stern continued to fester.

Out of necessity, Farhat enlisted the help of her eldest daughter, Muneeza, who was attending business school in Karachi at the time. Muneeza had taken the lead in managing IMG's affairs while Saifullah traveled to Afghanistan and was detained in Bagram. Muneeza worked on handling the company's expenses and handled audits of the company's financial records according to legal requirements. Muneeza's efforts took some pressure off Farhat so that the family matriarch could devote herself to the pursuit of justice for her husband and son. She was fiercely determined to vindicate them and to save her family.

Her primary targets were the Pakistani government and her husband's business partner. She was going to become the bane of their existence. With the Pakistanis, Farhat wanted to expose what she believed to be the government's collusion with the Americans in Saifullah's capture and detention. In addition to her local counsel in Karachi, Farhat retained a lawyer based in London, Akhtar Raja, who would serve as liaison with legal allies in the US, including Uzair's defense attorney. On August 19, 2003, Raja began sending letters demanding proof that Pakistani officials assisted in Saifullah's capture. His initial overtures were met with stubborn resistance. Farhat was frustrated but undeterred, navigating a tangled, international web.

She told a human rights advocacy organization at the time, "According to this letter [from the Pakistani government], the Foreign Office is in touch with the American Consulate in Islamabad and the State Department in Washington about the Saifullah Paracha case. The Thai Airlines showed the Sindh High Court the departure and arrival manifests with my husband's name included. This shows that he took the flight from Karachi and got off at Bangkok. . . . We have not received any other replies from anywhere."

As Farhat and her attorneys fought with the Pakistani government, they also used the Karachi courts to take on those who she believed had framed her son and husband. On September 15, 2003, which was only about a month after Farhat finally learned that Saifullah was taken to Bagram, she filed another lawsuit in the Sindh High Court. The following contemporaneous excerpt from a Karachi newspaper indicates how Farhat was proceeding to mount her offensive in court: "Filed through Advocate Nisar A. Mujahid, the plaintiff alleges that in order to advance his business interests, Charles Stern first involved her son, Uzair Paracha, in a case in New York and then invited her husband to Bangkok to facilitate his arrest by the American FBI."

Only a month before, Stern had even authorized Farhat to disseminate the following statement written in support for his partner, saying that Saifullah "very clearly knew I was Jewish. We had friendly talks on religion, and he never has shown any animosity at all to Jewish people or to America. The opposite—he spoke very highly of America. . . . I was shocked and scared by the allegations and find them very hard to believe. . . . Saif is my friend. And he knows it."

Despite Stern's supportive statement, by the following month the relationship between Stern and the Paracha family was completely severed. Farhat's lawsuit publicly accused Stern of working with the FBI to capture Saifullah, and the lawsuit was not just directed at Stern. It cast blame on a slew of people who Farhat had come to believe may have been complicit in efforts to frame Uzair and Saifullah. Among those she believed were involved were Stern's wife and even members of Farhat's own New York–based family. A Karachi newspaper reported, "Plaintiff Farhat Paracha alleged that the couple [Charles Stern and his wife], in collusion with Shahzad Paracha, Umer Haider, and Swaleh Khan and others, had also launched several identical concerns to usurp the business of the joint company. She seeks a number of injunctions against the couple, besides claiming . . . damages for harming her family business."

Farhat's lawsuit sought $470,000 from the Sterns. She claimed that the money represented profits owed to Saifullah by IMG. At this point, Farhat was out for blood from Stern and his wife.

CHAPTER 13

WELCOME TO GUANTANAMO BAY

Before her departure around September 2003, Agent Miller made a point to tell Saifullah that she was leaving Bagram and returning to New York. Uzair had some court dates coming up, and Agent Miller needed to refocus her efforts on that case. Despite learning that Uzair's prosecution would move forward, Saifullah expressed little concern about his son. Instead, he wanted to know how any of that affected *him* and demanded to know when he would be able to leave Bagram.

Agent Miller told him she could not answer either question. She asked if Saifullah was willing to continue meeting with investigators as they worked to sort out his case. Though he complained that he had already answered every question ad nauseam, Saifullah readily agreed.

Over the past month since Saifullah's capture, Agent Miller had gotten to know the elder Paracha quite well. She understood his quirks and idiosyncrasies. She knew what fired him up. He was now rather predictable. Agent Miller was even used to his condescending attitude and displays of pomposity.

The two had established an ongoing rapport. Saifullah trusted Agent Miller as much as one could under those circumstances. She proved to be his best advocate for complaints about his cell and treatment. They had spent hours upon hours and days upon days discussing everything from religion to business ethics. Saifullah was actually sorry to see her go.

With Agent Miller's exit, Saifullah entered a period of even greater uncertainty. After Agent Ruby's interruption back in mid-July 2003, the CITF agent stopped showing up. Saifullah never saw her again. Bob had lingered with Agent Miller for a few more sessions. But then, he also disappeared. Suddenly, Saifullah found himself being visited by a random cast of characters from the FBI and CITF. These investigators frequently stopped by to strike up conversation and ask questions. He always agreed to talk. The alternative was to remain in isolation in his cell. Having based his entire life and career on the ability to talk and communicate, Saifullah was certainly going to keep talking every time he had the opportunity.

A few investigators were aggressive. Others were more docile. Most of the agents did not have the same level of knowledge that Agent Miller possessed. They asked about explosives and al Qaeda links. They asked repeatedly about Saifullah's meeting with bin Laden. Majid Khan's name came up on a number of occasions. But Saifullah gave the same responses. His life became repetitive and mundane.

One agent asked if Saifullah was willing to take a lie-detector test. Saifullah agreed enthusiastically and was soon entering his meeting room to find a polygraph machine on the table. An FBI agent attached the cords to his body. The agent then asked a few questions. Was he a member of al Qaeda? His answer was a firm "no." Had he shipped explosives on behalf of al Qaeda? "No."

The polygraph was quick and to the point. Saifullah had passed, or so it seemed at first.

Law enforcement and intelligence officials later dismissed the polygraph results. They believed the test was ill-conceived and not properly conducted. The prevailing view was that the agent who administered the test was not familiar enough with Saifullah's case. The wording of the test questions was not precise enough. By including language such as "on behalf of al Qaeda," it gave Saifullah an easy out. Those who knew Saifullah well, such as Agent Miller, knew that he wasn't necessarily working for al Qaeda. But they remained convinced that Saifullah was providing expert advice and services for certain operatives—mainly KSM, Ali, and Majid Khan. Those at the FBI believed that the polygraph only complicated matters and emboldened Saifullah into sticking to his story.

Apart from the rehashing of old questions, FBI and CITF agents continued to ask Saifullah about his connections. They usually entered the room with a list and then inquired about names and phone numbers. Some of the individuals on the list seemed suspicious. Others might be tangentially connected to terrorism. The agents wanted to get to the bottom of it all.

One problem from the start was that there were just so many names. Saifullah had accumulated thousands of contacts, and he responded to nearly every inquiry that came his way. When an overzealous agent attempted to suggest that a contact was terrorist-related, Saifullah forcefully admonished the agent before pontificating about his status as a businessman, citing his extensive contacts as a necessary part of the job. Saifullah could be particularly cutting and condescending, saving his worst for agents he believed lacked respect or deference to his status.

Most of the names used by the agents came from his Casio electronic organizer. It documented all his successes through the vast array of names that Saifullah had accumulated over his career. Stored within the Casio's databanks was a veritable who's who of Pakistani society. The names reached to the top of the country's political establishment, as well as its business and charitable sectors. The Casio was, for all intents and purposes, representative of Saifullah's entire life.

The list of names used by the investigators may not have been complete. It is believed that the Casio was damaged when Saifullah was first captured and tossed into the van at the Bangkok airport. Technical experts at Bagram worked to repair the Casio to full functionality but had little luck. The most they were able to do was to get the Casio to briefly turn on for a few seconds before it shut itself off again. Bagram workers struggled to quickly record the names by hand before the Casio shut down. It was frustrating, labor-intensive work.

Some of the names contained in the Casio did appear suspicious. Individuals thought to have connections to nuclear and chemical programs were believed to be listed in the device. Those names only piqued investigators' interest considering KSM's admission that Saifullah had offered to assist in nuclear proliferation. In several instances, Saifullah was asked about an octogenarian Pakistani scientist "recruited by al Qaeda to develop chemical and biological weapons." But as always, when Saifullah was confronted with such information, he had a readily available response explaining why that person was a contact. Depending on how he was feeling that day, his answers could be arrogant and self-serving.

Ultimately, Bagram officials decided to send the Casio back to the United States. There, technical experts with more advanced equipment and facilities could work to fix the device. The Casio was packaged into a FedEx bag, which was common for certain types of evidence, and put out for delivery. Investigators were anxious to get a real look at the Casio's databank.

The package never arrived. Agents tried in vain to track down the Casio, believing it might have been lost somewhere near a US military base in Turkey. But they couldn't confirm. Somehow, Saifullah's Casio had gotten lost in the mail.

* * *

Hassan bin Attash was used to the routine Bagram soldiers used when preparing him in his cell for a departure. Ankles and hands were shackled. Uniformed Americans covered his eyes and ears before guiding Hassan to an unknown destination. It was September 22, 2004.*

Destinations didn't really matter for Hassan at this point. Ever since his capture on September 11, 2002, the Americans—including the CIA—had him frequently on the move. Although Hassan later claimed that he was tortured under the CIA's EIT program, CIA records appear to disprove that notion. Regardless, Hassan's movements for the next two years ultimately led him to Bagram Air Base.

Hassan had been captured in Karachi as part of the raid that netted 9/11 plotter Ramzi Binalshibh along with documents linking back to Saifullah Paracha. There's no record that Hassan had ever previously encountered Saifullah. Some law enforcement personnel suspect that Hassan may have been one of the mysterious, secretive men who had traipsed into the Karachi offices of IMG and Universal Broadcasting with KSM back in 2001.

Hassan was certainly close to KSM and his nephew Ali. When they tasked Majid Khan with preparations for the assassination of Pakistani

---

* Author interviews with military personnel and detainees involved in that day's movement described the mood.

President Musharraf, it was Hassan who constructed the suicide vest. Hassan was groomed to be a kind of explosives specialist for al Qaeda.

Like his older brother, Khallad bin Attash, Hassan was regarded as al Qaeda royalty. Khallad was the man who came up with the plan for hijackers to sneak box cutters onto passenger airplanes as part of the Planes Operation, and he was eventually captured with Ali as the pair sought to obtain explosives for a planned attack on the US Consulate in Karachi. There was no question that Hassan was in the same family business. An administrative board convened by the US military to review Hassan's continued detention would later state the following: "[Hassan] refused to acknowledge that he was affected by his extremist upbringing and indoctrination at an early age. [The board] . . . determined that continued law of war detention of the detainee remains necessary to protect against a continuing significant threat to the security of the United States."

Government records are inconclusive regarding Hassan's age and nationality. It is generally accepted that Hassan was born in either Yemen or Saudi Arabia sometime between 1982 and 1985. He might have been as young as seventeen years old when he was constructing Majid Khan's suicide vest.

Hassan was one of several detainees at Bagram who had previously been in CIA detention. The fate of men like Hassan and his former CIA-to-Bagram compatriots Ali al Haji Sharqawi and Sanad al-Kazimi was uncertain. Sharqawi was sort of al Qaeda's jack-of-all-trades, handling everything from recruitment to safe house management. Kazimi was a bodyguard for bin Laden. After 9/11, Kazimi joined USS *Cole* mastermind Abd al-Nashiri in efforts to attack targets in the United Arab Emirates. After their CIA interrogations ended, each of these men was handed over to the military for sporadic interviews. It was almost like the US government had run out of questions.

Pentagon officials reviewed their files, ultimately determining that their continued detention at Bagram was no longer feasible. The men were still considered dangerous based on their roles with al Qaeda. Hassan's level of danger to the US was obvious. He was a young man raised by terrorists who showed no interest in doing anything else but plotting to maim and kill. Sharqawi and Kazimi, for their part, were directly connected to bin Laden and other senior al Qaeda leaders. Pentagon leadership ultimately authorized the transfer out of Bagram for Hassan, Sharqawi, and Kazimi, as well as the transfer of seven others.

Ten men in all were moved out of their Bagram cells for transfer on September 22, 2004. Most of the ten detainees knew the drill, having been moved via airplane at some point during their detention, but this flight seemed to last a very long time before they finally experienced the familiar feeling of an airplane landing. Now on the ground, they were instructed to stand before being marched off the airplane. A rush of hot, humid air instantly hit their bodies. The blindfolds were still on, so they couldn't see their surroundings. The next hour or so was a confusing odyssey of vehicles, buildings, more vehicles, and one interlude that felt like a boat ride.

They were eventually led into a building. One by one, their blindfolds and ear coverings were removed. Medical personnel were on hand for another medical screening. Soon, each of the detainees was stripped naked. For the first time, they were able to view their surroundings, but their regained eyesight didn't reveal much. They were in another windowless military facility. Uniformed American soldiers were there. The fluorescent lighting was the same.

The ten naked men looked at each other to see if they recognized anyone. An Army officer interrupted them, entering the room with a flurry and shouting, "Welcome to Guantanamo Bay!" An interpreter shouted the same thing in Arabic. The detainees were then quickly dressed. Their eyes and ears were covered again. Soldiers led them to their new homes—cells in what was known as Camp 5, which was a maximum-security facility located just yards from the sparkling blue waters of the Caribbean—a site the detainees did not see because Camp 5 was a windowless structure.

Camp 5 had only recently opened. Modeled after a federal maximum-security prison in Terre Haute, Indiana, its cells were small, featuring a skimpy bed, a prayer mat, a Koran, and a toilet. While some Guantanamo Bay camps were communal facilities where detainees could regularly intermingle, those camps were for so-called "compliant" prisoners. Camp 5 was for the noncompliant detainees.

The new arrivals received very little information. The Army officer who welcomed them barked some rules and regulations that they were urged to follow. But the ten men were still in shock. Guantanamo Bay was an unknown destination. They could only wonder what kind of hell this was going to be.

Hassan was led to his small cell. So were Sharqawi and Kazimi. These were notoriously bad men, truly among the "worst of the worst." Hardly anyone in the outside world would make much of a fuss over the fate of these die-hard Jihadists.

As each of the new arrivals was directed to their new homes, one man was particularly in disbelief at this latest development in his life. He worried about his family. He fretted over his business. The man, after all, was almost sixty years old and in questionable health. He sat down on his new bed, which barely fit his wide frame. He wondered what was to become of him. This was, of course, Saifullah Paracha.

Upon arriving at Guantanamo Bay, he and the other detainees were not referred to by their names, as the author would learn on a later visit to Camp 5. In fact, most soldiers assigned to Joint Task Force-Guantanamo Bay (JTF-GTMO), the military entity charged with running the detention camps, never knew the names. Each detainee was assigned an Internment Serial Number, or ISN. Whatever number they had back at Bagram was now obsolete. The guards knew them by their ISNs.

Hassan bin Attash was now only known as ISN 1456. Kazimi was ISN 1453. Sharqawi became ISN 1457. Their real names were mostly relegated to the confines of classified documents that were tucked away in secret, locked file cabinets and classified computer databases. The ISNs were now the only way to identify each detainee.

At Guantanamo Bay, Saifullah's success in international business and the thousands of contacts he had made over the years meant nothing. On September 22, 2004, as ISN 1094, he was now one of hundreds of nameless men.

CHAPTER 14

MASTERS OF THE EARTH

Uzair and Saifullah Paracha were essentially accused of the same crime, which involved providing material support to al Qaeda. But the allegations against Saifullah were much more expansive than those against his son. As 2003 bled into 2004, it was still widely believed that Saifullah, KSM, and Ali were plotting to smuggle explosives and weapons of mass destruction into US ports. The Marriott bombing in Jakarta proved that terror plots were still proceeding even with some of the principal operatives in custody. And with Majid Khan complicit in the Marriott murders, another of several common denominators linking the Parachas to al Qaeda, tough times were certainly ahead for father and son.

Uzair and Saifullah's personal situations could not have been more different, due to the unique factual circumstances of their individual cases. Uzair was facing federal charges by virtue of his being arrested in New York. The charges stemmed from Uzair's role in assisting Majid Khan with his immigration problem, as well as his acceptance of al Qaeda funds for the Cliftonia investment. Uzair was not accused of being involved in the explosives and smuggling plot. Uzair was represented by experienced defense lawyers. He was permitted telephone calls home. New York–based family members were even allowed to visit with Uzair on a limited basis. It was hardly an ideal situation, but at least Uzair had some legal recourse.

Saifullah was alleged to be much more deeply involved with al Qaeda operatives, and he had none of those benefits afforded to his son. Due to his classification as an enemy combatant, the elder Paracha was being held in what was known as indefinite detention. No criminal charges were on the horizon. Release appeared increasingly unlikely. The US government reasoned that enemy combatants like Saifullah could be held until the end of the war. Since this conflict was known as the "Global War on Terror," who knew when that would end? Years? Decades?

"Uzair is doing better than his father," a nephew of Saifullah, who asked to remain anonymous, stated in early 2004. "Unlike his father, Uzair has been given a right to counsel. In spite of the fact that it is very tough on him, he is staying strong. Our family has only been able to see him once since he was detained ten months ago."

But life for Uzair was extremely complicated. In the past, when he had an issue, he could count on his father to intervene. With Saifullah locked away, Uzair was forced to confront matters on his own, and he had a terrible time dealing with legal woes and confinement.

Perhaps the most momentous decision of Uzair's life had come in October 2003. Uzair was offered a deal: a guilty plea in exchange for five years in federal prison. Uzair's lawyers advised him to take the deal and count his blessings. His defense attorneys reasoned that the evidence against him was solid. Prosecutors from the Southern District of New York (SDNY) had documentary evidence proving that Uzair had agreed to assist Majid Khan. Moreover, Uzair's statements to Agent Miller in late March 2003 had proven disastrous. She got him to admit that he knew Khan and Mustafa (a.k.a. Ali Abdul Aziz Ali) were al Qaeda operatives. A jury was likely to convict Uzair of supporting terrorism. And if the case went to a jury, he was likely to spend decades in prison.

But Uzair couldn't bring himself to accept his lawyers' advice. Perhaps it was the burger in him, but Uzair was unable or unwilling to admit guilt. He began telling his lawyers and family members that the FBI abused him. He recanted everything he told Agent Miller. He blamed her for coercing him into making a false confession. Uzair even equated his treatment in FBI custody with the perceived torture that many assumed his father was going through at the hands of the military. Uzair told his lawyers that he would not plead guilty. He wanted to take his chances with a jury. He believed that he could prevail, that they would see his side of the story, that he was just a businessman handling rudimentary tasks for a client. He believed that anyone could see he was not a terrorist. He had convinced himself that he was simply not guilty. The government was lying, not him.

His attorneys were alarmed. They could see that Uzair was not thinking rationally. But ultimately, the decision was his.

Uzair's lawyers tried everything they could to talk him into taking the deal. They even asked his family for help. Cousins and uncles begged Uzair to reconsider his decision. But Uzair flatly refused their entreaties.

"Basically, he did istikhara," a cousin said, referring to a religious practice where a person prays for guidance. "And the istikhara did not say to take the plea deal. Which, you know . . . we tried our best."

Uzair had made his decision, and it was now up to his lawyers to seek an acquittal. After the deal was rejected, the court scheduled a hearing for November 25, 2003, which was postponed until late February 2004. This would now be Uzair's life, bouncing from court date to court date as he careened toward a trial. His family hoped for the best. But their trust in the American system of justice had been shaken. Although they had urged Uzair to take the deal, they still fully believed that he was innocent of the crimes.

"Uzair has pleaded not guilty," the cousin stated. "The government's case is very weak against him. Insha'Allah we are just hoping for a fair trial. If he does receive a fair trial, he will be released. The bad part of this is it is an election year [2004] and we fear his case will get caught up in politics."

The plea deal was certainly a crucial decision for Uzair, but he also was forced to contend with life in jail, for which he was unprepared and unaccustomed. While he managed to keep his mind sharp by reading the books that were sent to him by relatives, an ever-changing group of cellmates cycling through his living quarters was rough. Being a spoiled rich Pakistani kid in a New York jail meant that conflicts between Uzair and his cellmates were frequent. Uzair may have thought he was tough in business, but jail was an entirely different world. It required a skill set he simply didn't possess.

The jail staff brought another new complication to his life a few months after Uzair rejected the plea deal. In December 2003, Uzair was placed under what are known as Special Administrative Measures, or SAMs. These are procedures governed by Federal Bureau of Prisons policy that allows for expanded security measures to be applied in certain cases. SAMs typically involve lengthy periods of solitary confinement. Communications with the outside world are placed under stricter limitations, as well. SAMs are common in cases involving international terrorists. Of course, Uzair and his family did not believe he was a terrorist. They believed the SAMs were punishment for his rejection of the deal.

"About one in [ten] guards treated us like human beings," Uzair later wrote. "About one in [ten] hated us with a passion and terrorized us at every opportunity."

Through 2004 and into 2005, Uzair counted down the time until he could have his day in court. Once that moment came, he believed that this nightmare would be over. But for his father, there were no criminal trials in his future. The situation looked bleak. At Guantanamo Bay, as mentioned previously, Saifullah was being held in indefinite detention, designated as an enemy combatant. The US government might as well have tossed him in a cell and thrown away the key.

Saifullah was a fighter and never one to wallow in self-pity. He knew Farhat was steadfast in her support. Between the two of them, they were committed to raising hell with a protracted struggle. Government officials would ultimately be forced to take notice of his case both in the US and Pakistan.

* * *

In early 2004, while Saifullah was still at Bagram, Farhat had taken her campaign for justice directly to the US judicial system, linking up with several US attorneys through an organization called the Center for Constitutional Rights (CCR). Farhat and Saifullah now had a US-based legal team whose mission was different from the British and Pakistani lawyers that were already retained. The CCR lawyers did not set out to address business matters or even to seek answers. Instead, the CCR lawyers took on the daunting and infinitely complex task of winning Saifullah's release and bringing him home.

The attorneys included Gaillard Hunt, a Maryland lawyer who initially made a name for himself during the 1960s and 1970s representing military conscientious objectors. Farhat referred to Hunt as a "gem of a man . . . [who] has been trying hard to help my husband get justice."

Also on the team was David Remes, a partner at the prominent law firm of Covington & Burling. Despite his elite legal pedigree, Remes proved himself to be a dyed-in-the-wool activist on behalf of detainees subject to indefinite detention.*

For Hunt and Remes, Saifullah was among the first of what would be many detainee-clients. The lawyers filed numerous lawsuits and writs of habeas corpus in federal courts on behalf of Saifullah. They demanded access to books and religious materials and filed an injunction on his behalf preventing military doctors from conducting medical procedures. But first and foremost, the lawyers demanded Saifullah's freedom.

The first demand for his freedom had been filed in early 2004, when Saifullah was still at Bagram. The lawyers argued that Saifullah was a lawful permanent resident; consequently, he should be afforded the same constitutional rights as other American citizens. The US government disagreed, refusing to release Saifullah. Instead, the government shipped him to Guantanamo Bay.

On the day of that transfer, Farhat had received a phone call in Pakistan. It was a representative from the Red Cross. The ICRC representative broke what would be absolutely devastating news at that point: Her husband was no longer at Bagram and had been relocated to Guantanamo Bay. She instantly called Gaillard Hunt and implored him to find a way to bring Saifullah home.

The wheels of justice moved slowly within the courts, and the responses from the federal judges were not sympathetic. Hunt decided that the lawyers needed to circumvent the federal courts. They had to deal directly with a complex administrative system, such as it was, at Guantanamo Bay. Hunt vowed to pursue every possible option to gain any advantage for Saifullah.

Meanwhile, Saifullah and Farhat continued to communicate through handwritten letters, the ICRC still being the conduit for these messages.

---

* A few years later, Remes resigned from Covington & Burling in disgrace. Evidently, he became so overzealous about the plight of his clients—particularly the strip searches that went on at Guantanamo Bay—that he held a news conference in Yemen where Remes removed his pants in front of dozens of stunned onlookers and cameras. In his resignation, an unapologetic Remes vowed to become a human rights lawyer full-time. "The reaction to what I did makes me very sad," he told the *Washington Post* at the time. "I wish people paid as much attention to the suffering and torment in Guantánamo as they paid to the way I sought to dramatize it."

Many of their letters complained about the slow delivery service. At least their family could share updates about their lives. The ICRC messages certainly had some emotional value. The following is a letter Saifullah sent to his family in mid-2005, almost six months after his transfer to Guantanamo Bay:

> Dear Mom, Farhat, Muneeza, Mustafa and Zahra,
>
> Assalam o Alaikum. I pray to Almighty God for your health and well being. May God always keep you safe and sound. I received your two letters dated Feb. 14 and 27. Happy Valentine's Day to you too. Here all days are same. By blessing of God my health is good, but you don't mention about your health. Please write in detail. Whenever you write place a carbon paper for your own record, I put you [sic] letters in front of me and reply, so you can also refer back to your copies in you [sic] record. I have replies [sic] Eid Activities, you must have received by now. Happy to know about kids are doing fine in their studies and other activities. Zahra's sport noted. It is good to know her participation. Zahra, keep it up! Delays in letters is not in our control, we have to live with it. But now it is getting efficient some what . . . May God keep you happy healthy, wealthy and long life. Allah Hafiz.
>
> Best Regards,
> Ma-Assalam (Peace be upon you)

* * *

Farhat's frantic phone call to Gaillard Hunt sent the Maryland human rights lawyer into overdrive. It was the fall of 2004, and she had just informed Hunt that Saifullah was now at Guantanamo Bay. The lawyer knew what this meant: a Combatant Status Review Tribunal (CSRT) would be coming up fast. A CSRT was not a court. Instead, it was an administrative function established for recent arrivals at Guantanamo Bay. The sole purpose of the CSRT was to determine whether an individual detainee met the standard for being classified as an enemy combatant. The standard itself essentially came down to whether a detainee was affiliated with al Qaeda or its associated forces, such as the Taliban.

Hunt was direct and to the point, instructing Farhat to gather a list of respectable associates of her husband. If these associates were amenable, Hunt would ask them to provide character references. The lawyer knew that the cards were stacked against his client. But if he could get a panoply of professionals to attest that Saifullah was as moderate and freedom-loving as they come, then perhaps he had a chance to prevail. While Hunt would not be able to represent Saifullah in person, he could still direct the narrative from afar.

Farhat readily agreed to the plan, which seemed easy to carry out at the time. Saifullah was revered in many circles of Pakistani society as an elite businessman and had many friends in high places. He was respected and his philanthropy was well known. Farhat assumed there would be many whose lives he had touched who would come forward to help rectify this gross miscarriage of justice.

She was wrong.

The Parachas had become radioactive. With Saifullah at Guantanamo Bay and Uzair in a New York jail, they had become what young Mustafa Paracha described as "that family." Friends and associates with long-standing ties to Saifullah kept their distance. Religious organizations that had greatly benefited from Saifullah's outreach ignored Farhat's pleas for assistance. She found suspicions and wariness about the family in all quarters.

A dismayed Mustafa Paracha described former allies' attitudes this way: "We don't know you. We don't want to know you. We don't care about you. We never knew you."

This widespread abandonment traumatized Farhat, who had been raised to believe that one could always count on friends and family for support. Those were certainly the values she and her husband had always operated on and raised their children to believe in. But the family quickly learned that any sort of link to a Guantanamo Bay detainee was an insurmountable stigma in social circles that had once celebrated Saifullah's success.

A Pakistani journalist based in Karachi, Zofeen Ebrahim, later recalled that [Farhat] "told me that she had gone through so much, that she was taking medical counselling, psychiatric help, she was in depression. But if you look at the family, they were such a normal family like yours or mine would be."

Despite the unforeseen resistance, Farhat doggedly pursued allies. Saifullah's longtime office manager, an elderly man named Syed Abul Mahasin, eagerly agreed to write a letter on Saifullah's behalf. Farhat also managed to get a letter of support from an employee of the Pakistan Television Corporation. A nephew and several Pakistani barristers also signed on. So did Khalid Khawaja, a retired Squadron Leader of the Pakistan Air Force and former Pakistani Inter-Services Intelligence (ISI) agent turned businessman. But Farhat really received a limited amount of support relative to what it could have been.

In November 2004, a few weeks prior to Saifullah's CSRT, Hunt submitted seven letters from those serving as character witnesses. Some were notarized. Others were on company letterhead. Another was in the form of an email. Each letter had a common theme. Saifullah was a good man and not a terrorist. Hunt reasoned as an attorney that if the government was going to submit the worst about Saifullah, then it was Hunt's obligation to share the best about his client.

Saifullah's office manager, Mahasin, described his boss as "an honest and true Muslim. He never keeps company with Alcohol and other trivialities. Lots of people lined his office every day, including people related to business and social welfare institutions. People used to take advantage of his philanthropy . . . [and] some used to get loans from him and never repaid."

Mahasin also described a financial situation that went against Saifullah's carefully crafted narrative of good fortune with his business endeavors. "His financial status is such that there is hardly any cash balance in his account. His own house is under mortgage. Still he would help his friends, even by taking loans. His alleged involvement in terrorist activities is baseless and without foundation. . . . Being a Muslim, his sympathy with Afghanistan and Iraq does not mean that he is involved in terrorism or supports terrorism." Mahasin went on to glowingly describe several of Saifullah's charitable endeavors. He somewhat facetiously ended his letter with the line: "You may draw your own conclusion about Mr. Paracha's character."

Another letter written by Saifullah's nephew, whose name was redacted from the official document, described Saifullah's visceral reaction to the 9/11 attacks. "On September 11th, 2001, I was right in front of the WTC when the first building collapsed. I was literally inches from losing my life.

Saifullah Paracha at Guantanamo Bay, photographed by a delegate of the International Committee of the Red Cross.
(*Miami Herald* / Contributor)

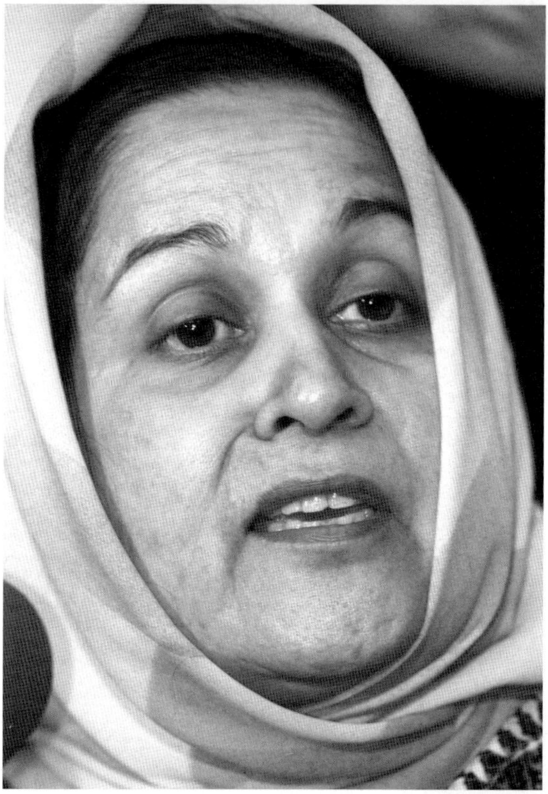

Farhat Paracha, matriarch of the Paracha family.
(Getty Images / Handout)

Uzair Paracha, CEO of Chenco (formerly International Merchandise Group).
(Getty Images / Handout)

Majid Khan at
Guantanamo Bay.
(MCT / Contributor)

Majid Khan at a Guantanamo Bay Military Commission hearing.
He's holding a written confession.
(MCT / Contributor)

GAY VICTIM TELLS OF VICIOUS ATTACK

SEE PAGE 7

STRAPPED TA RUNNING NEARLY EMPTY BUSES

SEE PAGE 6

SPORTS ★ ★ ★ ★ FINAL

DAILY NEWS

50¢ www.nydailynews.com NEW YORK'S HOMETOWN NEWSPAPER Monday, March 3, 2003

NABBED TERROR MASTERMIND PLANNED ATTACKS IN CITY, U.S.

JUST IN TIME

PAGES 2-3

Khalid Shaikh Mohammed after his arrest Saturday in Pakistan.

AP

Khalid Sheikh Mohammed's capture gained international attention.
(*New York Daily News* Archive / Contributor)

Hamid Gul, former director-general of Pakistan's Inter-Services Intelligence. (Robert Nickelsberg / Contributor)

9/11 conspirator Ramzi bin al-Shibh. (FBI / Handout)

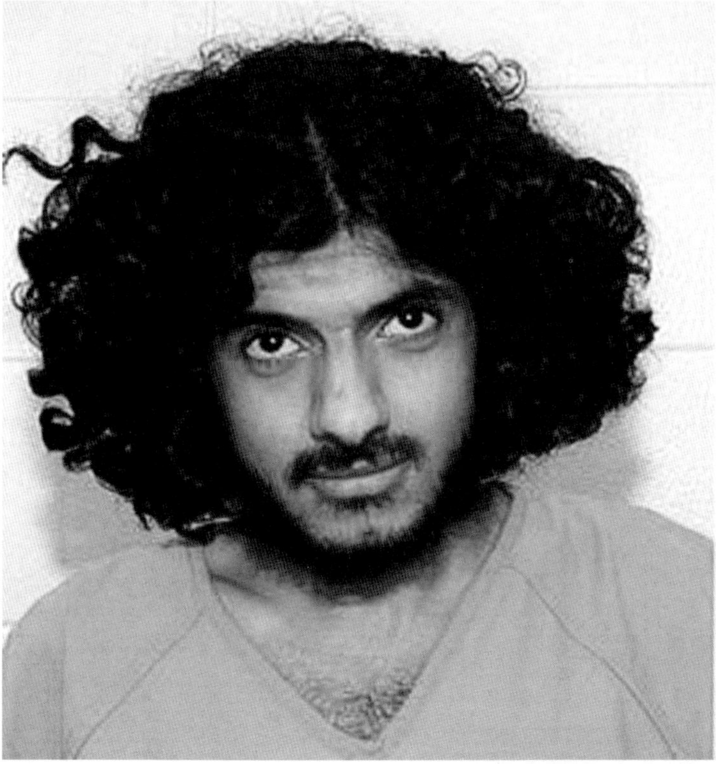

Hassan bin Attash at Guantanamo Bay. (MCT / Contributor)

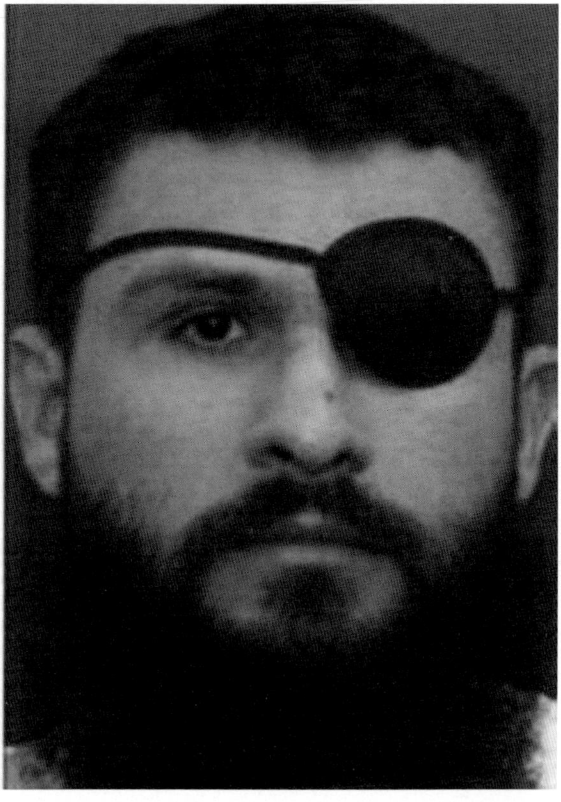

Abu Zubaydah, high-value detainee at Guantanamo Bay. (MCT / Contributor)

Khalid Khawaja following a 2007 arrest in Pakistan.
(Aamir Qureshi / Staff)

Abdul Qadeer Khan (left) recognized as the father of Pakistan's nuclear weapons program.
(Tanveer Mughal / Contributor)

Rear Admiral James McGarrah, director of the Guantanamo Bay Office of Administrative Review of Enemy Combatants.
(Mark Wilson / Staff)

As debris was falling down and hitting people, most people began to panic and start stampeding, thus many people lost their lives due to that. With my own eyes I saw people holding hands and jumping out of the window of the eighty-plus floors.

"I have discussed the events of September 11th with my uncle, and he was completely against what happened. He expressed sorrow and compassion for people who lost their lives, and agreed that nothing justified killing innocent people as bin Laden did that day. My uncle was into saving and helping people. He spent his time in charity work, building a hospital [and] schools in the poorest area of Pakistan, which is the Northwest Frontier. This area is next to Afghanistan, with which it shares a very porous border. If my uncle crossed into Afghanistan, it would have been in connection with this charitable work."

Some letters offering support for Saifullah were not as compelling. A missive from Khalid Khawaja, the retired Pakistani Air Force officer and security professional, was a particularly odd character-witness choice. Khawaja was an early associate of Usama bin Laden during the conflict against the Soviet Union in Afghanistan. Khawaja was frequently dogged by allegations of links to extremism. It is likely that Attorney Hunt was unaware of this reputation at the time. The CSRT tribunal did not reference Khawaja one way or another.

A very short letter written by Pakistani lawyer Khawaja Naveed Ahmed was also underwhelming, and he was misinformed about Saifullah's location. "It is certified that Mr. Saifullah Paracha is known to me for last three years. He is a businessman of good repute. To the best of my knowledge, he bears good moral character. I have been told that he has been detained in Kabul for last about sixteen months."

Hunt surely realized that the letters of support were a mixed bag. But it was the best he was going to get. Hunt's years of experience had exposed him to the challenge of stigma. So, he was not going to let any opportunity go by without advocating for his client—including submitting the character references themselves.

The letters were submitted to Rear Admiral James McGarrah of the now-defunct Office of Administrative Review of Enemy Combatants. Accompanying the letters were cover pages with Hunt's letterhead. Within these cover pages, Hunt appealed for common sense to prevail in this case. "Whatever indiscrete associations Mr. Paracha may have contacted in the course of his wide-ranging business and charity activities in Pakistan and Afghanistan, one thing is clear. Holding a moderate and sympathetic public figure like Mr. Paracha does a lot of harm to the American cause on the ground, where it matters, among our allies and supporters in Karachi and throughout Pakistan."

In another cover page for a different batch of support letters, Hunt took a more legalistic tack. "Since Mr. Paracha is a civilian far beyond military age, is a citizen of a country allied with the United States in the struggle with terrorism, and came under American control while peacefully traveling in civil aviation hundreds of miles from any war zone, he is not an enemy combatant. Any derogatory information American intelligence may have on him, if indeed there is any, will have to be dealt with in some way other than holding him under the metaphorical or fictitious label of enemy combatant. Confident that the Tribunal will carry out its orders with the objectivity and fairness my own experience with courts martial and military boards leads me to expect from American military officers, we anticipate Mr. Paracha's designation as not an enemy combatant, and look forward to his return to Pakistan, where he has been a voice for moderation and reason."

Hunt's tactics were creative in the context of the early CSRTs. But would that be enough? While the CSRT hearing itself would indeed be something of a disaster for Saifullah, as his lawyer, Hunt had reasoned that if the Tribunal took an objective look at the entire record, the decision could have come down in Saifullah's favor.

* * *

It was early December 2004, and Saifullah had been at Guantanamo Bay for two months when he was invited to attend a CSRT. It was a sham. No detainee had ever been released as part of the CSRT system, and while the system was ultimately reformed, the revised CSRTs—later named Periodic Review Boards, or PRBs—wouldn't be implemented until more than ten years later. In 2004, even having been at Guantanamo only a short time, Saifullah knew the true score with the CSRT, and he was in no mood for any of it. He was openly incredulous and snarky in the face of Americans who were treating him like a terrorist. Military officers held his fate in their hands, yet they had no concept of how international business functioned. Their facts were wrong. They just were not getting it.

"Is it possible to loosen my handcuffs?" Saifullah asked at the very first opportunity he had facing the CSRT Tribunal, his loud voice booming in the brightly lit conference room.

The lead military officer, an Air Force colonel known as the Tribunal President, refused. "It is standard practice in this situation [to wear handcuffs]," the colonel said. "You may be assisted in reading any documents by your Personal Representative, but this is standard practice for all Tribunals."

Saifullah gave the Tribunal President a hard stare, then just shook his head. He couldn't help being indignant at being subjected to such a farce.

The Tribunal consisted of three military officers. No lawyers. No judges. An officer known as a recorder served in the role of prosecutor, and the members of the Tribunal were often quick to point out that the CSRT was not a court. Without his attorneys, Hunt and Remes, in the room to argue for Saifullah, a military officer known as a personal representative was tasked with advocating on his behalf.

Despite the limited nature of the CSRT, the stakes couldn't have been higher. If the Tribunal determined that Saifullah was not affiliated with al Qaeda, then he would no longer be deemed an enemy combatant. If that happened, the US government would lose its legal justification for detaining Saifullah, and he would be released from custody and allowed to go home.

The members of the Tribunal had already read through Saifullah's file. They already knew about his meeting with Usama bin Laden. They had read Agent Miller's interview notes, and they'd even had access to the then-top-secret confessions of KSM, Ali, and Majid Khan—including their statements made subject to torture, for which the CSRT had no prohibitions. The Tribunal officers were also aware of Saifullah's assistance in holding $500,000 for KSM. They knew about KSM's and Ali's 222,000-euro investment in Cliftonia, and the Sharafuddin Shamim bank account. Saifullah's file also documented his assistance to Majid Khan and the plot to smuggle explosives and WMDs through his import/export business, including Saifullah's lone admission given before Agent Ruby interrupted that interview at Bagram.

The CSRT summarized the case against Saifullah as follows: "The [evidence] asserts that the detainee met and associated with high-level al Qaeda operatives, including Usama bin Laden, held large amounts of al Qaeda money, researched investment possibilities for al Qaeda money, helped locate homes for al Qaeda members, and used his media facilities to translate extremist materials into Urdu. The detainee also proposed the use of nuclear weapons against US troops and suggested a source for such weapons and discussed plans to smuggle explosives and chemicals into the borders of coalition members."

The hearing felt like a formality, and Saifullah doubted that these officers would seriously listen to him.

Underscoring his attitude of disdain, during Saifullah's first substantive statement to his Tribunal adjudicators, he began with a caustic joke about politics. "If I am allowed to tell a joke, this would only take two seconds. There were three professionals, and [they ask] which one is the oldest? One doctor, one engineer, and one politician. The doctor said he was the oldest [profession], because he founded the birth of Adam and Eve onto Earth. The engineer said he was the first profession, because he found chaos and confusion on Earth and rebuilt it. The politician said he was the oldest profession, because he was the one that started all the chaos and confusion in the first place."

The record does not reflect how Saifullah's joke was received, but he immediately went from telling his joke to pontificating about his many contacts—and repeating his contention that he alone could have stopped 9/11. He then went through each allegation and denied them all. "I have never been supportive of the Taliban or al Qaeda or its partners. I have never been involved in an al Qaeda plan to smuggle explosives into the United States. I have already given the FBI details of my business in Pakistan, and they have not found anything. I never held money for safekeeping for any al Qaeda operative. I never gave any research for any company for investment possibilities. I have never associated with any high-level al Qaeda operatives.

"I never recommended to al Qaeda [that nuclear weapons be used against US troops], or where the nuclear weapons would be available; I don't know, sir, where these are available. I have never assisted an al Qaeda member or family to find a place to rent; however, I did assist some people who said they were Pakistanis. I showed one Pakistani the area I lived and I showed another Pakistani how to find a place from the classifieds in the newspaper.

"I never offered al Qaeda media facilities or translation; I do have a news agency I own. . . . I gave this information to my interrogators. I did meet with Usama bin Laden in 1999 and 2000, two times. I never met two high-level al Qaeda officials that were wanted men, sir."

Once Saifullah finished denying the allegations, the Tribunal President asked if he had any other statements that he would like to make. Saifullah, of course, relished the opportunity to speak. He went on an extended, winding diatribe about the history of Pakistan. But the undertone of this history lesson was clear. Saifullah was making a case that he did not know that KSM and Ali (a.k.a. Mir and Mustafa, respectively) were terrorists: "The nation of Pakistan is over 140 million people; we are the most victimized of the Cold War between Russia and the US. During the late '70s, Russia invaded Afghanistan and Pakistan defended at that time along with France. President Carter did not pay much attention to that. When President Reagan was elected in 1980, Vice President Bush, a former CIA director, realized the importance of this invasion and the defense of Muslims.

"So, the US propagated jihad, called freedom fighting; freedom fighters, young rebellious radical Muslims were brought in to the Russians. It took almost ten years to win that war. Finally, Russia left. Those freedom fighters were left there, and are still there in thousands. Pakistan and Afghanistan share an unregulated, uncontrolled border. Many fled to Pakistan as refugees, and they are still there and have been there for twenty years. They have no family, parents, or brothers and sisters. They have not been accepted back to their home countries; terrorism has been harbored in Pakistan because of that situation. Pakistan has become a center of terrorism. They have become Pakistanis; they act like Pakistanis, eat the same food, look like Pakistanis, so no one can tell them apart. Anybody raised in Pakistan could come from anywhere, and nobody knows who's who. . . .

"When I met Usama, he delivered the Koran, and said he was a prophet. He said very nice things, very impressive. I asked him to speak about the terrorism program for an English program. We intended to make a program for my television station, and I claim that if people watched my station, that they will know the difference between Christianity and Islam. During the Cold War, Pakistan and Afghanistan have suffered the most. Afghanistan is poor people, and Pakistan is on the verge of bankruptcy. The only country with power is the United States. I swore to send up letters to President Bush about the situation there, but nobody paid attention. What I feel, sir, is the Lord Almighty plans slowly for the nations. Pakistan, US, and Russia, God forbid if they ever have direct conflict. They both have enough weapons of mass destruction to destroy the world 50 times. So the Lord planned for the Cold War to be ended with the least casualties. Yesterday, some were your soldiers, and today, they are being labeled as your enemy."

If Saifullah expected to get into a debate with the Tribunal, he was mistaken. The Tribunal President allowed Saifullah to make his speech without interruption, but when it was finished, the Tribunal President simply stated, "Thank you. I understand that concludes your statement."

After some procedural activities, the Tribunal officials began to ask questions. The nature of their questions demonstrated they were extremely skeptical of Saifullah's denials. One officer questioned why Saifullah would show KSM around the area.

"Are you a real estate agent?"

"He wanted me to show him the area I live, so I took him around," Saifullah replied. "He doesn't live in Karachi."

Another Tribunal member noted that some of Saifullah's initial denials of the allegations "were addressed in a cursory fashion." The officer went on to ask whether Saifullah knew of any plans to bring explosives or weapons into the US.

"No," Saifullah replied.

"So it didn't matter if it was al Qaeda or anybody else?" the officer asked.

"No, sir," Saifullah stated. "The allegation was specific, so I gave a specific answer, and in general terms, I don't know."

Saifullah perked up when asked about his specific business interests, and he reverted to his name-dropping and influence. In response to a question about a failed business, Saifullah put a positive spin on the matter. "That is a publicly traded company, and I own 96% of the shares. They manufacture bags, sugar, cement, fertilizer. . . . The governor of Pakistan offered a good incentive to put the business there, about one million dollars came from the

European Union and the US to establish it there to stop the poppy industry there. The government put the money somewhere else, but I invested a million dollars in that myself. It was in a remote area, and was not profitable . . . I wrote the American embassy that this could provide employment there to reduce the poppy business. It can never be eliminated, but it could be controlled. I have been trying to do this, and I know a lot of government officials."

Saifullah continued to advise the Tribunal that Agent Miller had all his exculpatory evidence, including his letters to President Bush and others. But Saifullah came across as slightly incredulous when it came to questions about IMG. It was obvious that the military officers were buying into the notion that Saifullah's import/export company was being used to smuggle explosives and weapons into the ports. Saifullah essentially told the Tribunal officers that they did not know what they were talking about.

"International Merchandise is a business where I am an equal partner with my friend in New York. We facilitate for Walmart, companies like that. We do not do shipping. We are a buying agent for garments and other merchandise from Pakistan. The shipment is from the factory straight to New York."

The Tribunal officers still weren't giving credence to the story. One officer asked, "There is an international shipping component to that business?"

"No, we are a buying agent only," Saifullah firmly replied, his voice rising. "We get a commission in the States, in which I get half from my partner."

If Saifullah's contempt for the proceedings wasn't evident before, it was about to make itself known. The questioning about his businesses, especially the incorrect impressions of IMG, were particularly infuriating. Saifullah pointedly asked about the legal justification for holding the CSRT in the first place. Despite being in military custody for more than a year, Saifullah was taken aback by what he perceived as a condescending, dismissive response from the Tribunal President.

"You do understand this is an administrative hearing, and this is not a legal proceeding," he stated. "I do know you had some questions about the legality of your detention. That would be referred to other organizations of the government, but you will be receiving more specific instructions shortly of how to bring your question to US courts."

"Your honor," Saifullah deadpanned. "I have been here over seventeen months. Would that be before I expire?"

This time, the Tribunal President showed just the hint of a smile and said, "I would certainly hope so, especially since you are under the care of the US government while you are here. As far as some of the other statements you made about jurisdiction, this is a US government executive decision in regard to the detention of enemy combatants. This is an administrative hearing being conducted to review, on an independent basis, the government's information and statements you provide us, to consider or reconsider whether you are an enemy combatant."

"Your honor," Saifullah stated, his voice booming now and seething with derision. "My question is . . . Is your Executive Order applicable around the Earth?"

"It is a global war on terrorism," the Tribunal President replied.

"I know sir, but you are not the master of the Earth . . ."

"No, but we are in a coalition with allied partners to fight this new war," the officer retorted.

This CSRT hearing was going about as well as Saifullah expected, which was not well at all. But he rarely went into negotiations empty-handed, and this situation was no different. He held back for a moment, believing he had another card to play.

* * *

The results of Saifullah Paracha's CSRT arrived shortly after his hearing concluded. Two sentences: "On 8 December 2004, the Tribunal determined, by a preponderance of the evidence, that Detainee #1094 is properly designated as an enemy combatant. . . . In particular, the Tribunal finds that this detainee is affiliated with al Qaeda."

A Navy lawyer's memorandum dated December 20, 2004, upheld the decision, noting that the CSRT was legally sufficient and also confirmed that the decision was unanimous. The next day, the director of the CSRT process, Rear Admiral McGarrah, signed a memorandum concurring with the Tribunal decision, confirming that the US continued to view ISN 1094 as an enemy combatant.

Saifullah was not going home, and his options were running out. He was now forced to rely on the federal courts for relief. Saifullah now believed that his best opportunity might be something that would have been unthinkable in any other situation. He wanted to be charged by a criminal court. Perhaps a jury would see the truth. Saifullah didn't know it then, but criminal charges at Guantanamo Bay held their own unique challenges, and he would have to wait his turn.

* * *

If Saifullah's CSRT was a disaster, then Uzair's criminal trial was to be an equivalent catastrophe. During the trial, Uzair elected to take the stand in his own defense. He had been thinking about this moment for more than two years, ever since he was arrested in March 2003. It was now November 2005, and he was in a federal courtroom in Manhattan. Uzair was going on trial for providing material support to al Qaeda.

Once again, Uzair thought he could explain away the past. But all he did was tell the jury that he was a liar. He said he lied to the FBI. He lied to his own attorneys. He lied to prosecutors. Uzair essentially recanted every derogatory statement he made to the FBI back in late March 2003. He told the jury that he lied about knowing that Majid Khan and Mustafa were members of al Qaeda. That he was on trial for his life after rejecting a generous plea deal made Uzair's testimony even more tragic.

Uzair tried to explain to the jury that he was simply a twenty-three-year-old who "panicked initially." He noted that when he had been picked up by the FBI in March 2003, he did not have a lawyer. Uzair lamented that the FBI took away his cell phone. He noted that he was traumatized by a strip search. Uzair even told the jury that he was threatened with jail if he tried to invoke his right to an attorney. "I had already told them the truth, and I did not go home. That is when I started lying. . . . If I had known these people were al Qaeda, I would not have helped them out."

Uzair went on to lament the fact that his father "put me into this situation," adding that he made some half-hearted efforts toward completing the tasks for Majid Khan "out of respect" for Saifullah. Uzair's story did not go over well with the jury. It went even worse when Agent Janelle Miller took the stand. She came across as extremely credible, and her testimony was backed by documentary evidence, including the fact that Majid Khan's credit cards and ID cards were in Uzair's possession. When Agent Miller flatly denied that Uzair was mistreated or threatened with jail if he asked for an attorney, the jury (and judge) believed her.

Uzair's defense was doomed to failure almost from the start. His best defense was to present then-classified evidence from Majid Khan, KSM, and Ali confirming that they hid their al Qaeda affiliations from Uzair. That evidence would have bolstered his argument that he had no knowledge that he was assisting members of al Qaeda. If he could have proven a lack of knowledge, then he would have been acquitted. But after some legal wrangling, the government was able to limit those statements to some unclassified summaries. The jury would never get the benefit of the full picture. They would not hear testimony from any of the detained operatives, including Ali and Majid Khan.

The summaries that Uzair's lawyers were permitted to read to the jury were quite favorable to Uzair. For example, Ali's written summary went into the record as follows: "Uzair Paracha was totally unwitting of Al-Baluchi's [Ali's] al Qaeda affiliation, or of Al-Baluchi's intention to use Saifullah Paracha for the broader operational plan involving Majid Khan. Uzair Paracha knows nothing about operations. Neither Al-Baluchi nor Majid Khan indicated to Uzair Paracha at any time that they were mujahidin or al Qaeda. Uzair Paracha did not complete the task involving Majid Khan."

Khan's summary was equally supportive of Uzair's claim that he had no knowledge of Khan's affiliation: "Majid Khan thought Uzair Paracha was a good person who was willing to help. Majid Khan might have been interested in recruiting Uzair Paracha once Majid Khan returned to the United States and had time to assess Uzair Paracha. Majid Khan would only give Uzair Paracha a five-to-ten-percent suitability assessment, citing the fact that Uzair Paracha had no extremist views and was not really a practicing Muslim."

The unclassified summaries certainly bolstered Uzair's strongest case because they supported his primary defensive argument. They also served to muddy the overarching picture about the Parachas and their role with al Qaeda, particularly pertaining to shipping and explosives. Advocates consistently cited those summaries as proof of Uzair and Saifullah's innocence.

In contrast, law enforcement never bought Ali and Khan's dismissal of Uzair and Saifullah's knowledge of their al Qaeda affiliation. At the end of the day, they reasoned, Saifullah handed bin Laden a business card, which caused the leader of al Qaeda to dispatch KSM to Saifullah's office. After 9/11, KSM introduced Saifullah to Ali, who in turn introduced the Parachas to Majid Khan. Saifullah remained in contact with Ali even after KSM was captured and his identity was revealed to the world. To law enforcement and prosecutors, these facts proved that Saifullah and Uzair must have had knowledge of Ali and Khan's ties to terrorism. Uzair's earlier confession that he helped Khan to protect the financial investment in the Cliftonia real estate project made the most sense.

But by the end of Uzair's trial, those unclassified statements didn't matter. Evidently, summarized statements that were stipulated by lawyers did not resonate with the jury, whereas Uzair's tangled web of lies did stand out. He was never able to overcome those missteps.

On November 23, 2005, the jury in New York found Uzair Paracha guilty on all counts. Eight months later, on July 20, 2006, the judge issued his sentence. Uzair was not going to get five years as he was previously offered. The judge sentenced him to thirty years in a maximum-security federal prison.

* * *

In late 2005, as Uzair was on trial in New York for assisting al Qaeda, a clandestine group was seeking the acquisition of two dirty bombs as the first of a two-part mission. During this step one, the group was to obtain the radioactive material necessary to build two bombs that combined conventional explosives with radioactive particles. Once obtained, the team would embark on the second part of the mission: to smuggle the radioactive material into the US through official border crossings.

This team was aware of Uzair and Saifullah Paracha. In fact, Saifullah's apparent failure to deliver on a shipment of conventional, nuclear, or radiological explosives had partially motivated these would-be dirty bombers, who—like Saifullah—were Americans. But they did not own an import/export business. Instead, their plan was to create a fake business that ostensibly worked in the field of radioactive material. If they could acquire enough radioactive material for two dirty bombs, the team planned the risky move of transporting the radioactive material into the US. The group's guiding principle was "that anyone can purchase small quantities of radioactive sources for stockpiling because suppliers are not required to exercise any due diligence in determining whether the buyer has a legitimate use for the radioactive sources."

One member of the group later described their first moves in carrying out their mission: "We produced counterfeit documents. . . . We found two NRC [Nuclear Regulatory Commission] documents and a few examples of the documents by searching the internet. We subsequently used commercial, off-the-shelf computer software to produce two counterfeit NRC documents authorizing the individual to receive, acquire, possess, and transfer radioactive sources."

With fake documents in hand, a member of the group filled out paperwork claiming that he represented a company located in Washington, DC. The document justified the need for radioactive material through some official nonsense about running a business calibrating personal radiation pagers. That member later reported, "The purchase was not challenged."

On December 14, 2005, the group dispatched two teams, one that was located in Canada and the other in Mexico. In both countries, the respective teams placed two containers of radioactive sources into the trunk of rented vehicles. A total of four containers full of material necessary for a dirty bomb were en route into the US. At that point, the US Customs and Border Protection (CBP) had no idea what was coming.

At the Canadian border, a rental truck containing dirty bomb material was met by CBP agents. An agent stopped the driver and his companion and informed them that the truck was going to be inspected. The agent motioned for the driver to pass through a special checkpoint equipped with a radiation monitor. As the driver passed the monitor, he watched intently as the CBP agent "look[ed] down and reach[ed] to his right side of his booth." The mission appeared to be over. The driver later recalled that he "assumed that the radiation portal monitors had activated and signaled the presence of radioactive sources."

The CBP agent again approached the truck driver and his passenger. He asked for identification and where they lived. Both produced passports indicating that they lived in the Washington, DC, area. The agent then asked what they were transporting. The driver replied, "Specialized equipment back to the United States."

A second CBP agent approached the truck and asked, "What else are you transporting?"

"Radioactive sources for the specialized equipment," the driver tried to explain, but the mission appeared to be compromised.

Both CBP agents were writing information into notebooks while looking over at the truck. The driver was ordered to park in a secondary inspection zone, one designed for further scrutiny. A new group of CBP agents approached the truck, soon demanding answers from the driver, who reached into the truck and pulled out the fake NRC document that his team had created on a computer. The driver also produced a counterfeit bill of lading for the radioactive material. The CBP agent inspected the documents and asked if he could make copies. The driver agreed. "Although the CBP inspector took the documents to the copier, [we] did not observe him retrieving any copies from the copier," the driver later recounted.

The CBP agents informed the duo that additional inspections needed to be performed. After several minutes of inspection, the agents approached the two team members once again. They were free to travel into the US with their cargo of radioactive material.

"At no time did the CBP inspector question the validity of the counterfeit bill of lading or the counterfeit NRC document," the driver subsequently reported. The dirty bomb material had indeed been permitted into the country through the northern border.

At the same time, the second two-person team drove their truck containing radioactive material and counterfeit documents through Mexico to the southern US border. They also were met by CBP agents. As with the team's counterparts at the northern border, the driver was ordered by CBP agents to pass through the radiation monitors. Again, the team "assumed that the radiation portal monitors had activated and signaled the presence of radioactive sources."

One of the CBP agents asked if the driver and passenger were American citizens. When the team produced state driver's licenses, a CBP agent inquired about their purpose in Mexico and if they were bringing anything back into the US. A team member recalled that "[we] told the CBP inspector that [we] were returning from a business trip in Mexico and were not bringing anything into the United States from Mexico."

At that point, the driver and passenger were ordered out of the vehicle. A CBP agent grabbed a radiation scanner and waved it around the outside of the vehicle. Another CBP agent confronted the two team members. The driver later recalled that he said they were transporting "specialized equipment." The CBP agent ordered him to open the back of the truck. When the back was opened, the driver made an admission, that they "were transporting radioactive sources in addition to the specialized equipment."

The CBP agents ordered the driver to move the truck to a secondary inspection zone, the same inspection routine encountered by the team at the northern border. The driver reported, "During the secondary inspection, the CBP inspector said he needed to verify the type of material [we] were transporting." The dirty bomb material was being stored in cardboard boxes in the back of the truck. The CBP agent's scanner confirmed the presence of that radioactive material.

The team was asked a second time about their purpose in Mexico. This time, the driver offered a somewhat convoluted excuse, that they "had used the radioactive sources in a demonstration designed to secure additional business for [their] company." The passenger then produced the counterfeit documents as proof for that assertion. A CBP agent took the fake paperwork and walked into the CBP station several yards away.

"He returned several minutes later," the driver recalled. The cardboard boxes were closed and secured in the back of the truck. The CBP allowed the team to enter the US at the southern border with the dirty bomb material and their fake documentation.

Fortunately, no radioactive material was released into the air and no dirty bombs exploded. The team members were not actually terrorists. They were undercover agents working for the US Congress. A Senate committee had requested a group of undercover investigators from the Government Accountability Office (GAO), a nonpartisan watchdog agency in the government's legislative branch, to assess radiation monitors at US ports of entry. The plot to smuggle dirty bombs into the US was the top of mind subject of their undercover operation. Senators wanted to know if the country was safe. The GAO proved that it was not.

Senator Carl Levin, a Michigan Democrat, referred to it as "a wake-up call." Norm Coleman, a Minnesota Republican, was aghast. "These issues must be addressed with a sense of urgency. It's just an indictment of the system that it's easier to get radiological material than it is to get cold medicine."

* * *

Uzair was sick of hearing the name Majid Khan. That person had been nothing but trouble ever since he first entered his life back in Karachi. Uzair's trial was over with the guilty verdict, and the ring he had proudly planned on presenting to his girlfriend would never adorn her finger. Uzair felt his life was over. All of this had happened because he became a brief acquaintance with Khan. Farhat described her son as "like any young twenty-something, with the world at his feet and a girlfriend by his arm. They were desperately in love and were just waiting for him to finish studies. She got married recently and I don't blame her, for she couldn't wait endlessly."

As he passed the time at the Supermax federal prison in Colorado, Uzair became solemn and withdrawn. His weight jumped to 170 pounds, and the once strong athlete avoided exercise because he didn't want to be strip-searched, a requirement before entering the fitness area. Uzair was content to just read books and pray regularly. Thirty years was a lifetime.

One day in late 2006, Uzair received a letter. It was from a representative of that louse who ruined his life. Majid Khan had a CSRT coming up. Majid had apparently been sent to Guantanamo Bay. The US military was set to determine whether Majid met the definition of an enemy combatant. Majid asked if Uzair would make a statement on his behalf. Uzair recoiled at the thought. He couldn't bring himself to get involved and just wanted to live in solitude reading his books.

Uzair didn't know it at the time, but Majid's personal life was also in shambles beyond just the loss of his freedom. While Uzair became withdrawn, Majid turned indignant and combative. After years of seclusion and abuse, Majid's good-natured attitude was gone. By late 2006, Majid was angry and started lashing out at his new captors at Guantanamo. In response, his guards punished him. They took away the comforts that he enjoyed, such as finger foods and recreational time with other detainees. The cycle of misbehavior and discipline only escalated.

Majid's main incitement was a letter provided by the ICRC in October 2006. He had only been at Guantanamo Bay for about a month. Accompanying the letter was evidence of a life now lost, a photo of Majid's daughter.

Back in 2003, Majid had been captured while his wife was at home, pregnant. At the time, Majid and his wife didn't know the sex of the baby. It was only after three years in captivity that he finally learned that the baby was a girl. In fact, he didn't even know if his wife had given birth until he received the ICRC letter. Majid became emotional. He took his daughter's photo back to his cell, but a guard considered it contraband and forcibly pulled the photo out of Majid's hands. "I went crazy and yelled for one hour and they ignored me as if they didn't know I was yelling," he later recalled.

After the conflict over the photo, Majid was at loggerheads with the guards. The result was typically the same: He lost his comfort items. "On November 2, 2006, they gave me new wrong-prescription eyeglasses to wear. Also wrong frame, which don't fit my nose. I took it and when I try to wear it, they made my eyes hurt and head spin. The prescription was way off. They knew I am practically blind without my glasses and knew exactly how to hurt me. Anyway, so I didn't wear it. I kept wearing the old one. After four days, they forcibly took my old glasses and made me wear new ones."

In early 2007, Majid went on a hunger strike. He was suicidal. Majid demanded "mails, newspaper, and my lawyer." The prison staff again took away his comfort items and confined him to a windowless cell. "The reason I was on hunger strike is that I wanted to go back to Pakistan or be charged," he said. "Until then, treat me with respect like CIA did in last ten months before my arrival [at Guantanamo Bay]. . . . Anyway, days passed like this, but eventually I got frustrated and chewed my artery which goes through my elbow on January 7, 2007."

Majid wasn't the only detainee to have been transferred out of CIA custody in 2006. In fact, nearly all the high-value detainees were flown to Guantanamo Bay. They were housed in a special detention facility often referred to as Camp 7. It was a building shrouded in secrecy. Even Camp 7 lawyers in later years had to seek court orders to visit the facility.

Nearly everyone directly and indirectly associated with Saifullah's al Qaeda connections was now on the same island. Bin Laden, of course, was still at large and hiding out during this time. And Uzair was in federal prison. But Majid, KSM, and Ali were in Camp 7 at Guantanamo Bay. They were joined by 9/11 plotters Ramzi Binalshibh, Mustafa al Hawsawi, and Khallad bin Attash, along with Hambali, Lillie, and Zubair, Majid's contacts with respect to the JW Marriott attack in Jakarta. Al Qaeda operative Abu Zubaydah, who was seized in a raid in Pakistan that netted documents linked to Saifullah, was also at Camp 7. Saifullah and the young explosives expert, Hassan bin Attash, were housed in Camp 5, on a separate part of the Guantanamo Bay naval base. Detainees in Camp 5 had no communication with those in Camp 7. The bin Attash brothers would never have an opportunity to see each other.

As was the case with Saifullah, the Camp 7 arrivals were afforded CSRT proceedings to determine whether they were enemy combatants. Some refused to participate. Others, like KSM, proudly admitted to their crimes. This was an infamous hearing in which KSM declared that he was responsible for the 9/11 attacks "from A to Z."

Ali, on the other hand, denied that he was affiliated with al Qaeda. Instead, Ali defended himself with testimony that was eerily similar to Saifullah's, although calmer and more polite. He was even deferential to the Tribunal members, hardly the demeanor one would expect for an accused 9/11 plotter. But like Saifullah, Ali had one major theme throughout his hearing, albeit without the grandstanding. Ali claimed he was just a businessman. "I am an entrepreneur with many personal contacts in different companies around the world. Because of my position, I am unable to accomplish tasks, whether administrative, monetary, buying, selling, advertising and customs through my own private resources. So it is normal that people use my outsourcing services."

Even with respect to his association with 9/11 hijacker Marwan al Shehhi, Ali coolly claimed that it was just innocent business. "When Marwan al Shehhi approached me, he never declared himself as 'hijacker Marwan al Shehhi.' He approached me the same way he approached other individuals and companies in the US; a man wanting to do business." Ali had the same answer for others, such as 9/11 plotter Ramzi Binalshibh. "Just was introduced through Khalid Sheikh Mohammad," Ali asserted. "If he needed any business help, which he didn't."

And his association with Majid Khan? "Just a person . . . introduced through KSM," he said.

A Tribunal officer asked him, "Did you help Majid Khan get into the United States or did you help him with any business matters or loans or anything like that?"

"No," Ali replied. "But, ah, he was from the States. So, he doesn't need any help going to States."

When asked about his ties to KSM, Ali stuck to his story. In some moments, it appeared that Ali might as well have been speaking for Saifullah. "If I was introduced to a person via Khalid Sheikh Mohammad, that does not necessarily mean that this person is a combatant or necessarily an al Qaeda supporter," he stated. "The people I met through my uncle are businessmen interested in trade, education, and travel. I am not aware of any links or animosity toward the United States or fighting against the United States."

There was plenty of documentary and other damning evidence to establish Ali's role in the 9/11 attacks, along with other terrorist activities. But it was notable that he relayed similar cover stories that KSM apparently provided to Saifullah in their dealings. "Mr. Khalid Sheikh Mohammad is my uncle by blood; he is my mother's brother," Ali explained. "He owned a honey trading company, and a henna distribution company. Additionally, he was also trying to work [in] Pakistan export and import. All these companies or activities were personal and belonged to no organization or party but [were] a source of income for his family members."

Through Ali's cover story, that familiar endeavor reappeared: "Export and import." It was now early 2007, yet the topic continued to come up. This time, Ali confirmed once again that KSM—who just days earlier proudly told his CSRT Tribunal that he accepted responsibility for the 9/11 attacks—was involved in "Pakistan export and import."

After making the reference, Ali quickly denied that he knew anything about smuggling or shipping explosives. He also denied knowing "the source of [the Tribunal's] information." Of course, just prior to Agent Ruby's interruption, Saifullah had admitted that Ali had at least considered the possibility of shipping explosives to Europe. Details of the plot continued to be murky. Notably, when offered the chance to specifically submit a supporting statement from businessman Saifullah Paracha, Ali declined.

Majid Khan, however, was happy to accept statements of support, including from Saifullah. These letters were mostly brief, self-serving, and full of denials. It was as if Majid's connections, as least those willing to assist, were maneuvering for self-defense.

Saifullah wrote that Majid was introduced to him by Ali. "I never knew Majid Khan was a member of al Qaeda. I never had any discussions with Majid Khan regarding any financial matters. . . . I am a businessman and I have a large business setup in Karachi. . . . All of my business details have already been provided. Have no way of judging Majid Khan's activities against the USA or its coalition partners at all."

A statement from Iyman Faris, the man whose discussions with Majid back in Baltimore motivated Majid to pursue Jihad, was even more contemptuous. "There was no discussions other than religious duty and what he liked to do in life, like work in construction and not in his father's business," Faris wrote from federal prison, adding that his purpose for visiting Majid's home was "to invest in the family business of gas stations."

Faris referred to allegations against him and Majid as "an absolute lie." When asked whether Faris was coerced, tricked, or deceived into making derogatory statements against Majid, Faris sarcastically replied with "all of the above."

The only exception to the outright defiance came from emotional statements submitted by Majid's father, Ali Khan. The father noted that he had attempted to travel to Guantanamo Bay to see his son, but the military refused to allow it. The last time the elder Khan spoke to his son in person, they were in a family quarrel, and he was attempting to keep young Majid out of harm's way. But with Majid now in military custody, the father was straightforward about the fact that he was 100 percent in his son's corner. He wrote, "You want to know whether my son is a terrorist? The answer is no. As I have said before publicly, I cannot accept these allegations against him. If you think that he did something wrong, show me the evidence. Charge him with a crime and give him a fair trial in a real court. This Tribunal is not a real court. It is not a legitimate proceeding. It is only for show, and the outcome has probably already been decided."

Ali Khan went on to protest Majid's treatment while in custody, including torture. He further lamented having been prevented from visiting his son: "This is not right. We expect much more in America. Particularly because Majid has political asylum here and grew up and went to high school here in Maryland. He has legal status in the United States."

If Ali's CSRT hearing was the model for calm and measured demeanor, Majid Khan's was the opposite. Majid was angry and indignant, venting his contempt for the proceedings. "I'm not satisfied with the . . . Tribunal process," he stated. "I would rather have a fair trial than have a Tribunal process. . . . I am not al Qaeda. To be al Qaeda, a person needs to be trained in Afghanistan and needs to take an oath in front of Usama bin Laden. I have never been to Afghanistan, and I have never met UBL. I cannot possibly be a member of al Qaeda. I admit I can't prove that I am not al Qaeda. It is very difficult to prove that [someone] is not al Qaeda. [The Tribunal] states that I was re-entering the States to commit a terrorist act. The only reason they assumed I was going to commit a terrorist act is because they made me al Qaeda in the first place. Their logic says I must be coming to commit a terrorist act. I am not al Qaeda. I am not an enemy combatant, and there were not any terrorist acts."

Majid then harshly downplayed the specific allegations against him, sometimes snarkily referring to Fox News as his source for all things al Qaeda: "After watching too much Fox News, I learned that to become al Qaeda, a person needs to go to Afghanistan for training and take an oath in front of Usama bin Laden for their cause. I've never been to Afghanistan or met UBL."

He also said, "I never called KSM my uncle. KSM is not my uncle. There was never any conversation between myself and Iyman Faris about meeting KSM." With respect to evidence extracted from Majid's laptop, he stated: "It is possible FBI intentionally put suspicious stuff on my hard drive. . . . Just because media was seized when I was captured does not mean that media belongs to me. You have to give me the benefit of doubt, please. If I was an extremist Muslim, why would I teach computers to Muslim and non-Muslims for free in Baltimore?"

Regarding his association with Uzair, Majid was even more adamant. In fact, Majid's comments about Uzair were rather striking because of how firm they were. "While visiting my new wife and family in Pakistan, my travel documents for return to the United States expired. As a fellow Pakistani, the Parachas agreed to help. Uzair Paracha is innocent; he is not a criminal. One ordinary citizen helping another ordinary citizen does not make them terrorists. Getting help from a criminal does not make me a criminal or, more importantly, an enemy combatant."

During questioning by Tribunal officials about the Parachas, there was one subject that made Majid rattled and evasive.

"Mr. Khan, I have one question," a military officer asked. "In Mr. Saifullah Paracha's statement, he said that you were introduced to him by Mr. Ammar al-Baluchi. What . . . what was your dealing with Mr. Baluchi?"

"I am not at—I can't answer that in this, ah—under these circumstances," Majid replied. "I'm not in position to tell you exactly what my association with that guy. . . . All I can tell you that the person, whoever it is, that, that I was introduced to him, in my opinion, that he is not al Qaeda, he's not Taliban, or associate forces who may be a threat to United States. And that's all I have to say about this person. Other than that, I can't comment."

The Tribunal ultimately determined that Majid Khan was indeed an enemy combatant. As expected, they made the same determination for all the other former CIA detainees. With the conclusion of the CSRT hearings, it was apparent that Majid, Ali, KSM, and Saifullah would be stuck indefinitely at Guantanamo Bay. Detainees and government officials then began setting their sights on a different type of proceeding: war crimes trials.

CHAPTER 15

LIES, SCHEMES, AND BETRAYAL

After 9/11, Khalid Sheikh Mohammad continued to help bin Laden achieve his dream of an American "Hiroshima." Toward this end, KSM and Ali began working with Saifullah Paracha in 2001 and continued until they were all captured in 2003. During that period, KSM had received a tempting offer. A group of Yemenis were in possession of "suitcase weapons." Those weapons of mass destruction were up for sale. A foreign government had recordings of those conversations. The recordings weren't shared until after KSM's capture.

On March 15, 2003, CIA agents had waterboarded KSM multiple times as they sought to learn more about the Yemenis and their suitcase weapons. KSM stuck to his story that no purchases were made. But the CIA persisted. They knew about Saifullah and his shipping business. CIA officials were aware of Paracha's Pakistani connections and his references to nuclear material. The waterboarding of KSM continued. A heavily redacted email from a medical official observing the interrogation described it like this: "During the waterboarding sessions that day, the application of the interrogation technique further evolved, with the interrogators now using their hands to maintain a one-inch deep 'pool' of water over KSM's nose and mouth in an effort to make it impossible for KSM to ingest all the water being poured. At one point, [CIA agents] waited for KSM to talk before pouring water over his mouth."

Eventually, the truth was revealed. The Yemeni offer was too good to be true. Al Qaeda operatives determined that the offer was a scam. Bin Laden and his men would have to look elsewhere for their "Hiroshima."

* * *

Saifullah was painfully anxious to get out of "shitmo," as he called it. Despite his legal setbacks, he remained desperately optimistic that he could come up with some sort of plan. As in his past life as a businessman, he was always scheming. He knew he needed to come up with something creative.

A potential opening presented itself in November 2006. At fifty-nine years old, Saifullah was the oldest detainee at Guantanamo Bay, and as described previously, his medical conditions were well known, including his diabetes, high blood pressure, and what he deemed a "weak heart." He constantly kept the medics busy as they ran test after test, and Saifullah frequently objected to being shackled during his medical appointments.

On one occasion, a doctor recommended that Saifullah undergo a procedure known as cardiac catheterization, a relatively common diagnostic test designed to locate any blockages and to gather exact blood pressure measurements. The procedure involved inserting a thin plastic tube into a vein or artery and threading it to the heart. The test was entirely precautionary. Although Saifullah was not in any imminent danger, based on the recommendation of doctors, Guantanamo Bay officials spent almost one million dollars to have an aircraft deliver a twenty-four-member team of cardiac specialists and equipment.

Saifullah usually had no issues with medical procedures. They had been a common occurrence in his life for many years. He also liked the idea of being the center of attention. But with this invasive medical procedure, Saifullah saw something different. He saw a possible ticket home.

He refused to undergo the procedure. Saifullah then contacted lawyers Hunt and Remes. Soon after, thanks in large part to his attorneys, a two-pronged assault took place. One was in the courtroom, and the other was in the media.

In a federal lawsuit, the lawyers argued that Saifullah's life might be in danger because Guantanamo Bay was not equipped to safely handle such a medical procedure. Their proposed remedy was for the court to order the federal government to send Saifullah to the US or Pakistan for treatment.

The media angle was perhaps more effective. Suddenly, Saifullah's name was making headlines for the first time since the 2003 port security scare went public. His supporters propagated a narrative describing Saifullah as old and frail, with a very serious heart condition. Fox News incorrectly reported that Saifullah had suffered a heart attack at Guantanamo Bay. Other media outlets copied the Fox News canard and disseminated it as fact. Soon, supporters were claiming that Saifullah also had suffered a heart attack way back at Bagram. Khawaja Khalid, Pakistan's chief coordinator for human rights issues, issued a statement to the media alleging that Saifullah was in "poor health and could die in detention if [he doesn't] receive treatment soon."

The US government was suddenly under pressure to send a sick and decrepit detainee home. The context of the actual, precautionary medical procedure had been lost. Instead, it had been elevated to dire terms such as "heart attack" and "dying." Guantanamo Bay already had a poor public reputation, which this turn of events exacerbated.

But the government pushed back hard. Camp officials and law enforcement believed that Saifullah's refusal to undergo the procedure was merely a ploy to get out of Guantanamo Bay. Common sense suggested that if Saifullah landed on US soil, he would invoke his status as a lawful permanent resident. In that scenario, Saifullah would never be sent back to Guantanamo.

Nobody in the government was willing to let him go. Agent Miller and others at the FBI were still perturbed by the Agent Ruby debacle years after her outrageous interruption. The official FBI position remained that Saifullah had provided KSM and Ali with some sort of practical information involving a plot to smuggle explosives and weapons of mass destruction. Agent Miller had come so close to extracting the details that, at this point, unless Saifullah came clean, there was absolutely no appetite at the FBI for letting him go.

Although public perception had labeled Saifullah's plight a travesty, the federal courts viewed his situation differently. A judge denied Saifullah's request to be sent to the US, ruling that he was not convinced that Saifullah was at risk of "irreparable injury" at Guantanamo Bay. In other words, this procedure was not full-blown heart surgery. The judge opined that the doctors and equipment that had been flown to Guantanamo could handle everything without any grave risk for the detainee patient.

For many years, the expensive equipment initially reserved for Saifullah's procedure languished—unused—at a Guantanamo Bay hospital. Saifullah never underwent the test. It had been his best shot to date at getting off the island, and it had almost worked. But in the end, like everything else he tried, it resulted in the government simply still considering him an enemy combatant.

After the medical evacuation ploy failed to get him out, Saifullah resumed his routine. Over the years, Saifullah had become the venerable elder statesman of Camp 5-Delta. He even sought to instill some pride among the detainees in their living conditions. Younger detainees referred to him as *chacha*, which is an Urdu word for "uncle."

It was a stark contrast to his earlier days at the camp. Back then, Saifullah frequently butted heads with other detainees with whom he had nothing in common. Many of those detainees only spoke Arabic, which was not Saifullah's forte. Detainees were all just angrier then, as well—they hadn't yet established a comfortable routine with each other. They verbally abused Saifullah on matters as petty as his choice of television shows, which were typically news programs.

By 2007, Saifullah had finally been accepted as the rich, old gentleman of Guantanamo. He organized business classes for his fellow detainees. He counseled them on the types of businesses they could start after they were released. Many of those detainees believed they were lucky to have such a shrewd and successful businessman in their midst. And Saifullah relished every opportunity to regale his fellow detainees with stories of his business exploits.

Saifullah also became what was known as a camp leader, a primary liaison between the detainees in Camp 5-Delta and the guard staff. He was granted occasional meetings with camp officials to advocate on behalf of the camp population. These meetings proved beneficial to everyone, including the guards, who appreciated Saifullah's calm presence and his ability to tamp down to some extent any detainee discontent. The detainees, for their part, had an experienced, trusted negotiator working for them. By all accounts, Saifullah's conduct in the camp was described as "exemplary." All the while, Saifullah never let up on his research and letter writing. While he enjoyed the adulation, he still wanted to go home.

To this end, Saifullah continued periodic meetings with FBI and CITF agents. Their questions were initially like those that were posed to him during his later days at Bagram, and his answers remained essentially the same.

"1094 is a lying fucker," exclaimed a sharp-tongued senior member of the now-defunct Joint Intelligence Group at Guantanamo Bay, in a 2010 meeting with the author. "The fucker knows about the explosives, and he knows that he was working with al Qaeda. It's pointless talking to him. He just feeds us bullshit."

With his life in greater limbo than ever before, it's true that Saifullah was wily, more than able to deceive and take advantage of his interviewers. One FBI agent, who had developed a good rapport with Saifullah, suggested, "He tests people. If he senses that someone isn't well prepared, he messes with their heads. Saifullah is a really smart man. He's a shark. If you're not prepared, he'll eat you alive." The FBI agent observed that Saifullah had successfully toyed with many investigators from the FBI and CITF over the years, and he had nothing to lose at any point between 2005 and those comments in 2012.

That agent, who happened to be African American, did add that Saifullah had something of a racist streak. "Saifullah is totally intimidated by black people," the agent said with a chuckle. "He tells racist jokes, too."

Racism aside, as time went by, the interview questions became less probing and substantive. With each passing year, the ominous explosives plot became less of a concern. Some law enforcement personnel believed that the plot was likely never in an advanced stage, after all. Based on their intelligence, many now believed that KSM's capture might have stopped the plan in its tracks. Others speculated that the various contradictory statements combined with documents seized in raids indicated that explosives and WMDs could have been stored in some unknown location; but al Qaeda was otherwise deprived of the means to ship them out.

None of this, of course, absolved Saifullah of his crimes, especially since investigators all agreed that he provided advice on this subject fraught with issues. But it did reduce the exigency in getting Saifullah to talk. Instead of discussing explosives and dirty bombs, agents began meeting with Saifullah just to check up on him. They discussed philosophy, religion, and business among other topics. The conversations were nonconfrontational, even laid-back. Life for Saifullah was calm, although he never ceased yearning to be released from imprisonment and what he still believed to be a gross miscarriage of justice.

In October 2009, Saifullah experienced what was the most momentous day since his arrival at Guantanamo Bay. He was allowed to see his wife's face in real time, thanks in large part to the Red Cross. Apart from human rights lawyers representing individual clients, the ICRC was the official conduit between Guantanamo Bay detainees and their families. For years, the ICRC sought to arrange video-telephone calls (VTC) so that detainees could not only speak to their loved ones, but also actually see them. Finally, in late 2009, the military acquiesced, and the VTCs were approved under stringent conditions.

Each detainee would be allotted VTCs with family members several times per year. The family members had to be on a list preapproved by the military to avoid terror-related communications. The calls were strictly limited in duration. Moreover, conversations were restricted to just general topics pertaining to family members and their lives, and not into more sensitive matters such as detainee treatment or camp procedures. ICRC delegates often traveled to homes overseas to deliver letters and set up the VTC links, and those delegates became like family for providing that lifeline.

To the Parachas, that first VTC in October 2009 was more than just a communication. It was their entire world. The family in Pakistan was finally able to see its patriarch for the first time since that day in July 2003 when Saifullah boarded the Thai Airways flight to Bangkok.

"I hadn't seen my father since I was fourteen," said Mustafa. "I saw him for the first time in six years through the VTC. While it cannot bridge the unbridgeable distance of thousands of miles between my father and our family, the video calls make the separation more bearable."

Farhat could not stop smiling after the first VTC. "We were so happy to see each other again," Farhat stated, her eyes beaming with newfound joy. "I told him as much as I could in one hour. Saifullah is missing his country and the outside world. The VTC reconnects him."

The news during VTCs wasn't always good, however. Saifullah learned that three of his siblings had died since his capture. But in the balance, the

VTC provided Saifullah with an outlet to be the jovial patriarch that he was before that fateful trip to Bangkok. When Mustafa told him that he was interested in renewable energy, Saifullah boasted that he had read an entire case study on the subject through periodicals in the camp library.

For Saifullah, the VTC privilege came along when he needed it most. Every ploy and legal argument he and his attorneys attempted had failed. But after six years, he still refused to admit that he did anything wrong. He was determined to stick to his story, even if it meant being stuck at Guantanamo forever. Even though nearly everyone at the Navy base knew him as ISN 1094, Saifullah believed that his name still meant something.

Meanwhile, prosecutors in New York and Guantanamo were quietly contemplating charges against Saifullah. Numerous factors were at play, including complicated and often competing political dynamics. Saifullah's reluctance to besmirch his name by directly linking it to al Qaeda was going to play an important role. It could even decide whether he lived or died far from home.

* * *

Farhat continued to carry on the fight and raise hell on all fronts. With Saifullah obviously not coming home anytime soon, she was forced into being the sole provider for her children. She was now a full-fledged business executive, a human rights advocate, a public relations maven, a plaintiff in US courts, and a vocal antagonist of the Pakistani government. Over the years, Farhat achieved an impressive number of victories. But her defeats were at times devastating.

One of the most pressing issues for her was financial. Saifullah's elderly office manager, Syed Mahasin, made the startling revelation during the 2004 CSRT that Saifullah did not have much cash in his bank accounts. Instead, his money was tied up in his various businesses. Farhat needed to keep the business alive to maintain the lifestyle to which she and her family were accustomed.

For a time, Farhat, with her eldest daughter Muneeza's assistance, managed to keep IMG afloat. But with the relationship between the Parachas and Charles Stern all but severed, it was impossible for them to keep running IMG anywhere near the profitable level it had in the past. At the same time, more of Saifullah's business ventures began running into trouble. Perhaps the biggest drag on the business was that Cliftonia real estate project in which Saifullah had invested so heavily.

After Saifullah's capture, a man of some limited acquaintance latched onto the family. At a time when the Parachas were becoming pariahs in their own neighborhood, the man's business acumen and assistance was very much appreciated. Farhat and Muneeza allowed him access to the office and their assets.

But at some point, after ingratiating himself, the man turned on the Parachas. He claimed that his associates had made a substantial investment in Cliftonia and wanted their money back in full. The amount in question: 220,000 euros, the same amount of money that KSM and Ali had invested and later helped convict Uzair in federal court.

Despite Farhat's vehement objections, the man announced that he was obligated to collect on the debt. Muneeza and Farhat arrived at the Karachi office one day to discover that it was completely cleaned out. All Saifullah's expensive media equipment from Universal Broadcasting was gone, as well. The man all but disappeared from the family's lives. His name was Khalid Khawaja, a suspected Pakistani terrorist who once boasted about being bin Laden's pilot and who had written the peculiar letter of support for the CSRT. Several years later, Khawaja was kidnapped and murdered by a Jihadist group that had a rivalry with al Qaeda.

Khawaja's betrayal devastated the family's financial situation. Farhat did not let up on her struggle to bring Saifullah home. She later waged a successful battle against the Pakistani government, suing for the failure to assist in the repatriation of her husband. She argued, in part, that Saifullah was subjected to "harsh treatment" at Guantanamo Bay. Ultimately, she convinced the Sindh High Court in 2006 to order the Pakistani government to provide quarterly reports on its progress of pushing for the release of all Pakistani detainees, including Saifullah. In other words, because of Farhat's efforts, the government was required to engage with the United States on bringing Saifullah home. This was a huge victory for Farhat. As the two countries were allies in the War on Terror—albeit in a shaky relationship—she believed that Pakistan could leverage some pressure on the Americans to let Saifullah come home.

Farhat also won compensation from the Pakistani government for families of Guantanamo Bay detainees. This victory assisted in her financial situation so that she could keep up the fight. But for every victory there seemed to be a setback or delay in progress. In 2010, the Sindh High Court found the Pakistani attorney general and foreign ministry secretary in contempt for failing to take concrete steps to secure the release of Pakistani citizens detained at Guantanamo Bay. Evidently, Pakistan was not doing much, if anything, to help Saifullah.

Of course, Farhat and Muneeza did not have much faith in the Pakistani government to begin with. After all, they believed that Pakistan assisted in Saifullah's capture by allowing Saifullah to depart the country. To this end, the family created a website called "FreeParachas.org." The goal was to raise awareness about Uzair's and Saifullah's situations. The site, which is defunct as of this writing, professed their innocence and was highly critical of the US government, and at the same time continued to perpetuate various falsehoods, including the notion that Saifullah had suffered "two heart attacks due to extremely harsh interrogations and torture."

Farhat's efforts did attract support from some unlikely sources. One early champion of Farhat's cause was Ernest "Fritz" Hollings, that longtime South Carolina senator who had urgently demanded that Congress provide funding for port security. As early as 2004, Hollings had singled out Saifullah's situation, urging action as follows in a speech he delivered on the House floor:

> Finally, the US government has failed to provide prompt notice to families of those captured that their family member is in custody, much less information about their health or whereabouts. In such cases, the families of individuals removed to such unknown locations have had no opportunity to challenge detentions that may continue for extended periods. For example, Saifullah Paracha, according to information his family received from the ICRC, has been detained at Bagram Air Force Base for more than 11 months. His wife and children remain in the dark, not only of the reason for his detention, but also when they can expect Mr. Paracha to be released or tried. Other individuals captured more than a year ago remain in

> detention at other undisclosed locations. The lack of information to family members about these detainees violates US legal obligations and sets a negative precedent for treatment that may be directed at US soldiers in the future.

Farhat's enduring achievement was her ability to keep the family together and thriving as much as possible, even through the period when the Parachas had become veritable pariahs in Pakistan. When young Mustafa started to underachieve at school, Farhat urged him to step it up. He recalled, "I made a resolve at that point in time . . . I'm going to work really, really super hard. I need to catch up with people studying at Harvard, because I'm going to hold myself to the same standards. My mom worked really hard to keep me in that school, to keep me going."

Muneeza likewise didn't let the failure of IMG bring her down. She finished business school and became a consultant specializing in financial and risk management. Ultimately, thanks in large part to their mother's insistence, Mustafa, Muneeza, and Zahra all graduated from college and established themselves in productive careers.

* * *

With Saifullah's refusal to participate in the cardiac catheterization procedure, he had a clear goal in mind. He wanted to go to the US, specifically to New York, where he had family, where he could once again be comfortable, where he'd had a base of operations for his business and personal interests over the years. He was confident that his presence in New York would facilitate the resolution of his predicament. And Saifullah and Farhat often dreamed of spending their golden, retirement years in New York.

John Cronan, a young and stylish federal prosecutor for the Southern District of New York, shared Saifullah's goal of getting him to New York, albeit for a different reason. Cronan wanted to send Saifullah to prison.

Cronan's background had prepared him well for his position. He had graduated from Yale Law School, serving as the editor of the *Yale Law & Policy Review*. Cronan began his career by obtaining highly sought-after judicial clerkships. Serious and hardworking, he was well liked and widely respected. He jumped onto the fast track at SDNY—the preeminent federal district that handled terrorism cases. At SDNY, Cronan successfully prosecuted several terrorist operatives. Notably, he was on the prosecution team that obtained a thirty-year prison sentence for Uzair Paracha.

In early 2009, the newly elected President Barack Obama issued an executive order designed to close the Guantanamo Bay camps. Most active military war crimes cases were halted, including the death penalty case against 9/11 plotters Khalid Sheikh Mohammad, Ramzi Binalshibh, Khallad bin Attash, Ali Abdul Aziz Ali, and Mustafa al Hawsawi. Attorney General Eric Holder then announced that the 9/11 case was going to be moved to federal court. The specific district where the proceedings were expected to take place was never in doubt. The case would be tried in Manhattan's SDNY.

The lead Assistant United States Attorney in the SDNY case was set to be David Raskin, perhaps the most accomplished terrorism prosecutor in the country at the time. Raskin had already begun preparations for bringing the 9/11 conspirators to justice. Tough and a bit prickly, Raskin was ready to take on that fight, but he needed a strong team of prosecutors to assist. Among the first names on his list was John Cronan.

The proposed transfer of the 9/11 detainees to New York was almost immediately mired in controversy. Republicans were up in arms and openly clashed with President Obama, calling him weak and irresponsible for attempting to close the Guantanamo camps and for ending the military trials. A significant number of congressional Democrats, not wanting to appear weak on national security issues, joined Republicans in opposing a New York–based trial. Eric Holder's plan to move the 9/11 conspirators was placed on hold for evaluation, and a decision would be made very reluctantly.

Other national security matters further complicated the picture. On Christmas Day 2009, a Nigerian named Umar Farouk Abdulmutallab attempted to blow up a passenger jet that was set to land in Detroit. The bomb was sewn into Abdulmutallab's underpants. The bomb failed to fully explode, although it did ignite inside the would-be terrorist's pants. Opponents of President Obama's closure order at Guantanamo Bay howled. They argued that Abdulmutallab needed to be interrogated by the military. They stated that his actions were a war crime. The FBI was said to be under too many constitutional restrictions to interrogate him in the US. Abdulmutallab was used as a case study for keeping Guantanamo Bay open.

A year later, in November 2010, a man named Ahmed Ghailani faced a New York jury over 285 charges pertaining to his involvement in the 1998 East Africa bombings that left 224 people dead. Ghailani's case was particularly notable because he had been formerly detained at Guantanamo Bay. In June 2009, Ghailani became the first and only detainee to be transferred from the naval base to the United States to face trial. The Obama administration's goals were quite clear. They wanted to use Ghailani's seemingly open-and-shut case as proof that the federal courts were well equipped to handle Guantanamo Bay matters, particularly the 9/11 case.

But the case was not destined to work out the way the administration hoped and expected.

The federal judge in Ghailani's case rejected the prosecutors' request to call an important witness, and things only deteriorated from there. In the end, on November 17, 2010, a New York jury found Ghailani guilty of just one charge—conspiracy to damage or destroy US property. Ghailani was acquitted of the 284 other charges. The judge later sentenced Ghailani to life in prison for the lone conviction, but by that time, the die had been cast as far as moving the 9/11 case to New York. Soon thereafter, David Raskin, the would-be lead prosecutor in the case, took a break from government service and joined a large law firm for the remainder of the Obama administration.

Meanwhile, after Ghailani's transfer to New York, Congress took further action to stifle plans to bring more Guantanamo Bay detainees to the US. Legislators included a provision within the National Defense Authorization Act—an annual major funding bill for military and defense spending—specifically prohibiting the expenditure of funds to move detainees from the naval base to the US. The cases and criminal process for Guantanamo detainees, including prospective cases, were suddenly in limbo. President Obama had stalled the military trials at Guantanamo, and Congress had forbidden those detainees from being transferred to the US for trial.

Despite this apparent legal and political paradox, prosecutors at Guantanamo Bay and New York continued to work. They believed that at some point, the impasse would end. Obama had initiated a task force to review the Guantanamo cases. The goal was to identify the following: detainees who could be sent home; detainees who would remain in indefinite detention but could not be prosecuted for legal or other issues; and detainees who could be prosecuted by the military. It was widely believed that once the task force concluded its work, military prosecutions at Guantanamo Bay would move forward.

The author was one of two military prosecutors assigned to the Saifullah Paracha military case. Shortly after taking over the case in 2009, I had read tens of thousands of pages of information linking Paracha to the Second Wave plot. Here was a Guantanamo Bay detainee involved in a plan to attack the US homeland, and one who had direct connections to Usama bin Laden and multiple 9/11 conspirators. Much of the evidence against him was untainted by torture. Early iterations of the military commissions had prosecuted detainees for much less dangerous offenses. Yet the Office of Military Commissions had demonstrated no rush to prosecute him. Successive chief prosecutors were reluctant to take on cases where detainees had been held by the CIA due to the legal morass of torture and harsh treatment. I pointed out that Paracha was mistakenly lumped in with the "black site" detainees. The circumstances of his capture and detention were vastly different. I argued that Paracha should be prosecuted in a military commission. I recall stating that "it would be a great injustice if Paracha dies a martyr at GTMO before being held accountable for his crimes."

During the summer of 2010, SDNY's Cronan welcomed me and another military prosecutor to his Manhattan office, complete with a window overlooking the skyline. The subject was the Saifullah Paracha case. This meeting must have been bittersweet for Cronan, who had designs to prosecute Paracha's case in New York. The military prosecutors were moving full speed ahead in preparation for prosecuting Saifullah at Guantanamo Bay. Although the military still did not have authorization to charge Saifullah, the military prosecutors were being proactive. They wanted to be ready as soon as they received the expected authorization to proceed.

At the meeting, the military prosecutors described how they envisioned presenting the case, as well as some evidentiary matters. For the most part, the military team and Cronan saw eye to eye on how the case should proceed. All things considered, the task of proving Saifullah's case was not particularly complicated. Unlike many other Guantanamo cases, evidence against Saifullah had already been entered into the record for Uzair's trial. That material included Pakistani financial records, as well as the Majid Khan documents. Therefore, admissibility would not be a problem in a military trial. Moreover, Saifullah had made several admissions during his interviews with Agent Miller and later during his CSRT hearing. Despite Farhat's claims that he was treated harshly and tortured, Saifullah himself stated on several occasions that his statements were being made voluntarily. Saifullah's words would be used against him.

Cronan wanted the case to be tried in SDNY. Based on the nature of the case and its evidence, he believed that federal court was the appropriate venue for Saifullah. But the political and legal landscape at the time made that impossible. A military prosecution was the only viable option, and even that was uncertain at best.

Even though the situation was distressing, Cronan was gracious throughout the meeting and in the days after. He was a straight shooter who respected the rule of law, steeling himself and agreeing to assist the military team with anything they asked. All Cronan asked in return was that the military prosecutors keep him apprised of their progress as they moved forward. The prosecutors had no problem with his request.

Soon thereafter, attorney Andy Patel joined Cronan and the military prosecution team for a meeting. Unlike human rights attorneys Hunt and Remes, Patel was a name that had not been closely linked to Saifullah. Patel was Saifullah's criminal defense attorney, and until now, he had had very little to do since no charges were pending or even authorized.

Patel was a jovial New York–based defense counsel. Despite being what he called a typical Jewish man, Patel joked that Indian mothers often tried to set him up with their daughters due to his last name. And while he was certainly affable by nature, Patel was no slouch as a lawyer. He was perhaps one of the top defense attorneys in the country with respect to federal terrorism cases. He also had experience working with suspects who were caught up in the fight between military and civilian custody. One of his clients was Jose Padilla, the alleged "dirty bomber."

The meeting with Patel was designed to look at a potential plea deal in Saifullah's case. Military prosecutors and SDNY's Cronan outlined a scenario where Saifullah could secure a reasonable sentence in exchange for pleading guilty. Patel indicated that his client was interested. Patel knew the score, and by all accounts, Patel was intrigued by the proposal. If things went well, Saifullah could indeed live out his twilight years at home with his wife and family. Of course, any plea deal would be contingent on President Obama and Attorney General Eric Holder finally authorizing the military to begin charging detainees in Guantanamo Bay military commissions.

Being the defense attorney that he was, Patel issued some preliminary demands. Specifically, he wanted to see all the evidence against his client. The prosecutors refused. They noted that there was enough already out there indicating that Saifullah was likely guilty. And if he wanted proof, Patel could simply look at what had happened to Uzair. Much of the same evidence that was used to convict the younger Paracha would be used to convict his father. Patel considered this and announced that they should continue moving forward with plea negotiations.

A few weeks later, Patel was invited to join the author and another military prosecutor on a flight to Guantanamo Bay. Patel was going to visit Saifullah in a camp meeting room. They would discuss the plea offer. For the first time in more than seven years, there was finally a real prospect for an end to this nightmare for Saifullah.

If Uzair was privy to the Guantanamo Bay plea negotiations, he likely would have urged his father to take the deal. After all, Uzair had his chance. Five years in exchange for admitting guilt. Uzair refused. A jury subsequently found him guilty, and the judge sentenced him to thirty years in federal prison.

Now it was Saifullah's turn. Prosecutors were not knocking down the doors of Guantanamo Bay bearing offers of plea deals. Only a few other detainees had deals in the works. This was a relatively rare opportunity.

The question was raised.

Would Saifullah take the deal, or would history repeat itself?

* * *

Majid Khan had aged considerably since his 2007 Combatant Status Review Tribunal. His hair was shorter. He no longer maintained a groomed beard and mustache. He was content with simple stubble. Most significantly, Majid was no longer angry.

By 2011, the young man who had behaved so defiantly by chewing his own artery and hunger striking was now a thirty-something prisoner full of sorrow and regret. Majid no longer butted heads with the guards. He peacefully read books and made use of all the time he had to think.

While one military prosecution team was looking forward to charging Saifullah, another group of prosecutors were looking into the possibility of charging a different set of Guantanamo Bay detainees. That prosecution team was known as the "JI Team." JI was shorthand for Jemaah Islamiyah, the Thailand-based terrorist organization responsible for the 2003 JW Marriott attack in Jakarta. Prosecutors at the time envisioned a joint trial involving Hambali, the JI leader, as well as his lieutenants Zubair and Lillie. Each of these men had been brought to Guantanamo Bay in 2006. Majid, as the man who was ordered by KSM to deliver $50,000 to Zubair for the attack, was also implicated.

Majid wanted no part of it. During the preceding years, he had taken stock of his life and didn't like what he saw. At some point, while sitting in his cell at Camp 7, Majid resolved to do better. He wanted to set things right. He sought redemption for his sins. His Jihad was over.

Through his lawyers, Majid was able to get the attention of military prosecutors and law enforcement officials. He had something to say. Not sure what to expect, prosecutors and FBI agents agreed to meet Majid in a room at Guantanamo Bay. What they found was an earnest, contrite man, smarter and more composed than he had been in years past. Majid told the group that he wanted to do the right thing and was ready to accept the consequences, which would be confinement for many years.

At that point, Majid proceeded to recant much of his statement that had been made to the CSRT. He described his path to Jihad and admitted to his dealings with KSM, including the plot to assassinate the Pakistani president. Majid confirmed that he delivered the $50,000 to Zubair that was ultimately used in the Marriott attack. Majid even opened up about KSM's nephew Ali and his prominent role with al Qaeda. During the CSRT, this had been a topic that Majid refused to address, and he said it felt good to make that admission. "Actions speak louder than words," he said. "That's what I'm trying to show by my cooperation."

Majid also discussed the Parachas. He confirmed that he didn't have any extensive dealings with them and wasn't in a position to discuss the shipment of explosives. Majid did acknowledge that he and KSM "discussed the possibility of opening an import/export company to move explosives to the United States." That discussion took place in March 2002, around the time investigators believed KSM and Saifullah were having similar conversations. Documents seized in the 2002 raids in Pakistan linking back to Saifullah also supported this contention, such that Majid's confession indirectly corroborated the case against Saifullah.

Majid reiterated that he sought Uzair's assistance on the immigration problem. Majid also confirmed that he had "attempted to recruit Uzair to officially work for al Qaeda." He added that Uzair refused. But again, Majid's admission supports the contention that by directly attempting to recruit Uzair, and eliciting Uzair's refusal, that Uzair at a minimum knew that Majid was an al Qaeda operative. That knowledge on Uzair's part would have met the legal standard for his material support to a terrorist organization.

Majid Khan continued to talk with prosecutors, and eventually, President Obama's task force completed its review of the Guantanamo Bay detainees. The military was now cleared to prosecute cases again. Majid agreed to plead guilty in a military commission. He accepted a deal that would keep him locked up for at least nineteen years. Majid knew what he had done. He was remorseful, and he offered his full cooperation, now on a path toward redemption.

Majid didn't ask for much from the government, but he did have one request. Before pleading guilty, he asked that he be permitted to call his father. He wanted to discuss it with him first. Majid didn't care who listened in on the call. He just wanted to hear his father's voice and possibly have the chance to win his approval. Until this point, the former CIA detainees being housed in the secretive Camp 7 were not permitted to make phone calls. They were held to a more restrictive policy than detainees held in Camp 5, where Saifullah resided. Prosecutors arranged the call. Majid was brought to the large courtroom at Guantanamo Bay's Camp Justice.

There, he spoke to his father for the first time in many years. It was an emotional call. Ali Khan offered his blessings for his son's plea deal.

Thinking about those people who were killed in the Marriott bombing was apparently the catalyst for Majid's change of heart. He was somehow still that kid from Owings Mills High School in Maryland and regretted what he had become as a man. There was no longer any hiding from the fact that he was a murderer. He referred to his actions as an al Qaeda operative as "grotesque and pernicious." He suggested that all he could do now was atone. "If it's any consolation, I would like to sincerely apologize to the family that I've either mentally or physically caused pain," he said. "I ask Allah to forgive me. Maybe Allah can put forgiveness for me in their hearts. Thanks to Allah the omnipotent and omniscient to give me courage to do the right thing."

He concluded by saying, "I obviously made some grotesque mistakes in my life. That's how I ended up here."

CHAPTER 16

WHO DID HE KILL?

Defense counsel Andy Patel's meeting with Saifullah Paracha in 2010 lasted several hours. When Patel finally emerged, he sat down privately with the author and his fellow prosecutor. Patel had some news. Saifullah was willing to testify to the fact that KSM was indeed the man who had worked out of his office.

The prosecutors were immediately dismissive. They didn't need Saifullah to confirm that bit of information. It was already well known, so there was no value in it. The prosecutors asked if Saifullah agreed to anything else. Patel could only shake his head in consternation. Saifullah did not agree to admit guilt in this case. He preferred to argue his case to a military jury. History appeared to be repeating itself yet again. Saifullah had learned nothing from his son's plight.

Patel offered to keep the lines of communication open. The military prosecutors agreed but were not optimistic. Aware of Saifullah's predilection toward toying with unprepared investigators, prosecutors viewed this as Saifullah merely playing more games. The line in the sand was clear. If Saifullah wanted a deal, he would have to accept culpability for his crimes. If not, there would be no deal.

The prosecutors brought the news back to Captain John Murphy, the chief prosecutor for the Guantanamo Bay military commissions. Murphy was assigned to the position in his capacity as a Navy reservist. In his civilian life, Murphy was a seasoned federal prosecutor. He asked the prosecution team to provide a presentation on the feasibility of taking Saifullah's case to trial. The team noted that it had the evidence needed to prosecute Saifullah. The case was relatively clean because Saifullah was treated well at Bagram and Guantanamo Bay. Other agencies with evidence to be used in the trial, such as the CIA and FBI, signed off on the team's litigation plan. The charges were already drafted. All the prosecutors needed now was the authorization to proceed, and Saifullah would finally face a criminal court.

After the prosecution team's presentation, Murphy noted that Saifullah's was part of a list of potential cases he was compiling. Once the military had authorization to begin prosecuting cases, matters that appeared on Murphy's list would be advised to proceed with charges. The 9/11 case and the case against Abd al-Nashiri, the suspected plotter behind the USS *Cole* attack, were already on the list. Majid Khan was ready to plead guilty. The JI case still needed some work. A few others were in various stages of preparedness. When the list finally came out, the first new name on it was Saifullah Paracha. Murphy intended to bring Saifullah to justice. All he needed was authorization from the Obama administration.

Something unforeseen happened several months later. Murphy was essentially fired by Jeh Johnson, then the Department of Defense General Counsel. Johnson (who later became Secretary of Homeland Security) had a dispute with Murphy over the way he was managing the 9/11 trial team. That case was ramping up, and Johnson did not believe that the trial team as then comprised could handle the rigors of death penalty litigation. Murphy was given an ultimatum: fire the prosecution team leads or be fired. Murphy, who was known as a decent and loyal man, refused to fire his people. Murphy was fired instead.

In the fall of 2011, Johnson named Brig. Gen. Mark Martins as the new military chief prosecutor. Martins was a West Point graduate and had earned his law degree from Harvard. His best friend was General David Petraeus, the soon-to-be CIA director, whom he served with as his legal counsel. His law school classmate was a young Barack Obama. Tall and physically fit, Martins held almost mythical status from his years in Iraq and Afghanistan as a Judge Advocate working in the province of rule of law. Martins had a reputation for only sleeping a few hours a night, and he was surely highly intelligent.

Upon Martins's arrival, it became clear that his priorities were different from his predecessor's. Martins was keenly aware of the poor reputation of the Guantanamo Bay cases. They were viewed as incompetent and unjust. Martins sought to improve public opinion of the military commission system. His plan included a policy of taking no risks, so Martins focused the office toward the high-profile and important 9/11 and USS *Cole* cases. Any other cases that had been contemplated for trial were now off the table. Saifullah's window of opportunity to have his day in court had slammed shut.

A military prosecutor asked Martins to reconsider his Paracha decision. Martins was not particularly receptive.

"Who did he kill?" he retorted.

Of course, Saifullah didn't directly kill anyone. That wasn't what his case was about. But Martins's response was indicative of how he viewed his role. The office would no longer prosecute seemingly "random" cases. Instead, the cases needed to be high-profile. And in Martins's view, that meant that any detainees headed toward trial would need to be accused of murder.

In addition, Martins did not like what he referred to as "the optics" of Saifullah's case. The military commissions previously got slammed in the media for bringing charges against Omar Khadr, a Canadian al Qaeda operative who was captured at the age of fifteen and eventually convicted of murdering a Special Forces soldier. With Saifullah, Martins did not like "the optics" of prosecuting the oldest detainee after the office's prosecution of its youngest. He also noted the health-related canards propagated by Farhat and other advocates. Although the "two heart attacks" narrative was false, they still contributed to the perception. If Saifullah had murdered someone, then perhaps the decision would have been different.

About a year later, Martins's decision to refrain from charging Saifullah proved prescient. An appellate court had ruled that the Guantanamo Bay prosecutors could not charge detainees with Material Support for Terrorism (MST). The court ruled that MST was not a traditional war crime, noting that the Guantanamo Bay cases were tasked only with adjudicating war crimes. MST was listed as a legitimate charge under the statute that created the military commission system, however. The problem was that the law hadn't been enacted until 2006. Any crimes of MST that had occurred prior to 2006 were considered *ex post facto*, meaning that because the charge didn't apply back then, the detainee couldn't be charged with it now. With respect to Saifullah, his alleged crimes occurred between 2000 and 2003. If he had been charged with MST as originally planned, those charges would have been thrown out. Ultimately, the law itself validated that Martins's initial refusal to prosecute Saifullah was the right decision.

So, did military prosecutors have any other angles to pursue? Yes. Saifullah was a lawful permanent resident of the United States. In fact, he was the only detainee at Guantanamo Bay to hold status as a US person (Majid Khan held refugee status, which was technically different). Saifullah's own lawyers in federal court made this claim numerous times. Legally, he was likely to have owed a duty of allegiance to the US. There was a charge that had been on the military justice books since 1950 called Aiding the Enemy. Moreover, since that time, Aiding the Enemy was permitted to be used in military commission cases. The Aiding the Enemy charge also contained the same elements as MST, for all intents and purposes, a viable equivalent.

This idea was brought to Martins's attention. Nothing else had changed with the evidence of the case. The charge sheet was simply modified to replace MST with Aiding the Enemy. Military prosecutors were then ready to go.

Martins still refused to prosecute Saifullah. It was too risky, he argued. Aiding the Enemy had never been used in this way, and Martins was reluctant to attempt a novel approach in this case. Again, Saifullah hadn't killed anyone. He was borderline elderly at this point. Martins feared that a setback in a "random" case could delegitimize the entire military commission system. The 9/11 and USS *Cole* cases were already experiencing significant problems. It was all about the optics. Justice was secondary.

Martins's decision was final. Saifullah would not be charged. He was now down to his last option. If Saifullah admitted guilt, he could be on the path toward going home. But if he continued to deny culpability, Saifullah was going nowhere.

CHAPTER 17

McVINDICATION

In 2018, Uzair Paracha was set back to a dismal square one. But as he put it, he was a much better person the second time around. And something unthinkable happened that July. Uzair was transferred from a maximum-security prison back to where his ordeal had started, the Metropolitan Correctional Center in Manhattan.

He was thirty-eight years old, with poor eyesight, thinning hair, and a growing waistline. Uzair suffered claustrophobia from his years in solitary confinement and lack of sunlight. But he had actually become content with his situation. Like Majid Khan, Uzair realized that he had a choice to make during his incarceration. He could let it kill him, or he could embrace it and grow as a man. Uzair had come to be somewhat embarrassed by the memory of his twenty-three-year-old self, his age at the time of his arrest. "I am not sure I would enjoy the company of my younger self," he said. "I have changed a lot."

He told a journalist that he did not regret his decision to turn down the plea deal, explaining, "Sometimes the loss is hard to bear but other times I have to remind myself that this was God's will and I benefited a lot from my time in prison." He added that the experience of incarceration became "a lesson in humility, patience, reliance on Allah, and other important lessons in life." Uzair did appear to find God and religion during his years in prison, which was common for many prisoners. But there was an element of irony that a man convicted of supporting al Qaeda found God *after* being convicted. It rarely, if ever, worked that way.

But Uzair realized that he had been misguided and devoted to the wrong things in life. He was indeed the quintessential burger. He was spoiled with values that placed too much emphasis on worldly possessions. His spirituality had not always been his first priority. Business and money led him onto the path toward prison. Now he was an aging man who sought knowledge and enlightenment.

While in prison, Uzair memorized the Quran. He worked to achieve a fluency in Arabic. He read every Islamic book in the prison library. By his estimate, Uzair read more than 50,000 pages on everything from Islamic jurisprudence to Quranic sciences. In 2016, he even self-published a book analyzing the causes of the most recent US economic recession. He wrote, "I am deeply grateful for the blessings that allowed it all to come to fruition. . . . [M]uch of it was due to opportunities far beyond my control."

That summer of 2018, an older, wiser Uzair was back at the New York jail. Ten years earlier, in 2008, his lawyers had filed a motion requesting a new trial. They had argued that new information coming from Guantanamo Bay justified the request and should invalidate Uzair's conviction. Not much happened after that. But here in July 2018, Judge Sidney Stein, the same judge who had sentenced Uzair to thirty years in prison, issued a shocking ruling. He agreed with Uzair's lawyers, and the conviction was voided.

The person Uzair had to thank for the decision was Majid Khan. The ruling essentially stated that new evidence unavailable during the trial cast doubt on Uzair's guilt. The judge specifically took note of Majid's vehement assertion during his 2007 CSRT that "Uzair Paracha is innocent; he is not a criminal." The judge cited a 2007 FBI interview with Majid that stated, "Uzair Paracha did not do anything, went to trial and got 30 years." The judge also noted that KSM, during his CSRT, failed to even mention the Parachas. The judge referred to this as a "glaring absence," and further stated, "From this new evidence, defendant could credibly ask the jury to infer Paracha's innocence and lack of involvement in the operations discussed."

The judge had finally come to believe that the CSRT statements supported Uzair's contention in court that he had no knowledge that Majid or Ali were al Qaeda operatives. And again, without such knowledge, Uzair could not be convicted of the crime of supporting terrorists. "The critical question in this case is now and has always been whether Paracha acted with knowledge that he was helping al Qaeda," Judge Stein wrote. "[T]he newly discovered evidence of exculpatory statements . . . would yield a fundamentally different trial and likely create a reasonable doubt favoring Uzair Paracha's theory of the case over the government's."

With Uzair's conviction reversed, he could no longer be incarcerated in a federal prison. He was transferred back to Manhattan. But he wasn't a free man. The judge's decision only vacated the conviction. It did not preclude the government from seeking a new trial. By all indications, that's what the government was going to do. Uzair had to start from the beginning, which included a bail hearing, although bail was soon denied. Uzair would have to wait for his trial—again.

Viewed objectively and contextually, the judge's decision is rather peculiar. During the 2007 CSRT, Majid Khan had lied. Several years later, when Majid sought to redeem himself, he finally told the truth. He voluntarily recanted his previous testimony. Majid had finally accepted responsibility.

Among his later confessions: He stated that he had "attempted to recruit Uzair to officially work for al Qaeda. Uzair refused." That statement left some room for interpretation. But it certainly diminished Majid's earlier declaration of innocence that the judge relied upon. The SDNY prosecutors certainly caught on. During Uzair's 2018 bail hearing, prosecutors cited Majid's guilty plea to make the case once again that Uzair knew that he was working with an al Qaeda operative. The prosecutor added that the government believed it had as strong a case as it did back in 2005.

Uzair was gearing up for another fight. But this time, he was indeed much wiser. At some point, he knew that he would get to go home. And when he did, Uzair would return a better person than he was before.

* * *

By 2019, both Uzair and Majid had found solace and redemption, each in his own way. This was sixteen years after the dramatic events of 2003 when they were captured and interrogated. Meanwhile, a military court had charged the 9/11 conspirators, including KSM and his nephew Ali, for the murders of 2,976 people. Charges had also been filed against Hambali,

Zubair, and Lillie—the men behind the Jakarta Marriott bombing. Something was happening for each of these men, but not for Saifullah. For the elder Paracha, his fate was as uncertain as it was in 2003 when the issue of port security and smuggling explosives and WMDs had become a national emergency.

The problem with Saifullah turned out to be Saifullah himself. Where Majid and Uzair found clarity and purpose while incarcerated, Saifullah never changed. Even when Saifullah turned seventy years old, he was still playing games. The evidence against him was substantial, infinitely greater than the case against Uzair. Yet Saifullah refused to come to terms with his situation.

Interestingly, Saifullah's fate may have turned out much differently if Agent Ruby had not interrupted his moment of weakness and confession. Saifullah was on the verge of admitting to the explosives plot. Had he done so, he would no longer have had a need or basis to hide this information. Eventually, the process might have played out differently such that a path home would have been feasible. But the reality was that Agent Ruby did undermine the interview. And therefore, Saifullah never got back to that point where he was willing to tell the truth.

Saifullah had numerous other chances to rectify his situation. Military prosecutors were more than willing to cut a plea deal. The one condition they had was that Saifullah accept responsibility for his crimes, and that he refused to do.

The old CSRT process was eventually modified into the Periodic Review Boards, or PRBs. Unlike the CSRTs, the reformed PRBs were not rubber stamps in favor of the government. They were instead designed to help clear the detainee population from Guantanamo Bay. Saifullah should have been a prime candidate at this point, and he had several opportunities to convince those boards that he was contrite. The PRBs made no secret about what they were looking for. Yet Saifullah refused to admit his culpability. He continued to believe that he still had cards to play with this business. But this wasn't *business*, and the PRB officers were not businessmen. They were not interested in playing any games. While other detainees were approved for release after participating in these parole-like hearings, Saifullah consistently was denied despite his age and health.

A June 2016 PRB issued the following decision:

> Saifullah Paracha (PK-1094) was a Pakistan-based businessman and facilitator on behalf of al-Qa'ida senior leaders and operational planners. He met Usama Bin Laden in 1999 or 2000 and later worked with external operations chief Khalid Shaykh Muhammad (KU-10024) to facilitate financial transactions and propaganda. Since his arrival at Guantanamo, Paracha has been very compliant with the detention staff and has espoused moderate views and acceptance of Western norms. Although there is no indication that he is in communication with extremists outside Guantanamo, Paracha's extensive extremist business contacts that he established before his detention could provide him opportunities to reengage upon release should he choose to use them. Second, he did not indicate a sense of responsibility for his involvement with al-Qa'ida or an awareness of the impact of his actions.

In response to that 2016 PRB decision, Saifullah offered to retire from his business activity. His human rights lawyer, David Remes, submitted a letter on Saifullah's behalf. In it, Remes wrote that "Mr. Paracha will wind down his business affairs and retire to Pakistan. Mr. Paracha resolved to retire even apart from the Board's concern. He accepts that he is too old and his health too precarious to go back into business. He feels the tug of family."

Neither Remes's effort, nor Saifullah's offer to shut down his business, had any effect on the PRB. All they wanted to hear was acceptance of responsibility. Instead, they got this still evasive and slightly infantile statement from Saifullah: "I deeply regret becoming involved with individuals who turned out to be al-Qaida. It horrifies me to think that I may have helped to enable indirectly, unwittingly to carry out their terrorist attacks on the US. This will haunt me for the rest of my life."

From the PRB's point of view, Saifullah's statement may as well have been, "I'm sorry for getting caught and I'm sorry you are too stupid to let me go." His attempt to express responsibility did not go over well. The PRB responded as follows:

> The Periodic Review Board, by consensus, determined that continued law of war detention of the detainee remains necessary to protect against a continuing significant threat to the security of the United States. In making this determination, the Board considered the detainee's past involvement in terrorist activities, including contacts and activities with Usama Bin Laden, Khalid Shaykh Muhammad and other senior al-Qa'ida members, facilitating financial transactions and travel, and developing media for al-Qa'ida. The Board also considered the detainee's continued refusal to take responsibility for his involvement with al-Qa'ida. The Board noted its inability to assess the detainee's mindset due to his complete lack of candor, and the significant inconsistencies between written submissions to the Board and the detainee's testimony concerning family support and future plans. Finally, the Board considered the detainee's indifference to the impact of his prior actions and the lack of evidence of significant mitigation measures.

In late 2018, a frustrated PRB doubled down on its position: "The detainee statements regarding his mindset and potential for re-engagement are not credible in light of his continued minimization of his interactions with al Qaeda, the change in justification for engaging with al Qaeda, failure to exhibit any remorse for the actions he does acknowledge, and dishonesty in his responses to Board questions."

For whatever reason, Saifullah did not seem to improve himself while in government custody. Meanwhile, his family back in Pakistan decided to move on from their old life. Although they still supported Saifullah, the family had made Farhat their unquestionable center. She was the rock that would keep the Paracha clan confident and successful, allowing them to reclaim their social standing and familial pride.

The family stopped their public relations campaign. The website advocating for Saifullah and Uzair's release was taken down. In 2018, Farhat sold their longtime home in Karachi and moved to a new city. Her divorce from Saifullah was finalized. The family had opted for a fresh start, and they were finally moving on. The future would be much better than the past. It had to be.

* * *

As the calendar rushed toward 2020, Farhat wasn't the only one moving on from the traumas inflicted by 9/11. Americans were, too. Consider pop culture. In 2005, Steven Spielberg directed a remake of the classic H. G. Wells alien invasion story *War of the Worlds*. The classic 1953 film served as an allegory to Cold War paranoia and nuclear anxiety. Spielberg's blockbuster remake was unabashedly an allegory to 9/11.

Terrence McSweeney, senior lecturer in film and television at Southampton Solent University, noted that Spielberg's movie is one of the ultimate pieces of pop culture born of the September 11, 2001, attacks: "I'd even suggest that it's a key film in the evolution of how America processed that day." The film's nod to 9/11 trauma was not subtle. In one scene where New York is under devastating attack, a young protagonist shouts, "Is it the terrorists?" Allegorical invasion films of that era such as *Cloverfield* and *The Mist* also depicted the shock and helplessness of surviving unknown threats in a post-9/11 world.

By 2018, pop culture had fully embraced a less grounded form of escapism. That year, superhero films *Avengers: Infinity War* and *Black Panther* dominated. McSweeney suggests that younger viewers today may not understand the trauma-based symbolism that arose after 9/11. "Two decades on, it's easy to gloss over the echoes of 9/11 in Spielberg's 2005 adaptation of H. G. Wells's classic novel. After all, we're now living in a time of superhero cinema domination: What are those movies forged in if not the iconography of that day? Toppling skyscrapers, plumes of smoke, rubble-strewn streets. *War of the Worlds'* 9/11-isms, by comparison, might not seem that remarkable to someone watching the film for the first time today."

America's increasing indifference to the 9/11 era would ultimately prove to have a profound impact on Saifullah Paracha and other detainees languishing at Guantanamo Bay.

* * *

While Saifullah continued with his games and bluster in Guantanamo, Uzair would pursue a hardball legal strategy in the attempt to secure his release from prison. After Uzair's original conviction was thrown out, he and his team knew they had an opening. Federal prosecutors were intent on avoiding a second trial. There simply was not enough time for prosecutors to review approximately 14,000 pages of classified documents before the trial date. Those prosecutors made it clear in court filings that Uzair was no longer a priority. They bristled at the idea of "diverting substantial resources from other important national security and law enforcement functions."

To avoid trial, prosecutors made several offers to Uzair. He could plead guilty to lesser charges to make a deal. The government even proposed that a guilty plea would result in Uzair's immediate return home to Pakistan. Just as he did before his first trial, Uzair rejected the overtures. But this time was different. He was listening to his lawyers, and he was now seeking something more—namely, vindication.

The government continued with various efforts to secure a lasting conviction against Uzair. They simultaneously dangled offers of immediate repatriation to Pakistan with court filings calling Uzair "an avowed al Qaeda supporter" whose release would pose a "serious danger to the public." Uzair scoffed at the characterization. He viewed it as a vestige from the past, and he wasn't about to back down from his quest for exoneration.

Uzair continued to hold out until March 2020. Almost seventeen years after Uzair's first meeting with Agent Miller in New York, he finally accepted a deal with prosecutors. The agreement was simple. Uzair agreed to give up his lawful permanent resident status; meaning he was no longer entitled to travel or live in the United States. In return, Uzair would be allowed to go home to Pakistan. Because his conviction was overturned, Uzair was indeed cleared of his criminal conviction, as he had hoped. As one of his lawyers put it, "Uzair's slate is clean, and he returns home to Pakistan a free and innocent man."

Uzair's return to Pakistan was a celebratory occasion. His family was waiting to greet him. Tears of joy were shed. Uzair was ready for the challenge of rebuilding his life. No longer that rich burger kid, he now possessed an inner strength and deep religious faith. "My prayers have been answered," Uzair said. "Still, it's hard for me to imagine life outside of prison, so I feel anxious but hopeful."

* * *

By 2021, as the world moved on from the 9/11 era, it also had moved on from Saifullah Paracha. Attention away from international terrorism had been gradually dwindling since the height of the Islamic State's power around 2016. Al Qaeda's efforts appeared aimed at reconstituting itself in Africa, far from the public's eye. The COVID-19 pandemic and the "Stop the Steal" campaign culminating in the January 6, 2021, events at the Capitol captured America's focus. For the roughly forty detainees still languishing at Guantanamo Bay, it seemed that nobody cared anymore.

The Biden administration embarked on what can best be described as a lackadaisical approach to Guantanamo Bay. On May 13, 2021, Paracha received a surprise notification. The Periodic Review Board had cleared him for release back to Pakistan. The PRB's two-sentence statement did not offer any substantive rationale. For all the drama and intrigue surrounding Paracha's capture and initial interrogations, the ending was so anticlimactic that it defied reality. It was just over. Or so it seemed.

Several years later, Paracha's lawyer, Gaillard Hunt, continued to express immense frustration with what happened immediately after the PRB decision—nothing. Paracha was not sent home. The Biden administration did not provide any information about his release. All Paracha had was a piece of paper clearing him to leave the detention facility. Without a plane ticket, he became a man with false hope.

In May and June 2021, Hunt "contented himself with self-congratulation and satisfaction that Paracha's long ordeal was over." That brief moment of validation soon turned to dread. "One issue I never understood is why they did nothing to release him after being cleared," Hunt lamented in a 2025 interview.

Documents and interviews from that period reveal a common theme of half-hearted government actions and confusion. Some speculated that Paracha's release was tied to the cases of brothers Abdul and Mohammed Rabbani. The Rabbani brothers had been detained at Guantanamo Bay since 2002 for assisting with al Qaeda safe houses and terrorist travel. Their release from the detention facility was delayed because there was some dispute over whether they were actually citizens of Pakistan, as intelligence documents suggested, as opposed to Saudi Arabia where they were born and raised. Others believed the delay was attributed to the notion that

Pakistan could not provide the US government with security assurances that Paracha would not revert to terrorism.

The Pakistani government's response to Paracha's PRB decision was cursory at best. On June 30, 2021—about a month and a half after Paracha was cleared for release, an advisor to Pakistani Prime Minister Imran Khan sent a letter to Secretary of State Antony Blinken asking "for discussions on repatriating Paracha." To Hunt, this was more ominous than helpful. "It seemed to be important and encouraging. But the revelation that such talks were not already under way was distressing."

By April 2022—nearly a year after being cleared for release—Paracha remained in detention at Guantanamo Bay. Hunt acknowledged feeling defensive about his own impatience. "There was no obvious way to move the process along and everyone had every reason to believe Paracha was on the way to release. As Paracha put it, 'I know I'll be home by Christmas. I just don't know which Christmas.'"

Things seemed to get worse when Pakistani Prime Minister Khan was removed from power in April 2022.

"When Prime Minister Khan was ousted, it is possible this connection worked against Paracha," Hunt recalled. "I could not help but remember my Kipling:

> At the end of the fight there's a tombstone of white,
> With the name of the dear deceased,
> And the epitaph drear, 'A fool lies here
> Who thought he could hustle the East.'"

Paracha insisted on fighting his ongoing detention in federal court. When his claims failed to gain traction, Hunt resumed a letter-writing campaign to anyone who could assist. "As soon as I heard of Ambassador Tina S. Kaidanow's possible appointment [to US ambassador to Pakistan], I drafted a letter to her dated July 21, 2022, suggesting that Paracha's family could get him home and that negotiations with Pakistan had never been necessary in the first place. She never acknowledged this letter, so I sent her several copies, including one I delivered in person to her address in Adams Morgan, DC."

On October 14, 2022, seventeen months after being cleared for release, Paracha finally received information. It was not from an official government source. Paracha—once a titan of industry who operated his own media company—was now content to rely on the rumor mill for news about his own freedom. Hunt described the dizzying flow of information like this: "Another detainee's lawyer called me to tell me that the other detainee had heard that Paracha had been told he would be leaving soon. On October 24, 2022, I was able to talk to Paracha by phone and Paracha confirmed this."

Where the legal system and government bureaucracy failed, the rumor mill turned out to be accurate. Hunt described the scene: "On October 29, 2022, a plane with at least 40 persons aboard, including a doctor and several corpsmen to look after Paracha, flew him to Islamabad. The Pakistani officials seemed to be expecting an invalid. When they saw that Paracha could get about on his own, they interviewed him briefly and then let him and his son Mustafa board a flight to Karachi. He was free at last."

* * *

More than two years after Uzair's return to Pakistan, Saifullah won his own opportunity to repatriate. When the occasion finally came to be, he gave a somewhat restrained smile for a camera, as Mustafa, the youngest of the four Paracha children, looked on. Saifullah's lawyer had been hoping to capture an image of Saifullah's trademark grin, that smile that lit up the room. The photo could serve as a victory of sorts. But Saifullah's return to Karachi was nothing as celebratory as his son's return had been. With eyes gleaming, Saifullah could only manage a half smile, with literally one side of his mouth turning up and the other side pursing down slightly.

This was late October 2022, and it was Saifullah's first photograph since he had been released from Guantanamo. If Saifullah had expected fanfare and a tear-filled family reunion, he did not receive that kind of reception. Instead, he was met by a subdued Mustafa and Saifullah's lawyer, Clive Stafford-Smith. Farhat wasn't there. Neither were Muneeza or Zahra. Uzair also chose to stay away from his father.

The Pakistani government issued a terse, official statement: "Mr. Saif Ullah Paracha, a Pakistani national, who was detained in Guantanamo Bay, has been released and reached Pakistan on Saturday, 29 October 2022."

Saifullah's photo was taken at a small table in a Karachi McDonald's fast-food eatery. The kitschy 1980s-era striped wall clashed with Saifullah's plain white T-shirt. He appeared much thinner, even gaunt, compared to the day he was captured about nineteen years earlier.

Saifullah never admitted culpability. In the end, he didn't need to. The world had moved on, and the US government was working to reduce the Guantanamo Bay detainee population. The endeavor had proven expensive and inefficient. In some ways, Saifullah's release was more of a one-sided business decision based on convenience, a bittersweet affair. He didn't receive the vindication he craved, just a plane ride to Karachi and then a meal at McDonald's.

* * *

On the surface, Saifullah Paracha's post–Guantanamo Bay life back in Pakistan was drastically different than it had been in years past. Gone was the palatial home in the gated Karachi neighborhood. His wife, Farhat, had remarried, and the kids had moved on with their lives. Pakistani society mostly shunned him. He was no longer the gregarious life of the party. In 2025, Saifullah preferred to speak through his attorney rather than put himself out there and rely on his own wits for this book.

But hints of the old Paracha still lingered with a new theory put forward about the explosives destined for US ports back in 2003.

Saifullah's longtime attorney, Gaillard Hunt, posited: "How much could he admit without facing bigger problems with the Pakistanis back home? All those questions about the explosives get into what is guilt."

Despite Saifullah's life in reclusion, he still possessed the inclination and wry twinkle of gamesmanship. Saifullah knew investigators long suspected that the explosives may have been procured and just waiting to be moved. He also understood that the term "explosives" was thought by some to have been code for Saifullah's suspected role in obtaining nuclear material on behalf of al Qaeda.

If he admitted to the location of the Second Wave explosives, then he would harshly run afoul of the Pakistani government. Same for confessing assistance with bin Laden's "Hiroshima" ambitions. But if he denied knowledge of the explosives and nuclear assistance, he faced American repercussions. Through his attorney, Saifullah ultimately put his faith in America.

"He was always pro-American," Hunt conveyed in answer to questions forwarded by this book's author. "He was not a typical prisoner. He had a thriving business empire that fell apart when he left. His entire family was impoverished since his incarceration. But again, what is guilt? He'd have bigger problems back home."

With Saifullah, it has always been difficult to ascertain and separate truth from fantasy. He was notorious within FBI circles for sly evasions and playing absurd games. But this new admission—if one calls it that—is tantalizing. Evidence surrounding the idea of missing explosives was what prompted the Paracha father and son manhunt in the first place. Janelle Miller's ill-fated Bagram interview had confirmed that Saifullah had something profound and deeply guarded to say about the Second Wave plot. He admitted to discussions with 9/11 conspirator Ali Abdul Aziz Ali about shipping explosives or chemical weapons.

In this new telling, Saifullah wasn't fighting over culpability for his own sake, but instead was struggling to decide whether admitting to the explosives plot would land him in Pakistani custody, or worse, lose him all those hard-earned contacts to Pakistani society. Paracha's interrogations had begun in 2003. In his hubris, he had no idea that everything he was hoping to protect would ultimately be destroyed over the next twenty years.

All that remained for him was a grudge. "What happened was just an abrogation of our entire Anglo-American tradition of habeas corpus," Hunt opined in a 2025 interview with the author. "You could be held without any reason. If Paracha could land in an airport in Islamabad or Karachi or anywhere else, he was prepared to be accepted."

Hunt posed the question once again. "How much could he admit? In the immortal words of Pontius Pilate, what is truth? Who do we believe?"

CHAPTER 18

SPIRALING TOWARD THE NEXT ATTACK

Mark Twain once famously said that "history doesn't repeat itself, but it often rhymes." An ominous rhyme of repetition comes to mind when considering our federal policies and lapses of vigilance just prior to 9/11 and similar actions and scenarios now playing out in 2026. Twenty-five years after the surprise attack on the World Trade Center and Pentagon, the US government appears to be falling into the perilous trap of complacency once again.

Recent threat assessments from the intelligence community are using similar language that was used in comparable reports during the 1999–2001 period. The many urgent post-9/11 policies implemented to defend against international terror threats have been scaled back. And the public's trust in lawful electronic surveillance techniques—often the first line of defense in fending off terrorist plots—has eroded over the years while priorities have shifted. In 2000, immigration issues were a key governmental security focus. In 2025 and into 2026, similar priorities have emerged. Counterterrorism and counterintelligence operations and information sharing were back then and now again no longer emphasized.

In 2006, the FBI's Inspector General publicly issued a report identifying deficiencies in the FBI's handling of intelligence information relating to 9/11 and subsequent Second Wave al Qaeda plots. The report stated, "Information was soon discovered that had been in the possession of the FBI and the Intelligence Community before September 11 that related to the hijacking of airplanes by extremists or that involved the terrorists who committed the September 11 attacks. The causes for these failures were widespread and varied, ranging from poor individual performance to more substantial systemic deficiencies that undermined the FBI's efforts to detect and prevent terrorism."

That FBI report offered several specific recommendations designed to prevent the next major terrorist attack. But recent priority shifts on combating international terrorism directly undercut those recommendations. The US is careening toward a pre-9/11 posture of vulnerability. The following graphic listing some of the FBI Inspector General recommendations illustrates this dichotomy of then and now in terms of lack of preparedness.

Recommendation: Improve the hiring, training, and retention of intelligence analysts.	**August 2025**: FBI reports losing more than 5,000 employees as a result of agents, analysts, and others taking severance or early retirement packages. Further, during a lengthy government shutdown, FBI special agents receive pay, but intelligence analysts are not paid. President Trump states that "[w]e got the people that we want paid, paid," leading to widespread concern over hiring, training, and retention of analysts.
Recommendation: Ensure effective management of analysts.	**August 2025**: The FBI Agents Association expresses concern over firings of senior leaders and reassignments, demotions, and dismissals of managers.
Recommendation: Require greater coordination and consultation between the operational and analytical units.	**September 2025**: FBI Director Kash Patel announces that the FBI's Joint Terrorism Task Forces will prioritize immigration enforcement and narco-terrorist groups. The Director references the October 7, 2023, Hamas terrorist attack on Israel, correlating it with "continued attempts of terrorist actors to infiltrate the United States as migrants."

Recommendation: Ensure that the FBI's information technology systems allow FBI employees to more readily receive, use, and disseminate highly classified information.	**July 2025**: A Department of Justice Inspector General report finds that the FBI is falling short in its efforts to adapt to novel adversarial threats enabled by technological transformation.
Recommendation: Improve dissemination of threat information.	**June–September 2025**: Orders from the executive branch prioritizing immigration and domestic threats raise concerns that the FBI is refocusing and re-prioritizing how it gathers and disseminates information involving international terrorism.
Recommendation: Ensure that field offices allocate resources consistent with FBI priorities.	**The Department of Justice's Fiscal Year 2026 budget summary** notes the following with respect to FBI priorities and allocation of resources: "Protecting the American people from the unprecedented flood of illegal immigration throughout the US will be a huge focus."

The US priority shift away from defending against international terrorism does not diminish the reality of potential, imminent peril. In August 2025, the North Atlantic Treaty Organization (NATO) issued a report stating that "[t]errorism is the most direct asymmetric threat to the security of the citizens of NATO countries, and to international peace and prosperity."

In September 2025, the US National Counterterrorism Center sent a memo to law enforcement agencies announcing that recent calls by al Qaeda for attacks against the US showed the group's continuing threat to the country. "Al Qaeda and its Yemen-based affiliate, al Qaeda in the Arabian Peninsula (AQAP), are likely seeking to leverage their media publications and global conflicts particularly where there is US support or military involvement, to inspire potential attackers."

While President Donald Trump's second administration has been prioritizing immigration over the enduring menace of foreign-based terrorism, that is a lapse that originated and has grown over several recent administrations. In 2022, the Chicago Council on Global Affairs, a nonpartisan, nonprofit organization, issued a report based on polling data revealing American complacency in this regard during recent years.

That report stated, "This concern has lulled because there has not been an international terrorist attack in the United States in a number of years. Also, Americans seem to think that the policies that the US government put in place since 2001 have been effective. Additionally, other concerns have overtaken international terrorism in recent years, such as the COVID-19 pandemic. . . . Chicago Council polling shows that Americans are more apt to express concern about internal (82%) versus external threats (17%), including home-grown violent extremist groups."

Since that 2022 report, more of the post-9/11 policies that Americans still believe are ongoing and effective have been diminished or repurposed to address other priorities. Meanwhile, the threat of international terrorism continues to exist. The Chicago Council noted that nine out of ten "Americans said they remember exactly what they were doing and where they were at the time of the [9/11] attacks." The trauma of such an attack is something that sears itself into the collective psyche. But those attacks—the kind that al Qaeda once referred to as "spectacular attacks"—do not occur in a vacuum or originate out of nowhere. They require meticulous and often long-term planning.

The Second Wave story is important in the present context and resonates in several ways. Beyond its historical footprint, it also serves as a warning. A major terrorist attack on the US homeland can certainly happen again. As in 1999 and 2000, the American public and government agencies are focused on other concerns. Lulling ourselves into a sense of security will only encourage international terrorists plotting against our US homeland.

* * *

On August 4, 2001—about five weeks before 9/11—investigators had a hijacker in custody at the Orlando airport. They also had in their possession the phone number for Mustafa al Hawsawi, who worked closely with

Ali Abdul Aziz Ali in plotting the 9/11 attack. A prepaid calling card available to those same investigators linked directly to 9/11 mastermind Khalid Sheikh Mohammad. They did nothing with this information. The data fell through the cracks. Their priority was immigration.

This breakdown highlights what can happen when priorities shift so far away from international terrorism toward immigration. A man named Mohammed al-Qahtani flew into the Orlando airport on a one-way ticket from Dubai. He was carrying about $3,000 in cash and spoke hardly any English. Qahtani's rudeness toward a female customs agent prompted a secondary interview in a confined room with an investigator. Apart from a vague excuse about being in the US for business purposes, a cagey Qahtani refused to say who he intended to meet with or where he was staying.

In those pre-9/11 days—like today—customs officials and investigators were hyper-focused on deterring illegal migration. Deemed to be a migrant by the investigator, Qahtani was given a choice. He could continue to be interviewed, or he could use his cash to purchase a ticket back to Dubai. Qahtani chose to leave.

What officials didn't know that day was that Qahtani was meant to be the twentieth and final 9/11 hijacker to arrive in the US. From the 9/11 Commission Report:

> The terrorists who hijacked three other commercial flights on 9/11 operated in five-man teams. They initiated their cockpit takeover within 30 minutes of takeoff. On Flight 93, however, the takeover took place 46 minutes after takeoff and there were only four hijackers. The operative likely intended to round out the team for this flight, Mohammed al-Qahtani, had been refused entry by a suspicious immigration inspector at Florida's Orlando International Airport in August.

Mohammad Atta, al Qaeda's 9/11 commander, was also at the Orlando airport. Atta waited four hours before using a prepaid calling card to inform 9/11 conspirator Hawsawi that Qahtani was a no-show. In fact, the airport investigator who interviewed Qahtani had in his hand a travel itinerary with Hawsawi's phone number listed as the contact. Qahtani's prepaid calling card was used to contact KSM. Vital clues were missed and an opportunity was lost. If Qahtani was scrutinized in the international terrorism context rather than the primary focus of that era—immigration—the 9/11 plot could have been exposed.

In 2002, Qahtani was detained at Guantanamo Bay after being picked up by US forces in Afghanistan along with about thirty other al Qaeda foot soldiers. A routine fingerprint scan on Qahtani led investigators to the pre-9/11 incident at the Orlando airport. From there, they pieced together his role as a would-be hijacker.

But like Saifullah Paracha's case where the public and government gradually lost interest, the same can be said for Qahtani. On June 9, 2021, the Periodic Review Board—a few weeks after addressing Paracha's detention—issued a three-sentence statement granting the would-be twentieth hijacker's release. It wasn't until March 2022—seven months before Paracha would be sent home—that Qahtani left Guantanamo for Saudi Arabia.

There were no protests and expressions of concern. It was just over. The public became ambivalent and America had moved on from 9/11. If a plot similar to what happened with Qahtani occurred today, history could very well repeat itself. Neither the United Arab Emirates (where Qahtani flew in from) nor Saudi Arabia (his nationality) is on the US travel or immigration ban list. In 2026, the government's stated priority is immigration. History remains relevant.

* * *

What if the Second Wave "explosives" plot meant nuclear or radiological bombs? It was known that bin Laden and KSM were working to obtain weapons of mass destruction. Pakistan was a newly minted nuclear power. Terrorist sympathies were prevalent within the Pakistani government. Al Qaeda operatives were cultivating relationships with Pakistani officials.

Enter Saifullah Paracha.

The timeline supports the narrative that Paracha's primary use to al Qaeda was facilitating shipments of nuclear or radiological explosives into US ports—not merely conventional explosives. Prior to 9/11, Paracha had met with bin Laden in Afghanistan. Several months later, bin Laden dispatched KSM—the al Qaeda leader trusted with the group's Planes Operation—to establish a relationship with Paracha. The 9/11 attack occurred, and KSM, along with Ali Abdul Aziz Ali, continued working with Paracha during the active Second Wave plotting. Paracha wasn't working with low-level operatives. His relationship went straight to the top of al Qaeda's hierarchy.

Breadcrumbs from Paracha's discussions with KSM and Ali further the idea of Paracha's possible role as a nuclear or radiological weapons facilitator. Paracha suggested to KSM "where these weapons might be obtained." Paracha told investigators that he had worked with Abdul Qadeer Khan, the father of Pakistan's nuclear weapons program and a known proliferator of nuclear technology. As corroboration, Qadeer Khan's contact information was stored in Paracha's beloved Casio organizer.

The Casio contained something else. According to FBI analysts, Paracha meticulously entered "information relating to military chemical warfare agents." Sarin. VX. Sulfur Mustard. Nitrogen Mustard. Each reference to explosives appeared among a list of names and what the FBI believe were telephone numbers. One disjointed entry looked like this:

> CHEMICAL/BIOLOGICAL DIVIDED INTO THREE
> 1ST NURVE AGENT - 5/1-GA/2GB 3-GD/4 GF&VX-DISTROY
> NURV SYS/LIFE KILLS 2ND - BOILS - 4 KINDS 1 HD 2
> HN LOCX BONS BODY/BOILS- PUSS
> 3RD BREATHING EFFECTX4 LUN GS-CORD
> 8 COUNTIRES/N M

Other evidence also supports the theory that Paracha may have been helping to arrange the shipment of weapons of mass destruction into US ports. With aviation under scrutiny, government officials and academics believed that hiding nuclear or radiological material in shipping containers was the most likely method of facilitating a nuclear or radiological attack in the US. Raids in Pakistan in 2002 revealed that al Qaeda was interested in shipping and establishing fictitious shell companies. Emails and documents linked directly to Paracha.

Perhaps the CIA's Paracha skeptics were right that the notion of smuggling "regular explosives" was an "op worthy of the lamentable knuckleheads." But that line of thinking focused on regular explosives using fertilizer or other conventional ingredients. Were those skeptics being shortsighted? Or just careful in how they worded things? The facts hint at something more sinister: bin Laden's "Hiroshima."

At the end of the day, only a handful of people may know the full extent of the Second Wave plot. Unfortunately, for the most part, those people are not talking due to classification and other constraints. While we do have tantalizing confirmations of the plot through statements made by KSM, we know those admissions were made under torture, and therefore, as indicated earlier, their credibility must be at least somewhat suspect.

Nevertheless, there were certainly snatches of reliable information scattered throughout the sequence of events in 2002 and 2003 involving the Parachas and others confirming that there was indeed an al Qaeda plot with at least serious ongoing discussions as far as smuggling explosives and WMDs under the cover of an import/export business. Saifullah appeared at a minimum to be the expert who would show the al Qaeda operatives how to carry out such a deadly plan.

Ray Kelly, the former New York Police Commissioner, unequivocally believed that the plot would have had dire consequences if not for the decisive work of Agent Miller and the Joint Terrorism Task Force. Kelly told Congress in 2006, "In Pakistan, [the Parachas] plotted with September 11th mastermind Khalid Sheikh Mohammad to use shipping containers controlled by that company to smuggle weapons and explosives into New York. Fortunately, they were arrested before that could happen."

Once Majid Khan sought to redeem himself, he discussed how KSM was ruminating over the idea of opening an import/export company to move contraband explosives to the US. Documentation pertaining to shell companies and import/export operations linked to Saifullah was seized in two separate al Qaeda safe houses. While Ali had denied any discussions regarding the smuggling of explosives, Saifullah had confirmed that such discussions did in fact take place during his interview with Agent Miller before being interrupted by Agent Ruby. All this evidence appears to confirm that something was going on. The only mystery that remains is exactly how far it went.

Perhaps the real legacy of Saifullah Paracha's involvement with al Qaeda has little to do with the actual plot, but rather more to do with the effects of the idea of such a Second Wave conspiracy. Ray Kelly suggested, "We are not certain if Paracha's plan would have included recruiting operatives to pick up the deadly cargo at its port of entry. What we do know, this task probably would have been accomplished easily, given the lax security check in place in our ports."

Security measures were subsequently fast-tracked with a focus on nuclear, WMD, biological, and chemical weapons detection. The pace of such reforms may have proceeded much more slowly without the impetus of fears stoked by Saifullah's interactions with KSM. By all accounts, the ports are still vulnerable to smuggling weapons and explosives into the country. But we are surely more secure now than we were prior to the 2003 scare, although that may be in jeopardy with newly entrenched complacency and misplaced focus hearkening back to pre-9/11 preparedness.

* * *

Another legacy outcome of the 2003 port security scare was our changing policy regarding torture as an extreme means to an end. Senior CIA officials were so alarmed by the prospect of such a sinister terrorist plot that they advocated for the torture of a fifty-six-year-old lawful permanent resident of the US. But for efforts by the FBI and the unique factual circumstances of Saifullah's case, this story may have turned out even darker.

A 2014 Senate report scrutinized the CIA's enhanced interrogation technique program. The goal of the report was to determine whether the EITs, or torture program as some people call it, was worth the trouble. Granted, the Senate report was a partisan effort, but its thorough reporting makes a compelling case against the viability of torture to gain information. The Senate report is notable here because one of its primary case studies pertains to the CIA's efforts to stop the plot to smuggle explosives into the US. The findings included the following statement:

> While being subjected to the CIA's enhanced interrogation techniques and afterwards, multiple CIA detainees fabricated information, resulting in faulty intelligence. Detainees provided fabricated information on critical intelligence issues, including the terrorist threats which the CIA identified as its highest priorities. At numerous times throughout the CIA's Detention and Interrogation Program, CIA personnel

> assessed that the most effective method for acquiring intelligence from detainees, including from detainees the CIA considered to be the most "high-value," was to confront the detainees with information already acquired by the Intelligence Community. CIA officers regularly called into question whether the CIA's enhanced interrogation techniques were effective, assessing that the use of the techniques failed to elicit detainee cooperation or produce accurate intelligence.

The Senate report went on to contradict, with examples, the CIA's contention that the agency would not have stopped the plot to smuggle explosives without the use of torture: The CIA disagreed, claiming that the enhanced interrogation techniques produced otherwise unavailable intelligence that led to the identification and/or arrest of Uzair Paracha and his father, Saifullah Paracha (a.k.a., Sayf al-Rahman Paracha). These CIA representations include gross inaccuracies and omit significant material information.

The report argued that Saifullah was already on the radar because his documents were seized in two al Qaeda safe houses. In fact, the FBI interviewed Saifullah's business partner, Charles Stern, after learning about those documents. Moreover, Agent Miller's expert ability to break down suspects such as Uzair and Saifullah Paracha through old-fashioned interrogation methods, as well as the Pakistani interrogator who initially interviewed Ali Abdul Aziz Ali with much success, proved that even ticking time bombs could be defused. The overall conclusion of the report is that the CIA torture program was unnecessary and perhaps counterproductive. The CIA continues to dispute this notion, and it has provided several examples of their own to support this contention.

Regardless, one thing is clear. The 2003 port security scare involving Saifullah and Uzair has had a lasting effect on the US in terms of law enforcement and intelligence gathering, as well as port security. Without the vigilant persistence of people like Agent Miller, combined with extraordinary efforts by military and CIA officers, this story could very well have ended in a much different way.

Senator Dianne Feinstein offered a compelling summation in the Senate report, stating, "Nevertheless, such pressure, fear, and expectation of further terrorist plots do not justify, temper, or excuse improper actions taken by individuals or organizations in the name of national security. The major lesson of this report is that regardless of the pressures and the need to act, the Intelligence Community's actions must always reflect who we are as a nation, and adhere to our laws and standards. It is precisely at these times of national crisis that our government must be guided by the lessons of our history and subject decisions to internal and external review."

* * *

Back in May 2001, FBI Deputy Director Thomas Pickard provided a routine update to members of the House. It was a perfunctory testimony with little fanfare. Pickard boasted about the FBI's Strategic Plan for 1998 through 2003. He identified key FBI priorities and goals. National and economic security was first on the list.

"Our highest national priority is the investigation of foreign intelligence, terrorist, and criminal activities that directly threaten the national and economic security of the United States," Pickard stated.

The controversy that followed the testimony forever marred Pickard's legacy and created one of the largest "what ifs" in American history.

The story itself is somewhat controversial. What is generally accepted is that an outspoken FBI agent named John O'Neill rubbed Pickard the wrong way. O'Neill wasn't just a random FBI agent. He was the special agent in charge of investigating the threat posed by Usama bin Laden and his al Qaeda network. O'Neill was convinced that al Qaeda was planning something big. If someone had to pick one expert on al Qaeda, O'Neill would be a safe bet.

The rift between Pickard and O'Neill had begun in 1998. Al Qaeda operatives detonated bombs at embassies in Kenya and Tanzania. Federal prosecutors in New York secured a sealed indictment against bin Laden. Typically, the district with the indictment gets to lead the investigation. In this instance, that would have been the FBI's New York office where O'Neill worked. But to Pickard and others in Washington, the names "bin Laden" and "al Qaeda" were obscure and mostly unknown. Pickard bristled at O'Neill's vocal insistence that the embassy bombings were orchestrated by such an obscure group.

Pickard had deep ties to the FBI's Washington, DC, field office. O'Neill's pleas to keep the investigation in New York were ignored. Pickard made the decision to move the investigation to Washington instead. O'Neill went over Pickard's head in protest, demanding that the investigation return to New York. Under pressure from then–Attorney General Janet Reno and others, Pickard relented. But in an act of pettiness, Pickard refused to let O'Neill travel to Kenya to pursue his belief that al Qaeda was behind the attack. Pickard never relented with his disdain for O'Neill.

In August 2001, O'Neill was forced to retire. Over the years, he had made some mistakes. He was believed to have had extramarital affairs and once allowed a girlfriend to enter an FBI safe house. In 2000, thieves briefly stole his briefcase, which contained sensitive documents. Investigators later determined that the documents were not accessed. O'Neill's expertise on al Qaeda continued to prove invaluable. In mid-2001, O'Neill remained passionately vocal about the al Qaeda threat.

Pickard, who at that point was Acting FBI Director, didn't see O'Neill's value. In August 2001, Pickard was believed to have leaked the year-old briefcase story to the *New York Times*. The implication was that Pickard wanted this outspoken expert to leave the FBI immediately, which is exactly what happened.

Shortly after, O'Neill took a job as head of security for the World Trade Center in New York. His remains were found ten days after the 9/11 attack in the rubble of the South Tower. O'Neill had been right all along. PBS's *Frontline* later dubbed him "The Man Who Knew." To this day, the questions remain: What if O'Neill wasn't forced to retire? Could he have stopped 9/11?

There is a haunting synergy between recent (as of this writing) FBI departures and Pickard's purported leak designed to force out the preeminent al Qaeda expert. In 2025 and into 2026, numerous FBI agents and senior leaders were reassigned, demoted, dismissed, or otherwise forced out. Lawsuits and public criticism contend that most of those personnel actions were political.

Moreover, it was reported in late 2025 that one-quarter of all FBI agents—about 3,000 in total—were reassigned to immigration enforcement. "The large number of reassignments . . . reflect a vast reshaping of the nation's premier law enforcement agency, which has focused on national security threats since the Sept. 11, 2001, terrorist attacks," the *Washington Post* reported at the time. "The intense focus on immigration has raised alarm among current and former FBI agents who say morale is low across the bureau as agents have less time to dedicate to the often-complex cases they were hired to work on."

With FBI agents stretched so thin, and other government agencies equally prioritizing immigration enforcement, the whole-of-government approach to investigating and stopping international terrorist plots is at risk. Nuggets of information may fall through the cracks. Data that only an expert could notice may be overlooked. What if one of those reassigned agents miss something that leads to the next major international terrorist attack?

* * *

The recent malaise of complacency over international terror threats can be traced back at least as far as 2016. A little-known Republican congressman from Staten Island, Dan Donovan, raised the alarm. The Second Wave conspiracy involved three factors: shipping, weapons of mass destruction, and sleeper agents. Thirteen years after Saifullah Paracha's capture, the conspiracy was raised once again on Capitol Hill.

The congressman lamented President Obama's proposed $500 million in budget cuts to Department of Homeland Security grants and issued a stark warning to a House committee on March 15, 2016: "Such threats aren't just theories—in the nearly fifteen years since the tragic attacks in 2001, law enforcement has thwarted sinister plots like these and more. Proposing cuts to the programs that keep the homeland safe would be foolish in any case, but they are particularly outrageous at a time when our threat level is the highest it has been since 2001. It would seem that either the President doesn't believe these threats exist or he doesn't care."

Donovan's words were directed at Obama. But as the complacency rooted itself over the years in the form of budget cuts and wavering focus, those words could easily be directed at the Democratic and Republican administrations that followed. To support his warning, Donovan ticked off a list of threats. In an era where the Islamic State (ISIS) was perceived as the primary threat to the US homeland, KSM's Second Wave plot received equal billing: "[Saifullah] Paracha worked with Khalid Sheikh Mohammad to devise a way to smuggle explosives—including possibly nuclear weapons—into the United States using the New York office of Paracha's import/export business."

Donovan went on to discuss Majid Khan's role in the "gas tank plot" and Khan's "complicity in a 2003 bombing of a Marriott hotel in Jakarta, Indonesia."

Donovan lasted two terms in Congress before losing his reelection bid in 2018. But his warning over cuts to DHS grants remain relevant ten years after his first warning, and twenty-five years after 9/11. Such cuts that began during the end of the Obama administration carried over and have increased exponentially into President Trump's second administration. The danger of complacency had set in and has become even more dire.

In late 2025 and early 2026, numerous cuts to DHS grants designed to defend against terror attacks were unveiled. For example, the Homeland Security Grant Program Funding was set to lose 86 percent of its counter-terrorism appropriations for New York.

"We are the #1 terrorist target," Congressman George Latimer noted. "They're defunding efforts to keep New Yorkers safe, while they continue to fund ICE operations that target and terrorize immigrant communities."

Around the same time, DHS grants were set to lose 90 percent of the funding for the Washington, DC, region. That funding was designed for responding to terrorist attacks. "[The funding] provides critical support to prepare for, prevent, and respond to terrorism and other threats in Washington, DC, and the National Capital Region," said Clint Osborn, director of the DC Homeland Security and Emergency Management Agency. "These funds are vital to the overall emergency preparedness and response capabilities where our threat level remains high, and where events designated as National Special Security events occur frequently."

In 2026, the Federal Emergency Management Agency (FEMA) also was set to lose about $300 million in funding for initiatives designed to help states and cities prevent and respond to acts of terrorism. In response to such funding cuts, DHS claimed that canceling funding for those grants is meant to "streamline federal resources and reduce the burden on the American taxpayer."

Complacency with respect to international terror threats goes beyond funding cuts. During the first Trump administration, two DHS task forces meant to combat complex threats such as terrorism were ended. In 2022, Congress passed a law requiring DHS to report why it started or ended a task force. But DHS under President Biden failed to provide any type of criteria for such decisions and had no measurable performance goals for the remaining task forces. In late 2025, DHS's Office of Intelligence and Analysis cut about half of its staff.

Around that same time, the nonpartisan Government Accountability Office provided a familiar warning about maritime security and DHS's shift in priorities.

"While there is increased attention to the southwest land border, criminal organizations continue to use maritime routes to smuggle people, drugs, and weapons into the United States," the GAO report stated. "Transnational criminal organizations and foreign terrorist organizations continue their efforts to smuggle people and contraband into our country. These organizations operate with immense capability, capacity, and nearly unlimited resources. Their smuggling operations are sophisticated, and they continually adjust their tactics, techniques, and routes to circumvent detection and interdiction by law enforcement."

Dan Donovan's short congressional career was largely unremarkable. But his 2016 warning about the threats the US faces in correlation with terrorism-related budget cuts marks an ominous milestone. It was an early explanation of why the Second Wave plot continues to resonate so ominously. It was a dire warning against complacency.

* * *

The US Attorney's Office for the Eastern District of Virginia (EDVA) is one of the nation's most prestigious federal court districts. Located just across the Potomac River from Washington, DC, EDVA is home to the Pentagon, CIA Headquarters, and numerous other high-profile federal buildings. EDVA prosecutors have handled cases involving Second Wave plotter Iyman Faris, "American Taliban" John Walker Lindh, and Zacarias Moussaoui, who had trained to be a pilot in the 9/11 attacks. Besides the Southern District of New York in Manhattan, no other jurisdiction prosecutes as many international terrorism cases as EDVA.

At the top of EDVA's counterterrorism team was Michael Ben'Ary. In 2012, Ben'Ary secured a thirty-year prison sentence for Amine El Khalifi for plotting to carry out a suicide bombing at the US Capitol on behalf of al Qaeda. In January 2025, Ben'Ary was appointed chief of the EDVA National Security Unit. At the same time, Ben'Ary was the lead prosecutor in the case against Mohammad Sharifullah, the only person charged in the United States for the 2021 Abbey Gate bombing in Afghanistan that killed thirteen US service members.

In October 2025, Ben'Ary was abruptly fired. A conservative social media influencer incorrectly linked Ben'Ary to internal divisions within the US Attorney's Office for the Eastern District of Virginia. Ben'Ary denied the accusations. He was forced out, nonetheless.

The EDVA US Attorney had recently been replaced by a former insurance industry lawyer with no criminal law experience. She was in no mood to listen to Ben'Ary's rebuttal. Solely based on an erroneous social media posting, EDVA's Chief of the National Security Unit was gone.

National security prosecutors do not merely try cases in court. They also build those cases and help lead investigations, all of which involves working with the intelligence community, law enforcement, Department of Treasury, State Department, and many others. National security investigations constitute a whole-of-government approach. Firing an experienced federal prosecutor at the tip of that spear makes the country more susceptible to attack from international terrorist groups. Firing experienced national security prosecutors based on erroneous social media postings is borderline government malpractice.

Before departing, Ben'Ary taped a one-page letter to his office door. It was addressed to his EDVA colleagues. In his letter, Ben'Ary recognized the danger to the US as an increasing number of experienced people left government: "The decisions to remove experienced career officials from US Attorneys Offices, the FBI, and other critical parts of DOJ undermines our country's ability to counter terrorist organizations, malign nation-state actors, and countless others that seek to harm our nation and its citizens. Justice for Americans killed and injured by our enemies should not be contingent on what someone in the Department of Justice sees in their social media feed that day."

Ben'Ary wasn't the only expert sounding the alarm. In late 2025, hundreds of former Department of Justice attorneys, FBI agents, and national security experts organized an advocacy group called the Justice

Connection. By their count, the Department of Justice experienced an "exodus of over 5,000 of us—draining the Department of priceless institutional knowledge and expertise, and impairing its historical success in recruiting top talent."

According to the group, remnants left from the exodus "cannot keep our country safe." In addition to the loss of experienced national security personnel, Justice Connection warned that the country's national security was in danger due to shifts in "highly trained special agents away from counterintelligence and counterterrorism." That warning is notable because it reflects government recommendations in the wake of 9/11 designed to prevent another major attack. Failing to prioritize international terrorist investigations is done at the nation's peril.

CHAPTER 19

"FIVE REPUBLICANS AND FIVE DEMOCRATS"

David Raskin has one fear. The longtime scion of national security prosecutions is afraid that KSM's 9/11 accomplices will be set free. During a 2025 interview with this book's author, Raskin said, "KSM is so infamous that he has an acronym, and everyone knows him. But other guys on the 9/11 charge sheet at GTMO are less widely known. Guys like Mustafa al Hawsawi. My concern is they will pull a Saifullah Paracha and claim to be sick, and nobody will give a shit and the politics will be such that some kind of deal will be cut and they will be released to a foreign country. This is not something we have to worry about for Zacarias Moussaoui, who has an Article III [federal court] conviction of life without parole. I will worry for the rest of my days that guys like Mustafa al Hawsawi will be free men. There will be little fanfare. It will just happen. It will be the greatest injustice in this country."

For many years, Raskin led the Southern District of New York (SDNY) unit tasked with prosecuting national security cases. Prior to 9/11, SDNY's organized crime unit indicted a then little-known terrorist named KSM for a multi-pronged assassination and airplane bombing plot known as "bojinka." After 9/11, Raskin traveled to Virginia to help prosecute Moussaoui, who to this day remains the only person convicted in the US for playing a role in the 9/11 attack. Raskin also supervised the case against Uzair Paracha. As such, Raskin knows a thing or two about KSM, 9/11, and the Second Wave plotting.

"I have no question that there was an explosives plot and Saifullah Paracha was up to no good," Raskin said. "Was he the worst terrorist we dealt with? Probably not. But KSM would have this sort of command of people and even if they didn't have the same level of evil in their hearts, they still did his bidding, and I think that's where Paracha came in, and Aafia Siddiqui and Majid Khan. They all knew what they were up to."

The post-9/11 time frame served as a transitional period for federal prosecutors and the FBI. The primary reason was that the government prioritized military and CIA operations over traditional FBI work. The results were mixed.

"The phone in SDNY didn't ring for a very long time," Raskin recalled. "There were changes in government policies. We stopped collecting evidence the way we had before 9/11 as the FBI didn't just tag along on the raids. We tried to make it work after the fact. There were a lot of cases that could never be brought to court. There was no chain of custody [for evidence]. No Miranda warnings. We got nothing very useful in building cases. This went on for a long time until things started looking a little less rosy in the military commissions at GTMO."

While complementing the work and tenacity of Guantanamo Bay prosecutors, Raskin highlighted Supreme Court decisions that effectively gutted those cases—or in his words, "GTMO cases became like a candy store for defense lawyers."

The torture program further diminished efforts to build cases against al Qaeda plotters, especially when compared to the work done by FBI agents like Janelle Miller.

"I wasn't there," Raskin said of the CIA's EIT interviews. "I read the cables. I've been in hundreds of law enforcement interviews with al Qaeda terrorists. For the most part, they were incredibly productive and that's because there were largely FBI agents who were really good at their job."

Raskin noted that things began to switch back to more traditional law enforcement investigations and prosecutions around 2008. That's when Second Wave plotter Aafia Siddiqui was arrested.

"One call I remember was Aafia Siddiqui. She had a pretty incredible story," Raskin said. "MIT student who disappeared in Pakistan and showed up at a police station with bomb notes. They called the FBI in Islamabad, and everyone was drinking tea in a room and Siddiqui, all of 80 pounds and without handcuffs, reached out behind a curtain, grabbed a loose rifle and started shooting at everyone. The craziness of it all really struck me because that was a true battlefield situation. She targeted not just FBI but the US military. That case should have been a military commission case, but they sent it back to Article III (federal) court. That's when cases started ramping up again."

The 2001 through roughly 2008 time frame is relevant today. Back then, the government refocused how it handled international terrorist plots. The federal court system was minimized in favor of military courts. The result was numerous failures to prosecute terrorists, lost evidence, and a general sense of confusion on typically fundamental issues of jurisdiction and investigative process.

"We learned a lesson back then," Raskin recalled. "We put our law enforcement toolbox aside immediately after 9/11 and focused on the military option. A big lesson is that system did not work as planned. So we brought out our law enforcement toolbox again. It's a method that achieved great success and had surmounted tremendous challenges. Until we find a better solution, it will be foolish to put it aside for several years again."

In 2026, the context has changed, but similar themes are playing out. The FBI is once again being refocused. Thousands of agents and analysts have been reassigned to support DHS immigration enforcement. Leading national security prosecutors have been fired, forced out, or otherwise felt compelled to quit. Raskin left the federal government in early 2025.

Meanwhile, international terrorist threats remain a prevalent force. In 2026, the US National Counterterrorism Center (NCTC) listed forty-eight active international terrorist groups. That list includes al Qaeda, ISIS, and numerous offshoots. Jemaah Islamiyah—the group Majid Khan and KSM assisted in attacking a Marriott hotel in Jakarta—is still active. A recent article from West Point's Combating Terrorism Center noted that remnants or offshoots of the Palestinian terrorist group Hamas—which has long plotted against Jewish targets in Europe—may turn their attention to terrorist attacks in the US. Hezbollah or other Iranian proxy groups also may target the US.

A document intended as a guide for the second Trump administration's agenda provided this warning: "African country-based terrorist groups like Boko Haram may currently lack the capability to attack the United States, but at least some of them would eventually try if allowed to consolidate their operations and plan such attacks." One such group, an al Qaeda affiliate called Jama'at Nasr al-Islam wal-Muslimin (JNIM), is on the march throughout Mali, Burkina Faso, Niger, Benin, and Togo. JNIM's expansion has similarities to ISIS's consolidation of territory, funding, and influence, a strategy that allowed ISIS to recruit operatives and plan attacks abroad. In mid-2025, General Michael Langley, then the head of US Africa Command, warned that "the Sahel region in Africa is now the epicenter of terrorism on the globe . . . with terror factions there having increased their presence dramatically in the past three years and ramping up their ability to launch attacks inside the US."

A number of governments and international organizations make it clear that there is no shortage of international terrorist threats in 2026. Indeed, the 9/11 Commission warned against complacency: "Because al Qaeda represents an ideology—not a finite group of people—we should not expect the danger to recede for years to come. No matter whom we kill or capture—including Usama bin Ladin—there will still be those who plot against us. Bin Ladin has inspired affiliates and imitators. The societies they prey on are vulnerable; the terrorist ideology is potent; and the means for inflicting harm are readily available. We cannot let our guard down."

Among the many recommendations contained in the 9/11 Commission Report: reform the FBI. "We need a stronger national security workforce within the FBI," the report reads. "What the FBI needs is a specialized and integrated national security workforce, consisting of agents, analysts, linguists and surveillance specialists. These specialists need to be recruited, trained, rewarded, and retained to ensure the development of an institutional culture with deep expertise in intelligence and national security."

Another post-9/11 reform proposal reads: "We need a better process for transitions involving national security officials, so that this Nation does not lower its guard every four or eight years."

Twenty-five years after the 9/11 attacks, a gradual slide toward complacency beginning at the end of the Obama administration has turned into a cascade. The 9/11 and Second Wave plots continue to be relevant in 2026. Lessons can be learned. But the warnings from history have aged.

"Carrying it forward today, no doubt there still is a threat," Raskin said. "It's a different threat. Al Qaeda, going back to bin Laden, was a ruthless and brilliant and horrific adversary. I think over time we dealt with that threat and it became something different, inspired by al Qaeda."

Although complacency has taken hold, there is some good news: unity, which is another lesson from history. This book is intended to be a reminder of what this country has experienced—and could experience again. But it's also a reminder of what Americans can accomplish when we work together for the common cause of national security and defense. History serves as a guide. The framework is already laid out throughout the past twenty-five years.

To that end, the author of this book now leaves you with a final quote to consider.

From the 9/11 Commission's 2004 testimony to Congress: "On that beautiful September day, we felt deep hurt, but we believed and acted as one nation. We united as Americans have always united in the face of a common foe. Five Republicans and five Democrats have come together today with that same unity of purpose. We file no additional views. We have no dissents. We have each decided that we will play no active role in the fall presidential campaign. We will, instead, work together in support of the recommendations in this report. We believe that in acting together, we can make a difference. We can make our nation safer and more secure."

PRINCIPAL CAST OF CHARACTERS

Ali Abdul Aziz Ali: Khalid Sheikh Mohammad's nephew and a 9/11 conspirator who assisted him in developing the Second Wave plot.

Hassan bin Attash: The younger brother of 9/11 conspirator Khallad bin Attash. Hassan assisted al Qaeda as an explosives expert.

Khallad bin Attash: A conspirator in the 9/11 attacks who developed a close relationship with Ali Abdul Aziz Ali during the Second Wave plotting.

Ramzi Binalshibh: A conspirator in the 9/11 attacks who was captured in a raid in Pakistan in 2002. During the raid, investigators recovered an email and phone number linked to Saifullah Paracha.

"Bob": A CIA employee who participated in the initial interrogations of Saifullah Paracha at Bagram Air Base.

Chief of Operations, CIA Counterterrorism Center: A CIA official who advocated for employing enhanced interrogation techniques against suspected al Qaeda detainees.

John Cronan: A federal prosecutor in the Southern District of New York.

Iyman Faris: A Columbus, Ohio, truck driver arrested for ties to al Qaeda, and a potential sleeper agent for the Second Wave plot.

Hamid Gul: Director of the Pakistani Intelligence Service and a purported contact of Saifullah Paracha.

Senator Ernest "Fritz" Hollings: A senator from South Carolina who led efforts to better fund security measures as US ports.

Gaillard Hunt: An attorney for Saifullah Paracha.

Majid Khan: A Maryland resident who was groomed by KSM for a prominent role in the Second Wave plot. He also was implicated in the Marriott bombing.

Khalid Khawaja: An acquaintance of Saifullah Paracha linked to al Qaeda and the Pakistani government.

Usama bin Laden: The leader of al Qaeda. In 2000, bin Laden met with Saifullah Paracha in Afghanistan. Shortly after that meeting, bin Laden dispatched KSM to Paracha's office in Pakistan.

Syed Abul Mahasin: Saifullah Paracha's office manager.

Mark Martins: Chief Prosecutor, Office of Military Commissions.

Rear Admiral James McGarrah: Director, Office of Administrative Review at Guantanamo Bay.

FBI Agent Janelle Miller: The lead FBI investigator into Saifullah and Uzair Paracha's role in the Second Wave plot.

Khalid Sheikh Mohammad (KSM): The architect of the 9/11 attacks and proponent of the Second Wave plot.

Nisar Mujahid: A Paracha family attorney based in Pakistan.

Captain John Murphy: Chief Prosecutor, Office of Military Commissions.

Encep Nurjaman, a.k.a. Hambali: The leader of Jemaah Islamiyah in Southeast Asia.

Jose Padilla: A US-based al Qaeda operative once believed to be planning to set off a radiological bomb, and a potential sleeper agent for the Second Wave plot.

Farhat Paracha: The wife of Saifullah Paracha and mother to Uzair. After Saifullah's disappearance, she filed lawsuits in the US and Pakistan while simultaneously taking over the family business.

Saifullah Paracha: A wealthy, lawful permanent resident of the United States who ran an import/export business with offices in New York and Pakistan. After meeting with al Qaeda leader Usama bin Laden and others, he was implicated in the Second Wave plot.

Uzair Paracha: The son of Saifullah Paracha. In 2003, Uzair was named CEO of his father's import/export company and subsequently moved to New York. Uzair was implicated in the Second Wave plot after agreeing to assist Majid Khan with regaining entry into the United States.

Andy Patel: A criminal defense attorney for Saifullah Paracha.

James Pavitt: CIA Deputy Director of Operations who participated in developing the enhanced interrogation technique program (EIT).

Akhtar Raja: A London-based attorney tasked as a liaison between the Paracha family and the United States.

David Remes: An attorney for Saifullah Paracha.

CITF Agent "Ruby": An Army non-commissioned officer who participated in the initial interrogations of Saifullah Paracha at Bagram Air Base.

Aafia Siddiqui: A Pakistani neuroscientist who eventually married Ali Abdul Aziz Ali. Siddiqui traveled to the US to assist Majid Khan in his effort to reenter the country for his role in the Second Wave plot. She was later arrested for shooting at Army soldiers during an interrogation.

Army Specialist "Smith": An Army soldier tasked with carrying out Saifullah Paracha's official transfer to military custody.

"Charles Stern": Saifullah Paracha's New York–based business partner who was suspected of assisting the FBI in luring Saifullah out of Pakistan to be captured.

Jafar al Tayyar: An al Qaeda operative being groomed to be a sleeper agent in the US during the Second Wave plotting.

Paul Wolfowitz: Deputy Secretary of Defense who signed a memorandum declaring Saifullah Paracha an enemy combatant prior to Paracha's capture.

Abu Zubaydah: An al Qaeda operative who was captured in a raid in Pakistan in 2002. During the raid, investigators recovered Saifullah Paracha's business card and an email from Saifullah referencing the creation of shell companies used for shipping merchandise.

AUTHOR'S NOTE ON SOURCES

As noted earlier in this book, I've played a small role in the Second Wave story. I was a longtime prosecutor in the Guantanamo Bay case against Khalid Sheikh Mohammad and his 9/11 confederates. I later was selected as a Department of Defense Special Trial Counsel where I handled separate Guantanamo Bay litigation in cases against the 9/11 plotters, an al Qaeda commander, and a mastermind behind the 2000 USS *Cole* bombing. I also led the military case against Saifullah Paracha. Those roles afforded me the opportunity to review nearly every document and every piece of evidence surrounding the 9/11 and Second Wave plots—classified and unclassified. I also had access to the people directly involved through interviews and meetings. I was one of the military prosecutors referenced in chapters 15 and 16. For many years, I lived the Second Wave plot.

The inside access conveyed in this book is not typically approved for publication. Based on my unique experiences at Guantanamo Bay, I sought special permission from the US government to tell the Second Wave story in full, taking into account my duty and obligation to protect classified information. Initially, as I've indicated, the government refused. They were uncomfortable having someone converting inside access into a book. But this story was too important not to be part of the historical record. The Second Wave plot holds a significant place within American wartime lore for the audacity put forth on all sides. The plot also serves as an important warning against complacency on many levels. After several years of negotiations, rejections, and more negotiation, the US government finally approved this book. That approval was largely in full and with minimal redactions.

The sourcing for this book is derived from several categories, detailed on the following pages.

Author Interviews

First are the personal interviews I conducted during and after my time at Guantanamo Bay. In most cases, I let interviewees speak about the nuances and small asides of the people involved. Additional background was supplemented through media reporting and documentation.

Each of the individuals listed below provided information used to tell the story of the Second Wave plot. For some sources, the government requested that I apply pseudonyms.

Sanad al-Kazimi
Haji Sharqawi
Majid Khan
Gaillard Hunt
David Remes
Andy Patel
FBI Agent "DT"
FBI Agent "Mae"
FBI Agent Janelle Miller
FBI Agent "JF"
FBI Agent "CS"
New York Police Department Detective "PL"
Army Specialist "Smith"
CIA Agent "Bob"
Individuals who participated in Paracha rendition
Various CITF agents
Director, Joint Intelligence Group

Personal Observations

As a Guantanamo Bay prosecutor, I had direct access to classified and unclassified evidence. In many instances, the prepublication review process cleared my conveyance of story details, but I had to forgo citing some specific underlying documentation. Regardless, documentation only tells part of the story. I also participated—either actively or as a passive observer—in the various processes at Guantanamo Bay.

ENDNOTES AND REFERENCES

When there are references in the text that are not cited in the endnotes, they derive from personal interviews or personal observations as described.

Chapter 1: Nuclear Threat

"Strategic goal of obtaining a nuclear capability": George Tenet, "The Worldwide Threat 2004: Challenges in a Changing Global Context," before the Senate Select Committee on Intelligence (February 24, 2004).

"Religious obligation": George Tenet, "The Worldwide Threat 2004: Challenges in a Changing Global Context," before the Senate Select Committee on Intelligence (February 24, 2004).

"Suggested where these weapons might be obtained": *Paracha v. Trump*, 453 F. Supp. 3d 168 (2020); Summary of Administrative Review Board Proceedings for ISN 1094, Guantanamo Bay, December 2006; "Detainee Statement," "Periodic Review Board Initial Hearing, Saifullah Abdullah Paracha, ISN 1094", Guantanamo Bay, March 8, 2016; Combatant Status Review Board, Department of Defense, November 10, 2004; *see also* Frank Davies, "Al-Qaeda nukes bid alleged," *Seattle Times*, February 11, 2005.

Chapter 2: The Big Fish

KSM and nuclear weapons: *Paracha v. Trump*, 453 F. Supp. 3d 168 (2020); Summary of Administrative Review Board Proceedings for ISN 1094, Guantanamo Bay, December 2006; "Detainee Statement," "Periodic Review Board Initial Hearing, Saifullah Abdullah Paracha, ISN 1094", Guantanamo Bay, March 8, 2016; Combatant Status Review Board, Department of Defense, November 10, 2004; *see also* Frank Davies, "Al-Qaeda nukes bid alleged," *Seattle Times*, February 11, 2005.

Jose Padilla: Senate Select Committee on Intelligence, "Study of the Central Intelligence Agency's Detention and Interrogation Program," December 3, 2014; CIA email from: [REDACTED]; to: [REDACTED]; subject: AZ information, July 10, 2002; SSCI Transcript "Detention of Jose Padilla," June 12, 2002.

Majid Khan: Majid Khan, "Unsworn Statement," read into court at Guantanamo Bay, October 28, 2021.

KSM: [REDACTED] 10985 (242351Z MAR 03). "Khalid Shaykh Muhammad's Threat Reporting - Precious Truths, Surrounded by a Bodyguard of Lies," IICT, April 3, 2003.

Deliberations and investigation: [REDACTED] Memorandum for the Record; subject: Meeting with Deputy Chief, [REDACTED], Counterterrorist Center ALEC Station; date: July 17, 2003; Senate Select Committee on Intelligence, "Study of the Central Intelligence Agency's Detention and Interrogation Program," December 3, 2014; Email from: [REDACTED] to: [REDACTED], [REDACTED], [REDACTED], [REDACTED], [REDACTED], [REDACTED], [REDACTED], [REDACTED], [REDACTED], [REDACTED], [REDACTED], subject: value of detainees, July 18, 2003; email from: [REDACTED] to: [REDACTED] DO_CTC_ALEC Chiefs Groups, [REDACTED], [REDACTED] ; cc: [REDACTED] ; subject: Re: value of detainee, July 18, 2003; CIA Memorandum for the Record, "Review of Interrogation Program on 29 July 2003," prepared by CIA General Counsel Scott Muller, dated August 5, 2003; briefing slides entitled, "*CIA Interrogation Program*," dated July 29, 2003, presented to senior White House officials; CIA Inspector General Special Review, Counterterrorism Detention and Interrogation Activities (September 2001–October 2003) (2003-7123-IG), May 7, 2004.

Chapter 3: A Family Business

"Charles Stern": *See, e.g.,* "Pakistani urged al-Qaeda to obtain nuclear weapons, authorities say," *Knight Ridder Newspapers*, February 10, 2005; "Detainee Statement," "Periodic Review Board Initial Hearing, Saifullah Abdullah Paracha, ISN 1094", Guantanamo Bay, March 8, 2016; Summary of Administrative Review Board Proceedings for ISN 1094, Guantanamo Bay, December 2006; various interviews with FBI Agents "DT," "Mae," "JF," "CS," and NYPD Detective "PL."

Paracha origins in Pakistan: Summary of Administrative Review Board Proceedings for ISN 1094, Guantanamo Bay, December 2006; interview with FBI Agent "Mae."

Court document: *Paracha v. Trump*, 453 F. Supp. 3d 168 (2020).

Paracha background in US: Summary of Administrative Review Board Proceedings for ISN 1094, Guantanamo Bay, December 2006.

Casio Organizer: Summary of Administrative Review Board Proceedings for ISN 1094, Guantanamo Bay, December 2006.

Tanzeem-e-Islami: Saba Imtiaz, "Forever Prisoners: Were a father and son wrongfully ensnared by America's war on terror?" *The Guardian*, December 13, 2018.

Cliftonia & Mustafa: *See, e.g., Paracha v. Trump*, 453 F. Supp. 3d 168 (2020); Summary of Administrative Review Board Proceedings for ISN 1094, Guantanamo

Bay, December 2006; "Detainee Statement," "Periodic Review Board Initial Hearing, Saifullah Abdullah Paracha, ISN 1094", Guantanamo Bay, March 8, 2016.

Ice cream parlor meeting: *See, e.g., Paracha v. Trump*, 453 F. Supp. 3d 168 (2020).

Business with Majid Khan: Stipulation of Fact, *United States v. Majid Khan*, Guantanamo Bay Military Commission, February 15, 2012; *Paracha v. Trump*, 453 F. Supp. 3d 168 (2020); Summary of Administrative Review Board Proceedings for ISN 1094, Guantanamo Bay, December 2006; "Detainee Statement," "Periodic Review Board Initial Hearing, Saifullah Abdullah Paracha, ISN 1094", Guantanamo Bay, March 8, 2016.

Khan continued to discuss Saifullah and Uzair Paracha: Stipulation of Fact, *United States v. Majid Khan*, Guantanamo Bay Military Commission, February 15, 2012; *US v. Uzair Paracha.*

CIA thinking at the time: 10740 (092308Z MAR 03).

Nuclear weapons: *Paracha v. Trump*, 453 F. Supp. 3d 168 (2020); Summary of Administrative Review Board Proceedings for ISN 1094, Guantanamo Bay, December 2006; "Detainee Statement," "Periodic Review Board Initial Hearing, Saifullah Abdullah Paracha, ISN 1094", Guantanamo Bay, March 8, 2016; Combatant Status Review Board, Department of Defense, November 10, 2004; *see also* Frank Davies, "Al-Qaeda nukes bid alleged," *Seattle Times*, February 11, 2005.

Al Qaeda structure: 9/11 Commission Report: Final Report of the National Commission on Terrorist Attacks Upon the United States," US Government, July 22, 2004.

"Found connections everywhere": *See, e.g.,* "Intelligence reports on historical background of Bin Ladin's army" (March 18, 1997); CIA Cable (January 3, 1997); *United States v. Bin Laden*, No. S(7) 89 Cr. 1023 (S.D.N.Y.) (case documents).

"Total chaos": Mary McCarthy, Fritz Ermarth, and Charles Allen briefing to 9/11 Commission (August 14, 2003).

Bin Laden's "Hiroshima": 9/11 Commission Report: Final Report of the National Commission on Terrorist Attacks Upon the United States," US Government, July 22, 2004; Testimony of George Tenet, "The Worldwide Threat 2004: Challenges in a Changing Global Context," before the Senate Select Committee on Intelligence (February 24, 2004).

Darunta and Herat WMD programs: *See, e.g.,* NSC memo, Benjamin to Berger and Steinberg (April 29, 1999); NSC email, Clarke to Berger (May 26, 1999).

"I offered him the moon": President Clinton meeting with the 9/11 Commission (April 8, 2004); see also State 073803, "Memorandum of the President's Conversation with Pervez Musharraf on March 25, 2000," (April 19, 2000).

ISID members were present: Samuel Berger interview with the 9/11 Commission (January 14, 2004).

Hidden shipments of explosives: 10984 (242351Z MAR 03), disseminated as [REDACTED].

KSM statements: CIA Directorate of Intelligence, "Khalid Shaykh Muhammad: Preeminent Source on Al-Qa'ida," dated July 13, 2004, faxed to the Department of Justice, April 22, 2005, entitled, "[REDACTED], Materials on KSM and Abu Zubaydah. [REDACTED]." This report was widely disseminated in the Intelligence Community and provided to the Senate Select Committee on Intelligence on July 15, 2004.

Iyman Faris: WHDC [REDACTED] (242226Z MAR 03); [REDACTED] 10983 (242321Z MAR 03).

Jose Padilla: Senate Select Committee on Intelligence, "Study of the Central Intelligence Agency's Detention and Interrogation Program," December 3, 2014; CIA email from: [REDACTED]; to: [REDACTED]; subject: AZ information, July 10, 2002; SSCI Transcript "Detention of Jose Padilla," June 12, 2002.

Majid Khan: Majid Khan, "Unsworn Statement," read into court at Guantanamo Bay, October 28, 2021.

KSM: [REDACTED] 10985 (242351Z MAR 03). "Khalid Shaykh Muhammad's Threat Reporting - Precious Truths, Surrounded by a Bodyguard of Lies," IICT, April 3, 2003.

Deliberations and investigation: [REDACTED] Memorandum for the Record; subject: Meeting with Deputy Chief, [REDACTED], Counterterrorist Center ALEC Station; date: July 17, 2003; Senate Select Committee on Intelligence, "Study of the Central Intelligence Agency's Detention and Interrogation Program," December 3, 2014; Email from: [REDACTED] to: [REDACTED], [REDACTED], [REDACTED], [REDACTED], [REDACTED], [REDACTED], [REDACTED], [REDACTED], [REDACTED], [REDACTED], [REDACTED], subject: value of detainees, July 18, 2003; email from: [REDACTED] to: [REDACTED] DO_CTC_ALEC Chiefs Groups, [REDACTED], [REDACTED] ; cc: [REDACTED] ; subject: Re: value of detainee, July 18, 2003; CIA Memorandum for the Record, "Review of Interrogation Program on 29 July 2003," prepared by CIA General Counsel Scott Muller, dated August 5, 2003; briefing slides entitled, "*CIA Interrogation Program*," dated July 29, 2003, presented to senior White House officials; CIA Inspector General Special Review, Counterterrorism Detention and Interrogation Activities (September 2001–October 2003) (2003-7123-IG), May 7, 2004.

Court document: *Paracha v. Trump*, 453 F. Supp. 3d 168 (2020).

"Burger": Saba Imtiaz, "Forever Prisoners: Were a father and son wrongfully ensnared by America's war on terror?" *The Guardian*, December 13, 2018; David Rohde, "Pakistani Detainee Enjoyed Deep US Roots," *New York Times*, August 18, 2003; "Interview with Zahra Paracha," *Cage International* (formerly *Cage Prisoners*), February 21, 2007.

Jamaica Estates: Carol Rosenberg, Happy Birthday? Pakistani captive at Guantanamo Bay turns 70, plans to write old neighbor President Trump," *Miami Herald*, August 17, 2017.

Casio Organizer: Summary of Administrative Review Board Proceedings for ISN 1094, Guantanamo Bay, December 2006.

Audience with Usama bin Laden: "JTF-GTMO Detainee Assessment," *Miami Herald*, December 1, 2008.

Chapter 4: Echoes of 9/11

"Suggested where these weapons might be obtained": *Paracha v. Trump*, 453 F. Supp. 3d 168 (2020); Summary of Administrative Review Board Proceedings for ISN 1094, Guantanamo Bay, December 2006; "Detainee Statement," "Periodic Review Board Initial Hearing, Saifullah Abdullah Paracha, ISN 1094", Guantanamo Bay, March 8, 2016; Combatant Status Review Board, Department of Defense, November 10, 2004; *see also* Frank Davies, "Al-Qaeda nukes bid alleged," *Seattle Times*, February 11, 2005.

"Second Wave": Intelligence report, interrogation of KSM, July 2, 2003; Intelligence report, interrogation of KSM, September 11, 2003.

Uzair Paracha: Saba Imtiaz, "Forever Prisoners: Were a father and son wrongfully ensnared by America's war on terror?" *The Guardian*, December 13, 2018; David Rohde, "Pakistani Detainee Enjoyed Deep US Roots," *New York Times*, August 18, 2003; "Interview with Zahra Paracha," *Cage International* (formerly *Cage Prisoners*), February 21, 2007; Huma Aamir Malik, "Father and Son Become Victims of the Global War on Terror," *Arab News*, February 25, 2006; *US v. Uzair Paracha.*

"Burger": Saba Imtiaz, "Forever Prisoners: Were a father and son wrongfully ensnared by America's war on terror?" *The Guardian*, December 13, 2018; David Rohde, "Pakistani Detainee Enjoyed Deep US Roots," *New York Times*, August 18, 2003; "Interview with Zahra Paracha," *Cage International* (formerly *Cage Prisoners*), February 21, 2007.

Jamaica Estates: Carol Rosenberg, Happy Birthday? Pakistani captive at Guantanamo Bay turns 70, plans to write old neighbor President Trump," *Miami Herald*, August 17, 2017.

Casio Organizer: Summary of Administrative Review Board Proceedings for ISN 1094, Guantanamo Bay, December 2006.

Audience with Usama bin Laden: "JTF-GTMO Detainee Assessment," *Miami Herald*, December 1, 2008.

FBI email about CITF: Email from [REDACTED] to Gary Bald, subject: Fwd. Impersonating FBI at GTMO, December 5, 2003.

KSM Mastermind of the 9/11 Attacks: "9/11 Commission Report: Final Report of the National Commission on Terrorist Attacks Upon the United States," US Government, July 22, 2004.

Abu Hafs, Nawaf al Hazmi, Khalid al Mindhar, Muhammad Atta, Ramzi Binalshubh: "9/11 Commission Report: Final Report of the National Commission on Terrorist Attacks Upon the United States," US Government, July 22, 2004.

9/11 Plot Timeline & Accomplices: Sworn Charge Sheet, Khalid Sheikh Mohammad, Walid Muhammad Salih Mubarak Bin Attash, Ramzi Binalshibh, Ali Abdul Aziz Ali, Mustafa Ahmed Adam al Hawsawi, *United States v. Khalid Sheikh Muhammad, et al*, Guantanamo Bay Military Commissions, April 4, 2012.

CIA Detainee Medical Care: Quarterly Review of Confinement Conditions for CIA Detainees, 1/28/03–4/30/03, May 22, 2003.

EIT Program: Senate Select Committee on Intelligence, "Study of the Central Intelligence Agency's Detention and Interrogation Program," December 3, 2014.

KSM March 24, 2003, Interview: [REDACTED] 10983 (242321Z MAR 03); [REDACTED] 10972 (241122Z MAR 03).

"KSM did not volunteer the purported smuggling plot": ALEC [REDACTED] (052230Z MAY 03); [REDACTED] 10985 (242351Z MAR 03). "Khalid Shaykh Muhammad's Threat Reporting - Precious Truths, Surrounded by a Bodyguard of Lies," IICT, April 3, 2003.

KSM admission of agreement to smuggle explosives: [REDACTED] 10984 (242351Z MAR 03); Senate Select Committee on Intelligence, "Study of the Central Intelligence Agency's Detention and Interrogation Program," December 3, 2014.

"KSM identified a mechanism . . . to smuggle explosives into the US": Email from: [REDACTED] to [REDACTED] cc: [REDACTED], [REDACTED], [REDACTED], [REDACTED] subject: re Addition on KSM/AZ and measures, February 9, 2004; Memorandum for: Inspector General; from: James Pavitt, Deputy Director for Operations; subject: re (S) Comments to Draft IG Special Review, "Counterterrorism Detention and Interrogation Program" (2003-7123-IG), February 27, 2004.

Senator Hollings port security bills: *see, e.g.,* Port and Maritime Security Act of 2001 (S. 1214); Maritime Transportation Security Act of 2002 (MTSA).

Pew Research: Hannah Hartig and Carroll Doherty, "Two Decades Later, the Enduring Legacy of 9/11," Pew Research Center (September 2, 2021).

Senator Hollings December 6, 2001, statement: Testimony of Senator Ernest F. Hollings, Committee on Governmental Affairs, Hearing on Seaport Vulnerability, December 6, 2001.

New York City Hall: *See, e.g.,* Michael Powell and Christine Haughney, "2 Killed at N.Y. City Hall," *Washington Post* (July 23, 2003); Michael Cooper, "Councilman Is Shot to Death in City Hall," *New York Times* (July 23, 2003); Al Baker and Kevin Flynn, "Shooting at City Hall: Security; City Hall Was Prepared, But Not for Act of Courtesy," *New York Times* (July 24, 2003).

Anthrax: *See, e.g.,* "Amerithrax or Anthrax Investigation," Federal Bureau of Investigation.

2003 changes: Elaine Kamarck, "9/11 and the reinvention of the US intelligence community," *Brookings* (August 27, 2021).

Global shipping: Review of Maritime Transport 2025, United Nations Committee on Trade and Development, September 24, 2025.

OECD Report: OECD Annual Report, Organization for Economic Cooperation and Development, April 29, 2003.

Sayed Abdul Malike: Testimony of Senator Jim Oberstar, Committee on Transportation and Infrastructure, Hearing on the Importance of America's Waterway Watch Program, September 14, 2007; Andy Newman, "Cabdriver is Arrested on Drug Charge, but Interest in Explosives Attracts Attention from F.B.I.," *New York Times*, May 22, 2003.

Megaports Initiative: *see, e.g.,* SAFE Port Act (Pub. L. 109–347) (2006).

Creation of maritime intelligence fusion centers: *see, e.g.,* National Security Act (2001); Maritime Transportation Security Act (MTSA) (2002).

Terrorist Screening Center: "New Terrorist Screening Center Established," FBI Press Release, September 16, 2003.

US cooperation partnership: Proliferation Security Initiative, US Department of State, July 2003.

Chapter 5: Moments of Truth and Terror

Majid Khan's life: Khan's story is captured in detail through two primary documents. Stipulation of Fact, *United States v. Majid Khan*, Guantanamo Bay Military

Commission, February 15, 2012; Majid Khan, "Unsworn Statement," read into court at Guantanamo Bay, October 28, 2021.

"America's Mayor": *See, e.g.,* Ina Jaffe, "Revisiting Guiliani's Role as 'America's Mayor,'" NPR, November 20, 2007.

"Either you are with us": George W. Bush, "Address to a Joint Session of Congress and the American People," White House, September 21, 2001.

Sikh fans in Cleveland: The author witnessed the events described at the NFL game. *See also,* "After the Attacks," Open Society: Soros Foundation Network News, Winter 2002 (this source is cited for purposes of independently noting that "[o]ne particularly public incident, broadcast on local news channels in Ohio, involved two US-born Sikhs being harassed and taunted at a Cleveland Browns football game").

Jafar al Tayyar: 10884 (182140Z MAR 03); Thomas Joscelyn, "Al Qaeda sleeper agent tied to 2009 NYC subway plot," *Long War Journal*, July 1, 2010.

Hafeez interaction with Majid Khan: Stipulation of Fact, *United States v. Majid Khan*, Guantanamo Bay Military Commission, February 15, 2012; Majid Khan, "Unsworn Statement," read into court at Guantanamo Bay, October 28, 2021; Transcript of Combatant Status Review Tribunal Hearing for ISN 10024, March 10, 2007.

Majid Khan indoctrination into al Qaeda: Stipulation of Fact, *United States v. Majid Khan*, Guantanamo Bay Military Commission, February 15, 2012; Majid Khan, "Unsworn Statement," read into court at Guantanamo Bay, October 28, 2021; Transcript of Combatant Status Review Tribunal Hearing for ISN 10024, March 10, 2007.

Majid Khan operational involvement: Sworn Charge Sheet, Majid Shoukat Khan, *United States v. Majid Khan*, Guantanamo Bay Military Commissions, February 13, 2012; *see also* Stipulation of Fact, *United States v. Majid Khan*, Guantanamo Bay Military Commission, February 15, 2012; Majid Khan, "Unsworn Statement," read into court at Guantanamo Bay, October 28, 2021.

Majid Khan tells his wife he may never return to their apartment: Stipulation of Fact, *United States v. Majid Khan*, Guantanamo Bay Military Commission, February 15, 2012.

Ali Abdul Aziz Ali interaction with Majid Khan: Stipulation of Fact, *United States v. Majid Khan*, Guantanamo Bay Military Commission, February 15, 2012; Majid Khan, "Unsworn Statement," read into court at Guantanamo Bay, October 28, 2021; Transcript of Combatant Status Review Tribunal Hearing for ISN 10024, March 10, 2007; Transcript of Combatant Status Review Tribunal Hearing for ISN 10018, March 30, 2007.

Garment District office: Huma Aamir Malik, "Father and Son Become Victims of the Global War on Terror," *Arab News*, February 25, 2006; *US v. Uzair Paracha*; *Paracha v. Trump*, 453 F. Supp. 3d 168 (2020); Summary of Administrative Review Board Proceedings for ISN 1094, Guantanamo Bay, December 2006; "Detainee Statement," "Periodic Review Board Initial Hearing, Saifullah Abdullah Paracha, ISN 1094", Guantanamo Bay, March 8, 2016.

KSM/Khan torture: *See, e.g.,* Majid Khan, "Unsworn Statement," read into court at Guantanamo Bay, October 28, 2021; [REDACTED] 10985 (242351Z MAR 03). "Khalid Shaykh Muhammad's Threat Reporting - Precious Truths, Surrounded by a Bodyguard of Lies," IICT, April 3, 2003; Senate Select Committee on Intelligence, "Study of the Central Intelligence Agency's Detention and Interrogation Program," December 3, 2014.

KSM March 24, 2003, Interview: [REDACTED] 10983 (242321Z MAR 03); [REDACTED] 10972 (241122Z MAR 03).

"Composed, stoic, and resigned": [REDACTED] 110983 (242321Z MAR 03); [REDACTED] 10974 241834Z Mar 03.

"Boxed in": [REDACTED] 10983 (24232 IZ MAR 03).

"KSM did not volunteer": ALEC [REDACTED] 052230Z MAY 03.

Ali Abdul Aziz Ali/Mustafa/Cliftonia: Stipulation of Fact, *United States v. Majid Khan*, Guantanamo Bay Military Commission, February 15, 2012; Majid Khan, "Unsworn Statement," read into court at Guantanamo Bay, October 28, 2021; Transcript of Combatant Status Review Tribunal Hearing for ISN 10024, March 10, 2007; Transcript of Combatant Status Review Tribunal Hearing for ISN 10018, March 30, 2007; *Paracha v. Trump*, 453 F. Supp. 3d 168 (2020); Summary of Administrative Review Board Proceedings for ISN 1094, Guantanamo Bay, December 2006; "Detainee Statement," "Periodic Review Board Initial Hearing, Saifullah Abdullah Paracha, ISN 1094", Guantanamo Bay, March 8, 2016; Affidavit of Janelle Miller, *US v. Uzair Paracha*, August 8, 2003.

2002 Evidence: ALEC [REDACTED] (222235Z DEC 02); DIRECTOR [REDACTED] (221835Z APR 02); DIRECTOR [REDACTED] (221835Z APR 02).

Abu Zubaydah: Senate Select Committee on Intelligence, "Study of the Central Intelligence Agency's Detention and Interrogation Program," December 3, 2014; "9/11 Commission Report: Final Report of the National Commission on Terrorist Attacks Upon the United States," US Government, July 22, 2004.

Front company for shipping explosives: Stipulation of Fact, *United States v. Majid Khan*, Guantanamo Bay Military Commission, February 15, 2012; Majid Khan, "Unsworn Statement," read into court at Guantanamo Bay, October 28, 2021.

FBI employer interview in New York: FBI WASHINGTON DC (271623Z MAR 03); ALEC [REDACTED] (191630Z MAY 03).

Ramzi Binalshibh: Senate Select Committee on Intelligence, "Study of the Central Intelligence Agency's Detention and Interrogation Program," December 3, 2014; "9/11 Commission Report: Final Report of the National Commission on Terrorist Attacks Upon the United States," US Government, July 22, 2004; Sworn Charge Sheet, Khalid Sheikh Mohammad, Walid Muhammad Salih Mubarak bin Attash, Ramzi Binalshibh, Ali Abdul Aziz Ali, Mustafa Ahmed Adam al Hawsawi, *United States v. Khalid Sheikh Muhammad, et al*, Guantanamo Bay Military Commissions, April 4, 2012.

"Terrorist financing activities": ALEC [REDACTED] (222235Z DEC 02); FBI WASHINGTON DC (271623Z MAR 03); ALEC [REDACTED] (191630Z MAY 03); CIA [REDACTED] (040123Z DEC 02)/[REDACTED]; CIA [REDACTED] (040123Z DEC 02)/ [REDACTED]; ALEC [REDACTED] (222235Z DEC 02).

Paracha Imports: Senate Select Committee on Intelligence, "Study of the Central Intelligence Agency's Detention and Interrogation Program," December 3, 2014.

Mustafa al Hawsawi; Khallad Bin Attash: "9/11 Commission Report: Final Report of the National Commission on Terrorist Attacks Upon the United States," US Government, July 22, 2004; Sworn Charge Sheet, Khalid Sheikh Mohammad, Walid Muhammad Salih Mubarak bin Attash, Ramzi Binalshibh, Ali Abdul Aziz Ali, Mustafa Ahmed Adam al Hawsawi, *United States v. Khalid Sheikh Muhammad, et al*, Guantanamo Bay Military Commissions, April 4, 2012.

Chapter 6: Al Qaeda's Plot Thickens

Majid Khan's travel: Khan's story is captured in detail through two primary documents. Stipulation of Fact, *United States v. Majid Khan*, Guantanamo Bay Military Commission, February 15, 2012; Majid Khan, "Unsworn Statement," read into court at Guantanamo Bay, October 28, 2021.

Majid Khan missions with al Qaeda: Stipulation of Fact, *United States v. Majid Khan*, Guantanamo Bay Military Commission, February 15, 2012; Majid Khan, "Unsworn Statement," read into court at Guantanamo Bay, October 28, 2021; Transcript of Combatant Status Review Tribunal Hearing for ISN 10024, March 10, 2007.

Ali Abdul Aziz Ali interaction with Majid Khan & travel documents: Stipulation of Fact, *United States v. Majid Khan*, Guantanamo Bay Military Commission, February 15, 2012; Majid Khan, "Unsworn Statement," read into court at

Guantanamo Bay, October 28, 2021; Transcript of Combatant Status Review Tribunal Hearing for ISN 10024, March 10, 2007; Transcript of Combatant Status Review Tribunal Hearing for ISN 10018, March 30, 2007.

Aafia Siddiqui: Stipulation of Fact, *United States v. Majid Khan*, Guantanamo Bay Military Commission, February 15, 2012; Majid Khan, "Unsworn Statement," read into court at Guantanamo Bay, October 28, 2021; *United States v. Aafia Siddiqui*; Declan Walsh, "Guantánamo files paint Aafia Siddiqui as top al-Qaida operative," *The Guardian*, April 26, 2011; *Paracha v. Trump*, 453 F. Supp. 3d 168 (2020).

I-131 evidence: *Paracha v. Trump*, 453 F. Supp. 3d 168 (2020); *US v. Uzair Paracha*.

Ali knew another person who could help: Stipulation of Fact, *United States v. Majid Khan*, Guantanamo Bay Military Commission, February 15, 2012; Majid Khan, "Unsworn Statement," read into court at Guantanamo Bay, October 28, 2021; Transcript of Combatant Status Review Tribunal Hearing for ISN 10024, March 10, 2007; Transcript of Combatant Status Review Tribunal Hearing for ISN 10018, March 30, 2007.

Uzair/Majid comparison: Saba Imtiaz, "Forever Prisoners: Were a father and son wrongfully ensnared by America's war on terror?" *The Guardian*, December 13, 2018; Majid Khan, "Unsworn Statement," read into court at Guantanamo Bay, October 28, 2021.

Uzair/Majid meeting and conversations: Stipulation of Fact, *United States v. Majid Khan*, Guantanamo Bay Military Commission, February 15, 2012; Majid Khan, "Unsworn Statement," read into court at Guantanamo Bay, October 28, 2021; Transcript of Combatant Status Review Tribunal Hearing for ISN 10024, March 10, 2007; Transcript of Combatant Status Review Tribunal Hearing for ISN 10018, March 30, 2007; *Paracha v. Trump*, 453 F. Supp. 3d 168 (2020); *US v. Uzair Paracha*; Summary of Administrative Review Board Proceedings for ISN 1094, Guantanamo Bay, December 2006; "Detainee Statement," "Periodic Review Board Initial Hearing, Saifullah Abdullah Paracha, ISN 1094", Guantanamo Bay, March 8, 2016; Affidavit of Janelle Miller, *US v. Uzair Paracha*, August 8, 2003.

Uzair/Majid/Saifullah/Mustafa meeting and conversations: Stipulation of Fact, *United States v. Majid Khan*, Guantanamo Bay Military Commission, February 15, 2012; Majid Khan, "Unsworn Statement," read into court at Guantanamo Bay, October 28, 2021; Transcript of Combatant Status Review Tribunal Hearing for ISN 10024, March 10, 2007; Transcript of Combatant Status Review Tribunal Hearing for ISN 10018, March 30, 2007; *Paracha v. Trump*, 453 F. Supp. 3d 168 (2020); *US v. Uzair Paracha*; Summary of Administrative Review Board Proceedings for ISN 1094, Guantanamo Bay, December 2006; "Detainee Statement,"

"Periodic Review Board Initial Hearing, Saifullah Abdullah Paracha, ISN 1094", Guantanamo Bay, March 8, 2016; Affidavit of Janelle Miller, *US v. Uzair Paracha*, August 8, 2003.

Cliftonia: *Paracha v. Trump*, 453 F. Supp. 3d 168 (2020); Summary of Administrative Review Board Proceedings for ISN 1094, Guantanamo Bay, December 2006; "Detainee Statement," "Periodic Review Board Initial Hearing, Saifullah Abdul lah Paracha, ISN 1094", Guantanamo Bay, March 8, 2016; Affidavit of Janelle Miller, *US v. Uzair Paracha*, August 8, 2003.

Uzair/Saifullah phone call: *Paracha v. Trump*, 453 F. Supp. 3d 168 (2020); *US v. Uzair Paracha*.

Majid Khan admission to CIA about Uzair: Senate Select Committee on Intelligence, "Study of the Central Intelligence Agency's Detention and Interrogation Program," December 3, 2014.

Ali Abdul Aziz Ali's role in 9/11: "9/11 Commission Report: Final Report of the National Commission on Terrorist Attacks Upon the United States," US Government, July 22, 2004; Sworn Charge Sheet, Khalid Sheikh Mohammad, Walid Muhammad Salih Mubarak bin Attash, Ramzi Binalshibh, Ali Abdul Aziz Ali, Mustafa Ahmed Adam al Hawsawi, *United States v. Khalid Sheikh Muhammad, et al*, Guantanamo Bay Military Commissions, April 4, 2012.

Chapter 7: The Witness

10,000 casualties: "9/11 Commission Report: Final Report of the National Commission on Terrorist Attacks Upon the United States," US Government, July 22, 2004.

Aum Shinrikyo impact on US: "9/11 Commission Report: Final Report of the National Commission on Terrorist Attacks Upon the United States," US Government, July 22, 2004.

Ben Bonk meeting with President-elect Bush: Ben Bonk interview with 9/11 Commission, January 21, 2004; Jim McLaughlin interview with 9/11 Commission, January 21, 2004.

Clinton/Bush meeting: President Clinton meeting with 9/11 Commission, April 8, 2004; President Bush and Vice President Cheney meeting with 9/11 Commission, April 29, 2004.

Doomsday Clock: "Doomsday Clock Timeline," *Bulletin of the Atomic Scientists*, available at the bulletin.org.

"Hundreds of thousands of dead and injured": Matthew Bunn, "Twenty years after 9/11, terrorists could still go nuclear," *Bulletin of the Atomic Scientists*, September 16, 2021.

"Any one of those weapons would likely be brought into the US in a ship": William J. Broad, Stephen Engleberg and James Glanz, "A Nation Challenged: The Threats; Assessing Risks, Chemical, Biological, Even Nuclear," *New York Times*, November 1, 2001.

March 28, 2002, raid evidence: ALEC [REDACTED] (222235Z DEC 02); DIRECTOR [REDACTED] (221835Z APR 02); DIRECTOR [REDACTED] (221835Z APR 02).

Abu Zubaydah: Senate Select Committee on Intelligence, "Study of the Central Intelligence Agency's Detention and Interrogation Program," December 3, 2014; "9/11 Commission Report: Final Report of the National Commission on Terrorist Attacks Upon the United States," US Government, July 22, 2004.

Garment District office: Huma Aamir Malik, "Father and Son Become Victims of the Global War on Terror," *Arab News*, February 25, 2006; *US v. Uzair Paracha*; *Paracha v. Trump*, 453 F. Supp. 3d 168 (2020); Summary of Administrative Review Board Proceedings for ISN 1094, Guantanamo Bay, December 2006; "Detainee Statement," "Periodic Review Board Initial Hearing, Saifullah Abdullah Paracha, ISN 1094", Guantanamo Bay, March 8, 2016.

FBI employer interview in New York: FBI WASHINGTON DC (271623Z MAR 03); ALEC [REDACTED] (191630Z MAY 03).

CIA comment about March 28, 2003: FBI WASHINGTON DC (271623Z MAR 03); ALEC [REDACTED] (191630Z MAY 03); Senate Select Committee on Intelligence, "Study of the Central Intelligence Agency's Detention and Interrogation Program," December 3, 2014.

Agent Miller enters office: Affidavit of Janelle Miller, *US v. Uzair Paracha*, August 8, 2003; *US v. Uzair Paracha* (case documents).

Request for Pakistani assistance: ALEC [REDACTED] (222235Z DEC 02).

March 2003 CIA interviews: Senate Select Committee on Intelligence, "Study of the Central Intelligence Agency's Detention and Interrogation Program," December 3, 2014.

"My father was very, very distraught": Saba Imtiaz, "Forever Prisoners: Were a father and son wrongfully ensnared by America's war on terror?"; David Rohde, "Pakistani Detainee Enjoyed Deep US Roots," *New York Times*, August 18, 2003; "Interview with Zahra Paracha," *Cage International* (then called *Cage Prisoners*), February 21, 2007; "Interview with Farhat Paracha," *Cage International* (then called *Cage Prisoners*), December 14, 2003.

"We had no idea what a material witness was": Huma Aamir Malik, "Father and Son Become Victims of the Global War on Terror," *Arab News*, February 25, 2006.

Saifullah Paracha began working the phones: Saba Imtiaz, "Forever Prisoners: Were a father and son wrongfully ensnared by America's war on terror?"

Hamid Gul: Bruce Riedel, "Terror's godfather," Brookings, August 20, 2015.

Proposed torture of an American permanent resident: Email from: [REDACTED] to: [REDACTED], [REDACTED]; subject: For coordination - DCI Highlight on Paracha, July 7,2003; [REDACTED] from: [REDACTED], May 6, 2003; Senate Select Committee on Intelligence, "Study of the Central Intelligence Agency's Detention and Interrogation Program," December 3, 2014.

Uzair's demeanor: Saba Imtiaz, "Forever Prisoners: Were a father and son wrongfully ensnared by America's war on terror?"; David Rohde, "Pakistani Detainee Enjoyed Deep US Roots," *New York Times*, August 18, 2003; "Interview with Zahra Paracha," *Cage International* (then called *Cage Prisoners*), February 21, 2007; "Interview with Farhat Paracha," *Cage International* (then called *Cage Prisoners*), December 14, 2003.

Janelle Miller background: Robert Gavin, "Upstate native first woman to head Albany FBI office, *Times Union*, May 17, 2018; "Sports Hall of Fame," Buffalo Academy of the Sacred Heart, 2025.

Agent Miller / Uzair Paracha interviews: Affidavit of Janelle Miller, *US v. Uzair Paracha*, August 8, 2003; *US v. Uzair Paracha* (case documents); *Paracha v. Trump*, 453 F. Supp. 3d 168 (2020).

Acting on behalf of al Qaeda: Affidavit of Janelle Miller, *US v. Uzair Paracha*, August 8, 2003; *US v. Uzair Paracha* (case documents); *Paracha v. Trump*, 453 F. Supp. 3d 168 (2020).

Khan evidence in Uzair's possession: Affidavit of Janelle Miller, *US v. Uzair Paracha*, August 8, 2003; *US v. Uzair Paracha* (case documents); *Paracha v. Trump*, 453 F. Supp. 3d 168 (2020).

Chapter 8: American Torture

"Dynamite": Email from: [REDACTED] to: [REDACTED], [REDACTED]; subject: For coordination - DCI Highlight on Paracha, July 7,2003; [REDACTED] from: [REDACTED]; May 6, 2003; Senate Select Committee on Intelligence, "Study of the Central Intelligence Agency's Detention and Interrogation Program," December 3, 2014.

"Enhanced measures": Senate Select Committee on Intelligence, "Study of the Central Intelligence Agency's Detention and Interrogation Program," December 3, 2014.

Jose Padilla: Senate Select Committee on Intelligence, "Study of the Central Intelligence Agency's Detention and Interrogation Program," December 3, 2014; CIA email from [REDACTED]; to: [REDACTED] subject: AZ information, July 10, 2002; SSCI Transcript "Detention of Jose Padilla," June 12, 2002.

Ali Saleh al-Marri: Senate Select Committee on Intelligence, "Study of the Central Intelligence Agency's Detention and Interrogation Program," December 3, 2014; [REDACTED], Memorandum for the Record; subject: Meeting with Deputy Chief, Counterterrorist Center ALEC Station; date: 17 July 2003).

Yasser Hamdi: *see, e.g., Hamdi v. Rumsfeld*, 542 US 507 (2004).

EIT deliberations for Saifullah Paracha: Email from: [REDACTED] to: [REDACTED], [REDACTED]; subject: For coordination - DCI Highlight on Paracha, July 7, 2003; [REDACTED] from: [REDACTED]; May 6, 2003; Interview of [REDACTED], by [REDACTED], Office of the Inspector General, August 5, 2003; Senate Select Committee on Intelligence, "Study of the Central Intelligence Agency's Detention and Interrogation Program," December 3, 2014.

Explosives evidence: Stipulation of Fact, *United States v. Majid Khan*, Guantanamo Bay Military Commission, February 15, 2012; Majid Khan, "Unsworn Statement," read into court at Guantanamo Bay, October 28, 2021; DIRECTOR [REDACTED] (181929Z JUN 03), disseminated as [REDACTED]; [REDACTED] 39239 (301600Z MAY 03); Senate Select Committee on Intelligence, "Study of the Central Intelligence Agency's Detention and Interrogation Program," December 3, 2014.

Saifullah Paracha citizenship status: Email from: [REDACTED] to: [REDACTED], [REDACTED]; subject: For coordination - DCI Highlight on Paracha, July 7, 2003; [REDACTED] from: [REDACTED]; May 6, 2003; Interview of [REDACTED], by [REDACTED], Office of the Inspector General, August 5, 2003; Senate Select Committee on Intelligence, "Study of the Central Intelligence Agency's Detention and Interrogation Program," December 3, 2014.

James Pavitt: Senate Select Committee on Intelligence briefing, November 7, 2001; *see also* transcript of Senate Select Committee on Intelligence staff briefing, December 11, 2001.

Nuclear weapons: *Paracha v. Trump*, 453 F. Supp. 3d 168 (2020); Summary of Administrative Review Board Proceedings for ISN 1094, Guantanamo Bay, December 2006; "Detainee Statement," "Periodic Review Board Initial Hearing, Saifullah Abdullah Paracha, ISN 1094", Guantanamo Bay, March 8, 2016; Combatant Status Review Board, Department of Defense, November 12, 2004; *see also* Frank Davies, "Al-Qaeda nukes bid alleged," *Seattle Times*, February 11, 2005.

Wolfowitz memorandum: Paul Wolfowitz, "Memorandum—Enemy Combatant Declaration," May 2003.

Ali Abdul Aziz Ali / Khalid bin Attash capture: "9/11 Commission Report: Final Report of the National Commission on Terrorist Attacks Upon the United States," US Government, July 22, 2004; Sworn Charge Sheet, Khalid Sheikh Mohammad, Walid Muhammad Salih Mubarak bin Attash, Ramzi Binalshibh, Ali Abdul Aziz Ali, Mustafa Ahmed Adam al Hawsawi, *United States v. Khalid Sheikh Muhammad, et al*, Guantanamo Bay Military Commissions, April 4, 2012; Senate Select Committee on Intelligence, "Study of the Central Intelligence Agency's Detention and Interrogation Program," December 3, 2014.

"Described Ali as 'chatty'": [REDACTED] 14291 (021645Z MAY 03); ALEC [REDACTED] (142334Z MAY 03); [REDATED] 19647 [REDACTED] 04); Senate Select Committee on Intelligence, "Study of the Central Intelligence Agency's Detention and Interrogation Program," December 3, 2014.

Ali Abdul Aziz Ali / Khalid bin Attash partners in crime: 9/11 Commission Report: Final Report of the National Commission on Terrorist Attacks Upon the United States," US Government, July 22, 2004; Sworn Charge Sheet, Khalid Sheikh Mohammad, Walid Muhammad Salih Mubarak bin Attash, Ramzi Binalshibh, Ali Abdul Aziz Ali, Mustafa Ahmed Adam al Hawsawi, *United States v. Khalid Sheikh Muhammad, et al*, Guantanamo Bay Military Commissions, April 4, 2012; Senate Select Committee on Intelligence, "Study of the Central Intelligence Agency's Detention and Interrogation Program," December 3, 2014.

Universal Broadcasting: *Paracha v. Trump*, 453 F. Supp. 3d 168 (2020); Summary of Administrative Review Board Proceedings for ISN 1094, Guantanamo Bay, December 2006; "Detainee Statement," "Periodic Review Board Initial Hearing, Saifullah Abdullah Paracha, ISN 1094", Guantanamo Bay, March 8, 2016.

"Planes Operation": 9/11 Commission Report: Final Report of the National Commission on Terrorist Attacks Upon the United States," US Government, July 22, 2004; Sworn Charge Sheet, Khalid Sheikh Mohammad, Walid Muhammad Salih Mubarak bin Attash, Ramzi Binalshibh, Ali Abdul Aziz Ali, Mustafa Ahmed Adam al Hawsawi, *United States v. Khalid Sheikh Muhammad, et al*, Guantanamo Bay Military Commissions, April 4, 2012; Senate Select Committee on Intelligence, "Study of the Central Intelligence Agency's Detention and Interrogation Program," December 3, 2014.

Ali Abdul Aziz Ali links: Senate Select Committee on Intelligence, "Study of the Central Intelligence Agency's Detention and Interrogation Program," December 3, 2014; Stipulation of Fact, *United States v. Majid Khan*, Guantanamo Bay Military Commission, February 15, 2012; Majid Khan, "Unsworn Statement," read into court at Guantanamo Bay, October 28, 2021; Transcript of Combatant Status Review Tribunal Hearing for ISN 10024, March 10, 2007; Transcript of Combatant Status Review Tribunal Hearing for ISN 10018, March 30, 2007; DIRECTOR [REDACTED] (181929Z JUN 03), disseminated as [REDACTED]; [REDACTED] 39239 (301600Z MAY 03).

KSM holding back information: Senate Select Committee on Intelligence, "Study of the Central Intelligence Agency's Detention and Interrogation Program," December 3, 2014.

May 20, 2003, CIA communication: ALEC [REDACTED] (022012Z MAY 03).

CIA pressed Pakistan to hand over Ali Abdul Aziz Ali: Senate Select Committee on Intelligence, "Study of the Central Intelligence Agency's Detention and Interrogation Program," December 3, 2014.

CIA Deputy Chief email: Email from: [REDACTED]; to: [REDACTED], [REDACTED], [REDACTED],[REDACTED], [REDACTED], [REDACTED], cc: :[REDACTED]; subject: KSM and Khallad Issues, October 16, 2003.

CIA officer noted in June 2003: ALEC [REDACTED] (302258Z JUN 03).

CIA communication: [REDACTED] 14291; Senate Select Committee on Intelligence, "Study of the Central Intelligence Agency's Detention and Interrogation Program," December 3, 2014.

"US interests": [REDACTED] 14291; Senate Select Committee on Intelligence, "Study of the Central Intelligence Agency's Detention and Interrogation Program," December 3, 2014.

May 2, 2003, conversation: [REDACTED] 14291; Senate Select Committee on Intelligence, "Study of the Central Intelligence Agency's Detention and Interrogation Program," December 3, 2014.

May 20, 2003: Senate Select Committee on Intelligence, "Study of the Central Intelligence Agency's Detention and Interrogation Program," December 3, 2014.

Inquiries into how explosives shipping could be done: DIRECTOR [REDACTED] (181929Z JUN 03), disseminated as [REDACTED]; [REDACTED] 39239 (301600Z MAY 03).

"Unwittingly being used": DIRECTOR [REDACTED] (181929Z JUN 03), disseminated as [REDACTED]; [REDACTED] 39239 (301600Z MAY 03); Senate Select Committee on Intelligence, "Study of the Central Intelligence Agency's Detention and Interrogation Program," December 3, 2014.

March 2003 KSM statement: email from: [REDACTED]; to: [REDACTED]; cc: [REDACTED], [REDACTED], [REDACTED], [REDACTED]; subject: re Addition on KSM/AZ and measures, February 9, 2004; Memorandum for:

Inspector General; from: James Pavitt, Deputy Director for Operations; subject: re (S) Comments to Draft IG Special Review, "Counterterrorism Detention and Interrogation Program" (2003-7123-IG), February 27, 2004; attachment, February 24, 2004; Memorandum re Successes of CIA's Counterterrorism Detention and Interrogation Activities; Senate Select Committee on Intelligence, "Study of the Central Intelligence Agency's Detention and Interrogation Program," December 3, 2014.

"Again, another ksm op worthy of the lamentable knuckleheads": Email from: [REDACTED; to: [REDACTED], [REDACTED], [REDACTED], [REDACTED, subject: see highlight: again, another ksm op worthy of the lamentable, March 25, 2003.

Bending the truth: Senate Select Committee on Intelligence, "Study of the Central Intelligence Agency's Detention and Interrogation Program," December 3, 2014.

Heathrow Airport plot: ALEC [REDACTED] 172242Z JUN 03; DIRECTOR [REDACTED] (241921Z MAR 02); Senate Select Committee on Intelligence, "Study of the Central Intelligence Agency's Detention and Interrogation Program," December 3, 2014.

"May be true": Email from: [REDACTED; to: [REDACTED], [REDACTED], [REDACTED], [REDACTED, subject: see highlight: again, another ksm op worthy of the lamentable, March 25, 2003.

Saifullah Paracha working the phones: Saba Imtiaz, "Forever Prisoners: Were a father and son wrongfully ensnared by America's war on terror?"; David Rohde, "Pakistani Detainee Enjoyed Deep US Roots," *New York Times*, August 18, 2003; "Interview with Zahra Paracha," *Cage International* (then called *Cage Prisoners*), February 21, 2007; "Interview with Farhat Paracha," *Cage International* (then called *Cage Prisoners*), December 14, 2003.

"I was horrified": "Interview with Farhat Paracha," *Cage International* (then called *Cage Prisoners*), December 14, 2003.

Farhat Paracha comments: Zofeen Ebrahim, "Pakistan: 'Gitmo is Like Being Alive in Your Own Grave,'" Inter Press Service, December 14, 2006; Interview with Farhat Paracha," *Cage International* (then called *Cage Prisoners*), December 14, 2003.

Saifullah Paracha businesses were a priority: Zofeen Ebrahim, "Pakistan: 'Gitmo Is Like Being Alive in Your Own Grave,'" Inter Press Service, December 14, 2006; Interview with Farhat Paracha," *Cage International* (then called *Cage Prisoners*), December 14, 2003; "Interview with Zahra Paracha," *Cage International* (then called *Cage Prisoners*), February 21, 2007; Summary of

Administrative Review Board Proceedings for ISN 1094, Guantanamo Bay, December 2006; "Detainee Statement," "Periodic Review Board Initial Hearing, Saifullah Abdullah Paracha, ISN 1094", Guantanamo Bay, March 8, 2016.

Abson Industries: *Paracha v. Trump*, 453 F. Supp. 3d 168 (2020); Summary of Administrative Review Board Proceedings for ISN 1094, Guantanamo Bay, December 2006; "Detainee Statement," "Periodic Review Board Initial Hearing, Saifullah Abdullah Paracha, ISN 1094", Guantanamo Bay, March 8, 2016.

Council of Welfare Organizations: *Paracha v. Trump*, 453 F. Supp. 3d 168 (2020); Summary of Administrative Review Board Proceedings for ISN 1094, Guantanamo Bay, December 2006; "Detainee Statement," "Periodic Review Board Initial Hearing, Saifullah Abdullah Paracha, ISN 1094", Guantanamo Bay, March 8, 2016.

Cliftonia: *Paracha v. Trump*, 453 F. Supp. 3d 168 (2020); Summary of Administrative Review Board Proceedings for ISN 1094, Guantanamo Bay, December 2006; "Detainee Statement," "Periodic Review Board Initial Hearing, Saifullah Abdullah Paracha, ISN 1094", Guantanamo Bay, March 8, 2016; Affidavit of Janelle Miller, *US v. Uzair Paracha*, August 8, 2003.

Chapter 9: Setting a Trap

"Agreed to smuggle explosives into the United States": [REDACTED] 10984 (242351Z MAR 03).

CIA pitch: Email from: [REDACTED; to: [REDACTED], DO_CTC_ALEC Group Chiefs, REDACTED], REDACTED], REDACTED], REDACTED], REDACTED], REDACTED], [REDACTED], cc: REDACTED], subject: subject: Re: value of detainees; date: July 18, 2003; Senate Select Committee on Intelligence, "Study of the Central Intelligence Agency's Detention and Interrogation Program," December 3, 2014.

Agent Miller / Uzair Paracha interviews: Affidavit of Janelle Miller, *US v. Uzair Paracha*, August 8, 2003; *US v. Uzair Paracha* (case documents); *Paracha v. Trump*, 453 F. Supp. 3d 168 (2020).

"Described Ali as 'chatty'": [REDACTED] 14291 (021645Z MAY 03); ALEC [REDACTED] (142334Z MAY 03); [REDATED] 19647 [REDACTED] 04); Senate Select Committee on Intelligence, "Study of the Central Intelligence Agency's Detention and Interrogation Program," December 3, 2014.

Internal, interagency deliberations: The author viewed various correspondence and documentation, in addition to interviews on this topic. However, pursuant to the prepublication review process, citations to those documents have been omitted. *See also*, Senate Select Committee on Intelligence, "Study of the Central Intelligence Agency's Detention and Interrogation Program," December 3, 2014 ("according to CIA records . . . , Saifullah Paracha's eventual capture and rendition to US military custody was complicated by [REDACTED]. According to emails within CTC Legal, Paracha was [REDACTED").

Kmart ruse: Zofeen Ebrahim, "Pakistan: 'Gitmo Is Like Being Alive in Your Own Grave,'" Inter Press Service, December 14, 2006; Huma Aamir Malik, "Father and Son Become Victims of the Global War on Terror," *Arab News*, February 25, 2006; Interview with Farhat Paracha," *Cage International* (then called *Cage Prisoners*), December 14, 2003; "Interview with Zahra Paracha," *Cage International* (then called *Cage Prisoners*), February 21, 2007; Summary of Administrative Review Board Proceedings for ISN 1094, Guantanamo Bay, December 2006; "Detainee Statement," "Periodic Review Board Initial Hearing, Saifullah Abdullah Paracha, ISN 1094", Guantanamo Bay, March 8, 2016; *Paracha v. Federation of Islamic Republic of Pakistan* (2003); "SHC Directs Constitution of Medical Board: Medical Treatment of Guantanamo Bay Detainee's Wife," APNAKARACHI.COM, June 2, 2010; Saba Imtiaz, "Forever Prisoners: Were a father and son wrongfully ensnared by America's war on terror?" *The Guardian*, December 13, 2018; *Paracha v. Trump*, 453 F. Supp. 3d 168 (2020) ("[s]o the United States turned to ["Charles Stern"] Mr. Paracha's US-based business partner, to execute a scheme that lured Mr. Paracha [REDACTED] under the pretense of a business opportunity"); the author also viewed various correspondence and documentation pertaining to the ruse planning and implementation, in addition to interviews on this topic. However, pursuant to the prepublication review process, citations to those documents have been omitted.

July 5, 2003: "Interview with Farhat Paracha," *Cage International* (then called *Cage Prisoners*), December 14, 2003; "Interview with Zahra Paracha," *Cage International* (then called *Cage Prisoners*), February 21, 2007; Huma Aamir Malik, "Father and Son Become Victims of the Global War on Terror," *Arab News*, February 25, 2006; Summary of Administrative Review Board Proceedings for ISN 1094, Guantanamo Bay, December 2006; "Detainee Statement," "Periodic Review Board Initial Hearing, Saifullah Abdullah Paracha, ISN 1094", Guantanamo Bay, March 8, 2016; *Paracha v. Federation of Islamic Republic of Pakistan* (2003); "SHC Directs Constitution of Medical Board: Medical Treatment of Guantanamo Bay Detainee's Wife," APNAKARACHI.COM, June 2, 2010; Saba Imtiaz, "Forever Prisoners: Were a father and son wrongfully ensnared by America's war on terror?" *The Guardian*, December 13, 2018; *Paracha v. Bush* (habeas corpus petition filed by Farhat Paracha) (November 17, 2004); the author also viewed various correspondence and documentation pertaining to implementation of the ruse, in addition to interviews on this topic. However, pursuant to the prepublication review process, citations to those documents have been omitted.

Thai Airways Flight TG502: *Paracha v. Federation of Islamic Republic of Pakistan* (2003); "SHC Directs Constitution of Medical Board: Medical Treatment of Guantanamo Bay Detainee's Wife," APNAKARACHI.COM, June 2, 2010; Interview with Farhat Paracha," *Cage International* (then called *Cage Prisoners*), December 14, 2003; "Interview with Zahra Paracha," *Cage International* (then called *Cage Prisoners*), February 21, 2007; *Paracha v. Bush* (habeas corpus petition filed by Farhat Paracha) (November 17, 2004).

"Quite perturbed at Charles' insistence": "Interview with Farhat Paracha," *Cage International* (then called *Cage Prisoners*), December 14, 2003; "Interview with Zahra Paracha," *Cage International* (then called *Cage Prisoners*), February 21, 2007; Huma Aamir Malik, "Father and Son Become Victims of the Global War on Terror," *Arab News*, February 25, 2006.

Car service in Bangkok: "Interview with Farhat Paracha," *Cage International* (then called *Cage Prisoners*), December 14, 2003; "Interview with Zahra Paracha," *Cage International* (then called *Cage Prisoners*), February 21, 2007; Huma Aamir Malik, "Father and Son Become Victims of the Global War on Terror," *Arab News*, February 25, 2006; *Paracha v. Bush* (habeas corpus petition filed by Farhat Paracha) (November 17, 2004).

Mood was tense: Saba Imtiaz, "Forever Prisoners: Were a father and son wrongfully ensnared by America's war on terror?" *The Guardian*, December 13, 2018.

Saifullah kissed Farhat goodbye: "Interview with Farhat Paracha," *Cage International* (then called *Cage Prisoners*), December 14, 2003; "Interview with Zahra Paracha," *Cage International* (then called *Cage Prisoners*), February 21, 2007; Huma Aamir Malik, "Father and Son Become Victims of the Global War on Terror," *Arab News*, February 25, 2006; Saba Imtiaz, "Forever Prisoners: Were a father and son wrongfully ensnared by America's war on terror?" *The Guardian*, December 13, 2018; *Paracha v. Bush* (habeas corpus petition filed by Farhat Paracha) (November 17, 2004).

Pakistani Federal Investigation Agency Exit Control List: *Paracha v. Bush* (habeas corpus petition filed by Farhat Paracha) (November 17, 2004); *Paracha v. Federation of Islamic Republic of Pakistan* (2003).

Saifullah's doubts about taking the flight: "Interview with Farhat Paracha," *Cage International* (then called *Cage Prisoners*), December 14, 2003; "Interview with Zahra Paracha," *Cage International* (then called *Cage Prisoners*), February 21, 2007; Huma Aamir Malik, "Father and Son Become Victims of the Global War on Terror," *Arab News*, February 25, 2006; Saba Imtiaz, "Forever Prisoners: Were a father and son wrongfully ensnared by America's war on terror?" *The Guardian*, December 13, 2018; *Paracha v. Bush* (habeas corpus petition filed by Farhat Paracha) (November 17, 2004); FREEPARACHAS.ORG (a now defunct website run by the Paracha family that chronicled the events leading to his capture and its aftermath); "Who Are the Guantanamo Detainees? Case Sheet 22," Amnesty International, October 2007 ("he rang one of his daughters just before boarding his flight but he never arrived at the meeting").

Chapter 10: Rendition and Darkness

Wolfowitz memorandum: Paul Wolfowitz, "Memorandum—Enemy Combatant Declaration," May 2003.

Explosives evidence: Stipulation of Fact, *United States v. Majid Khan*, Guantanamo Bay Military Commission, February 15, 2012; Majid Khan, "Unsworn Statement," read into court at Guantanamo Bay, October 28, 2021; DIRECTOR [REDACTED] (181929Z JUN 03), disseminated as [REDACTED]; [REDACTED] 39239 (301600Z MAY 03); Senate Select Committee on Intelligence, "Study of the Central Intelligence Agency's Detention and Interrogation Program," December 3, 2014.

Saifullah Paracha citizenship status: Email from: [REDACTED] to: [REDACTED], [REDACTED]; subject: For coordination - DCI Highlight on Paracha, July 7, 2003; [REDACTED] from: [REDACTED]; May 6, 2003; Interview of [REDACTED], by [REDACTED], Office of the Inspector General, August 5, 2003; Senate Select Committee on Intelligence, "Study of the Central Intelligence Agency's Detention and Interrogation Program," December 3, 2014.

It happened so quickly: The author viewed various correspondence and documentation pertaining to the specific details of Saifullah Paracha's capture and rendition, in addition to interviews of those directly involved in the rendition. However, pursuant to the prepublication review process, citations to those documents have been omitted. For corroboration and Paracha's perspective, *see, e.g.,* Summary of Administrative Review Board Proceedings for ISN 1094, Guantanamo Bay, December 2006; "Detainee Statement," "Periodic Review Board Initial Hearing, Saifullah Abdullah Paracha, ISN 1094", Guantanamo Bay, March 8, 2016; *Paracha v. Federation of Islamic Republic of Pakistan* (2003); "SHC Directs Constitution of Medical Board: Medical Treatment of Guantanamo Bay Detainee's Wife," APNAKARACHI.COM, Jun. 2, 2010; Saba Imtiaz, "Forever Prisoners: Were a father and son wrongfully ensnared by America's war on terror?" *The Guardian*, December 13, 2018; *Paracha v. Bush* (habeas corpus petition filed by Farhat Paracha) (November 17, 2004); "Interview with Farhat Paracha," *Cage International* (then called *Cage Prisoners*), December 14, 2003.

"I reached Bangkok International Airport": *Paracha v. Bush* (habeas corpus petition filed by Farhat Paracha) (November 17, 2004); Summary of Administrative

Review Board Proceedings for ISN 1094, Guantanamo Bay, December 2006; "Detainee Statement," "Periodic Review Board Initial Hearing, Saifullah Abdullah Paracha, ISN 1094", Guantanamo Bay, March 8, 2016; Combatant Status Review Tribunal for ISN 1094, November 2004.

"Pocket litter": Senate Select Committee on Intelligence, "Study of the Central Intelligence Agency's Detention and Interrogation Program," December 3, 2014 (defining pocket litter as "material acquired on a person upon a search and may include notes, identification cards, tickets, phone numbers, computer tiles, photographs, or any other material in the person's possession").

Pocket litter evidence: *See, e.g., Paracha v. Trump*, 453 F. Supp. 3d 168 (2020).

Farhat Paracha working the phones: "Interview with Farhat Paracha," *Cage International* (then called *Cage Prisoners*), December 14, 2003; "Interview with Zahra Paracha," *Cage International* (then called *Cage Prisoners*), February 21, 2007; Huma Aamir Malik, "Father and Son Become Victims of the Global War on Terror," *Arab News*, February 25, 2006; Saba Imtiaz, "Forever Prisoners: Were a father and son wrongfully ensnared by America's war on terror?" *The Guardian*, December 13, 2018; *Paracha v. Bush* (habeas corpus petition filed by Farhat Paracha) (November 17, 2004); FREEPARACHAS.ORG (a now defunct website run by the Paracha family that chronicled the events leading to his capture and its aftermath, available at http://web.archive.org/web/20080219151328/http://www.freeparachas.org/).

Anger with "Charles Stern": "Interview with Farhat Paracha," *Cage International* (then called *Cage Prisoners*), December 14, 2003; Huma Aamir Malik, "Father and Son Become Victims of the Global War on Terror," *Arab News*, February 25, 2006; *Paracha v. Federation of Islamic Republic of Pakistan* (2003) Const. P. 926/2003 (D.B.) Principal Seat Karachi (Pak.). 40; *See also* SHC Directs Constitution of Medical Board: "Medical Treatment of Guantanamo Bay Detainee's Wife," APNAKARACHI.COM (Jun. 2, 2010), http://www.apnakarachi. com/SHC-directs-constitution-of-medical-board.html.

Thai Airways Flight TG502: "Interview with Farhat Paracha," *Cage International* (then called *Cage Prisoners*), December 14, 2003; "Interview with Zahra Paracha," *Cage International* (then called *Cage Prisoners*), February 21, 2007; Huma Aamir Malik, "Father and Son Become Victims of the Global War on Terror," *Arab News*, February 25, 2006; Saba Imtiaz, "Forever Prisoners: Were a father and son wrongfully ensnared by America's war on terror?" *The Guardian*, December 13, 2018; *Paracha v. Bush* (habeas corpus petition filed by Farhat Paracha) (November 17, 2004); FREEPARACHAS.ORG (a now defunct website run by the Paracha family that chronicled the events leading to his capture and its aftermath, available at http://web.archive.org/web/20080219151328/http://www.freeparachas.org/).

"To not inform us of his whereabouts": "Interview with Farhat Paracha," *Cage International* (then called *Cage Prisoners*), December 14, 2003.

Petition in the Sind High Court on July 25, 2003: *Paracha v. Federation of Islamic Republic of Pakistan* (2003) Const. P. 926/2003 (D.B.) Principal Seat Karachi (Pak.).40.

Chapter 11: The Interviewer, a Notetaker, and a Story

CITF: Memorandum of Understanding between Federal Bureau of Investigation and the Department of Defense Criminal Investigative Task Force, 2004.

Bagram interview preparations: See, e.g., *Paracha v. Trump*, 453 F. Supp. 3d 168 (2020) (case documents).

Obaidullah: *See* "Guantanamo Detainee Profile," *New York Times*, November 23, 2015.

Interagency process: The author viewed various correspondence and documentation, in addition to interviews on this topic. However, pursuant to the prepublication review process, citations to those documents have been omitted. *See also*, Senate Select Committee on Intelligence, "Study of the Central Intelligence Agency's Detention and Interrogation Program," December 3, 2014 (referencing emails from CIA officials dated July 7, 2003, which was shortly after Saifullah Paracha's capture).

Paracha rendered to military custody: [REDACTED] 86058 [REDACTED]; Senate Select Committee on Intelligence, "Study of the Central Intelligence Agency's Detention and Interrogation Program," December 3, 2014 ("On July 5, 2003, Saifullah Paracha was detained in [REDACTED], in an operation orchestrated by the FBI. Shortly thereafter, Saifullah Paracha was rendered to US military custody at Bagram Air Force Base. At Bagram, Saifullah Paracha was questioned by an FBI special agent").

Believed that explosives might be on their way: *See, e.g.,* "Protecting America," Customs and Border Patrol Strategic Plan 2005 (noting an "al Qaeda plot to smuggle explosives in containers to the United States was revealed in 2003 with the detainment of Saifullah Paracha, a Pakistani businessman who ran an import/export business in New York").

Saifullah and Uzair Paracha treatment and interview process: See, e.g., *Paracha v. Trump*, 453 F. Supp. 3d 168 (2020) (case documents).

FBI interrogation strategy, Bagram meeting room, personnel in the room, and Saifullah Paracha Bagram interviews: The author viewed various correspondence and documentation, in addition to interviews on this topic. However, pursuant to the prepublication review process, citations to those documents have been omitted. *See also, Paracha v. Trump*, 453 F. Supp. 3d 168 (2020) (case documents).

"Sitting on the ground, blindfolded with ear coverings on": *Paracha v. Trump*, 453 F. Supp. 3d 168 (2020) (case documents).

Bob and Agent Ruby: The author viewed various correspondence and documentation, in addition to interviews on this topic, corroborating the account of Bob and Agent Ruby's participation in the interviews. However, pursuant to the prepublication review process, citations to those documents have been omitted. *See also, Paracha v. Trump*, 453 F. Supp. 3d 168 (2020) (case documents).

Paracha's pontificating and statements: The author viewed various correspondence and documentation, in addition to interviews on this topic. However, pursuant to the prepublication review process, citations to those documents have been omitted. *See also, Paracha v. Trump*, 453 F. Supp. 3d 168 (2020) (case documents); Summary of Administrative Review Board Proceedings for ISN 1094, Guantanamo Bay, December 2006; "Detainee Statement," "Periodic Review Board Initial Hearing, Saifullah Abdullah Paracha, ISN 1094", Guantanamo Bay, March 8, 2016; Combatant Status Review Tribunal for ISN 1094, November 2004.

Paracha meeting Usama bin Laden: *Paracha v. Trump*, 453 F. Supp. 3d 168 (2020) (case documents); Summary of Administrative Review Board Proceedings for ISN 1094, Guantanamo Bay, December 2006; "Detainee Statement," "Periodic Review Board Initial Hearing, Saifullah Abdullah Paracha, ISN 1094", Guantanamo Bay, March 8, 2016; Combatant Status Review Tribunal for ISN 1094, November 2004.

Bin Laden declaration of war: Usama bin Laden, "Declaration of War Against the Americans Occupying the Land of the Two Holy Places" 1996; *see also* Usama bin Laden, "Declaration of the World Islamic Front," 1998.

Bin Laden public statement: Usama bin Laden, "The Nuclear Bomb of Islam," *International Islamic Front for Fighting Jews and Crusaders*, 1998.

Mir: *Paracha v. Trump*, 453 F. Supp. 3d 168 (2020) (case documents); Summary of Administrative Review Board Proceedings for ISN 1094, Guantanamo Bay, December 2006; "Detainee Statement," "Periodic Review Board Initial Hearing, Saifullah Abdullah Paracha, ISN 1094", Guantanamo Bay, March 8, 2016; Combatant Status Review Tribunal for ISN 1094, November 2004.

Sharafuddin Shamim alias: *Paracha v. Trump*, 453 F. Supp. 3d 168 (2020) (case documents).

First Interim 9/11 Commission Report: Thomas H. Kean and Lee H. Hamilton, "First Interim 9/11 Commission Report," 9/11 Commission, July 8, 2003.

Mustafa: *See, e.g., Paracha v. Trump*, 453 F. Supp. 3d 168 (2020); Summary of Administrative Review Board Proceedings for ISN 1094, Guantanamo Bay, December 2006; "Detainee Statement," "Periodic Review Board Initial Hearing, Saifullah Abdullah Paracha, ISN 1094", Guantanamo Bay, March 8, 2016.

July 17, 2003: The author viewed various correspondence and documentation, in addition to interviews on this topic. However, pursuant to the prepublication review process, citations to those documents have been omitted. *See, also*, [REDACTED] 13588 (171505Z JUL 03); *Paracha v. Trump*, 453 F. Supp. 3d 168 (2020) (case documents).

Bob dispatch: [REDACTED] 13588 (171505Z JUL 03).

"We need to take a break": This account was corroborated by interviews with Bob and Agent Miller.

Chapter 12: A Bomb and a Missing Man

Suspecting "Charles Stern's" role in apprehension: "Interview with Farhat Paracha," *Cage International* (then called *Cage Prisoners*), December 14, 2003; "Interview with Zahra Paracha," *Cage International* (then called *Cage Prisoners*), February 21, 2007; Huma Aamir Malik, "Father and Son Become Victims of the Global War on Terror," *Arab News*, February 25, 2006; Saba Imtiaz, "Forever Prisoners: Were a father and son wrongfully ensnared by America's war on terror?" *The Guardian*, December 13, 2018; *Paracha v. Bush* (habeas corpus petition filed by Farhat Paracha) (November 17, 2004); *Paracha v. Federation of Islamic Republic of Pakistan* (2003) Const. P. 926/2003 (D.B.) Principal Seat Karachi (Pak.).40; FREEPARACHAS.ORG (a now defunct website run by the Paracha family that chronicled the events leading to his capture and its aftermath, available at http://web.archive.org/web/20080219151328/http://www.freeparachas.org/); "Karachi: Paracha's wife sues US partners," *Dawn*, September 13, 2003.

"Hate mails": "Interview with Farhat Paracha," *Cage International* (formerly *Cage Prisoners*), December 14, 2003.

Nisar Mujahid: *Paracha v. Federation of Islamic Republic of Pakistan*, (2003) Const. P. 926/2003 (D.B.) Principal Seat Karachi (Pak.).40; "Karachi: Paracha's wife sues US partners," *Dawn*, September 13, 2003.

"Enforced disappearance": *Paracha v. Federation of Islamic Republic of Pakistan*, (2003) Const. P. 926/2003 (D.B.) Principal Seat Karachi (Pak.).40; Amnesty International, "Denying the Undeniable: Enforced Disappearances in Pakistan," *Amnesty International Publications*, 2008.

Farhat tried to make sense of this theory: "Interview with Farhat Paracha," *Cage International* (formerly *Cage Prisoners*), December 14, 2003.

Habeas corpus petition in Karachi: *Paracha v. Federation of Islamic Republic of Pakistan* (2003) Const. P. 926/2003 (D.B.) Principal Seat Karachi (Pak.).40.

Amnesty International speculation: Amnesty International, "Pakistan: Human rights ignored in the 'war on terror,'" 2006.

NBC News story: Lisa Myers, NBC News, August 5, 2003; *see also* Dan Eggen, "US to File Terrorism Charges Against Pakistani Detainee," *Washington Post*, August 5, 2003 (confirming that NBC News first broke the story).

August 23, 2003: "Interview with Farhat Paracha," *Cage International* (formerly *Cage Prisoners*), December 14, 2003; *Paracha v. Federation of Islamic Republic of Pakistan* (2003) Const. P. 926/2003 (D.B.) Principal Seat Karachi (Pak.).40.

Mohammed Jabarah: "Terror Informant for FBI Allegedly Targeted Agents," *Washington Post*, January 19, 2008; Department of Justice documents on Mohammed Mansour Jabarah, including Jabarah's "Sentencing Memorandum"; Senate Select Committee on Intelligence, "Study of the Central Intelligence Agency's Detention and Interrogation Program," December 3, 2014.

Jemaah Islamiyah: *See, e.g.,* Sworn Charge Sheet, Encep Nurjaman, Mohammed Nazir bin Lep, Mohammed Farik bin Amin, Guantanamo Bay Military Commissions, October 8, 2019; Senate Select Committee on Intelligence, "Study of the Central Intelligence Agency's Detention and Interrogation Program," December 3, 2014; Senate Select Committee on Intelligence, "Study of the Central Intelligence Agency's Detention and Interrogation Program," December 3, 2014.

Hambali, Zubair, Lillie: *See, e.g.,* Sworn Charge Sheet, Encep Nurjaman, Mohammed Nazir bin Lep, Mohammed Farik bin Amin, Guantanamo Bay Military Commissions, October 8, 2019.

KSM, Majid Khan, Ali Abdul Aziz Ali role in Marriott bombing: *See, e.g.,* Sworn Charge Sheet, Encep Nurjaman, Mohammed Nazir bin Lep, Mohammed Farik bin Amin, Guantanamo Bay Military Commissions, October 8, 2019; Majid Khan, "Unsworn Statement," read into court at Guantanamo Bay, October 28, 2021; Stipulation of Fact, *United States v. Majid Khan*, Guantanamo Bay Military Commission, February 15, 2012.

Majid Khan's thinking: Stipulation of Fact, *United States v. Majid Khan*, Guantanamo Bay Military Commission, February 15, 2012.

Rusman Gunawan role in Marriott bombing: [REDACTED] 87551 (150731Z AUG 03); [REDACTED] 87552 (150738Z AUG 03); [REDACTED] 15108 (161148Z AUG 03); ALEC [REDACTED] (181711Z AUG 03); [REDACTED] 15173 (251117Z AUG 03); ALEC [REDACTED] (011729Z SEP 03); and [REDACTED] 15243 (020259Z SEP 03).

Aafia Siddiqui: Stipulation of Fact, *United States v. Majid Khan*, Guantanamo Bay Military Commission, February 15, 2012; Majid Khan, "Unsworn Statement," read into court at Guantanamo Bay, October 28, 2021; *United States v. Aafia Siddiqui*; Declan Walsh, "Guantánamo files paint Aafia Siddiqui as top al-Qaida operative," *The Guardian*, April 26, 2011; *Paracha v. Trump*, 453 F. Supp. 3d 168 (2020).

"Mr. Farooq": Stipulation of Fact, *United States v. Majid Khan*, Guantanamo Bay Military Commission, February 15, 2012; Sworn Charge Sheet, Encep Nurjaman, Mohammed Nazir bin Lep, Mohammed Farik bin Amin, Guantanamo Bay Military Commissions, October 8, 2019 (listing "Mr. Farooq as a known co-conspirator).

Noordin Mat Top, Mohammed Ikhwan, Dr. bin Hussein Azahari, Asmar Latin Sani: Stipulation of Fact, *United States v. Majid Khan*, Guantanamo Bay Military Commission, February 15, 2012; Sworn Charge Sheet, Encep Nurjaman, Mohammed Nazir bin Lep, Mohammed Farik bin Amin, Guantanamo Bay Military Commissions, October 8, 2019.

Briefing slide: Briefing for Chief of Staff to the President Josh Bolten: CIA Rendition, Detention and Interrogation Programs, May 2, 2006.

Farhat Paracha had a reoccurring dream: "Interview with Farhat Paracha," *Cage International* (formerly *Cage Prisoners*), December 14, 2003.

ICRC information: "Interview with Farhat Paracha," *Cage International* (formerly *Cage Prisoners*), December 14, 2003; FREEPARACHAS.ORG (a now defunct website run by the Paracha family that chronicled the events leading to his capture and its aftermath, available at http://web.archive.org/web/20080219151328/http://www.freeparachas.org/).

"No criminal record whatsoever": "Interview with Farhat Paracha," *Cage International* (formerly *Cage Prisoners*), December 14, 2003; FREEPARACHAS.ORG (a now defunct website run by the Paracha family that chronicled the events leading to his capture and its aftermath, available at http://web.archive.org/web/20080219151328/http://www.freeparachas.org/).

ICRC letter: Zofeen Ebrahim, "Pakistan: 'Gitmo Is Like Being Alive in Your Own Grave,'" Inter Press Service, December 14, 2006; "Interview with Farhat Paracha," *Cage International* (formerly *Cage Prisoners*), December 14, 2003.

Uzair letters: "Interview with Farhat Paracha," *Cage International* (formerly *Cage Prisoners*), December 14, 2003; FREEPARACHAS.ORG (a now defunct website run by the Paracha family that chronicled the events leading to his capture and its aftermath, available at http://web.archive.org/web/20080219151328/http://www.freeparachas.org/).

Effect on children: "Interview with Farhat Paracha," *Cage International* (then called *Cage Prisoners*), December 14, 2003; "Interview with Zahra Paracha," *Cage International* (formerly *Cage Prisoners*), February 21, 2007; Huma Aamir Malik, "Father and Son Become Victims of the Global War on Terror," *Arab News*, February 25, 2006; Saba Imtiaz, "Forever Prisoners: Were a father and son wrongfully ensnared by America's war on terror?" *The Guardian*, December 13, 2018; FREEPARACHAS.ORG (a now defunct website run by the Paracha family that chronicled the events leading to his capture and its aftermath, available at http://web.archive.org/web/20080219151328/http://www.freeparachas.org/).

"Psychologically, it has devastated our whole family": "Interview with Farhat Paracha," *Cage International* (then called *Cage Prisoners*), December 14, 2003.

Out of necessity: Saba Imtiaz, "Forever Prisoners: Were a father and son wrongfully ensnared by America's war on terror?" *The Guardian*, December 13, 2018.

Akhtar Raja: "Interview with Farhat Paracha," *Cage International* (then called *Cage Prisoners*), December 14, 2003; *Paracha v. Federation of Islamic Republic of Pakistan* (2003) Const. P. 926/2003 (D.B.) Principal Seat Karachi (Pak.).40.

Another lawsuit: "Karachi: Paracha's wife sues US partners," *Dawn*, September 13, 2003; *see also* "Interview with Farhat Paracha," *Cage International* (then called *Cage Prisoners*), December 14, 2003; Huma Aamir Malik, "Father and Son Become Victims of the Global War on Terror," *Arab News*, February 25, 2006; *Paracha v. Federation of Islamic Republic of Pakistan* (2003) Const. P. 926/2003 (D.B.) Principal Seat Karachi (Pak.). 40; SHC Directs Constitution of Medical Board: "Medical Treatment of Guantanamo Bay Detainee's Wife," APNAKARACHI.COM (June 2, 2010), http://www.apnakarachi. com/SHC-directs-constitution-of-medical-board.html.

Collusion allegation: "Karachi: Paracha's wife sues US partners," *Dawn*, September 13, 2003.

Chapter 13: Welcome to Guantanamo Bay

Agent Miller's relationship with Saifullah Paracha: See, e.g., *Paracha v. Trump*, 453 F. Supp. 3d 168 (2020) (case documents).

Random cast of characters: *See, e.g., Paracha v. Trump*, 453 F. Supp. 3d 168 (2020) (case documents); Summary of Administrative Review Board Proceedings for ISN 1094, Guantanamo Bay, December 2006; "Detainee Statement," "Periodic Review Board Initial Hearing, Saifullah Abdullah Paracha, ISN 1094", Guantanamo Bay, March 8, 2016; The author viewed numerous reports from each interview session that occurred between investigators and Saifullah Paracha over the course of his detention. Pursuant to the prepublication review process, citations to those documents have been omitted.

Polygraph: Summary of Administrative Review Board Proceedings for ISN 1094, Guantanamo Bay, December 2006; The author viewed reports involving the polygraph test. Pursuant to the prepublication review process, citations to those documents have been omitted.

Casio organizer: Summary of Administrative Review Board Proceedings for ISN 1094, Guantanamo Bay, December 2006; *Paracha v. Trump*, 453 F. Supp. 3d 168 (2020) (case documents).

Octogenarian Pakistani Scientist: Scott Shane & Benjamin Weiser, "Dossier Shows Push for More Attacks After 9/11," *New York Times*, April 25, 2011 (describing a classified assessment noting that Saifullah Paracha told investigators that he had worked with Abdul Qadeer Khan, considered to be the father of Pakistan's nuclear weapons program and a major proliferator of nuclear technology).

Hassan bin Attash: *See, e.g.*, "Guantanamo Detainee Profile, ISN 1456," Department of Defense, June 5, 2020; Stipulation of Fact, *United States v. Majid Khan*, Guantanamo Bay Military Commission, February 15, 2012; The author viewed numerous reports and the case file for this detainee. Pursuant to the prepublication review process, citations to those documents have been omitted.

Khalid bin Attash: 9/11 Commission Report: "Final Report of the National Commission on Terrorist Attacks Upon the United States," US Government, July 22, 2004; Sworn Charge Sheet, Khalid Sheikh Mohammad, Walid Muhammad Salih Mubarak bin Attash, Ramzi Binalshibh, Ali Abdul Aziz Ali, Mustafa Ahmed Adam al Hawsawi, *United States v. Khalid Sheikh Muhammad, et al*, Guantanamo Bay Military Commissions, April 4, 2012; Senate Select Committee on Intelligence, "Study of the Central Intelligence Agency's Detention and Interrogation Program," December 3, 2014.

Hassan bin Attash administrative board: "Unclassified Summary of Final Determination," Department of Defense, October 11, 2016; Combatant Status Review Board, Department of Defense, November 9, 2004.

Ali al Haji Sharqawi: *See, e.g.*, Periodic Review Board, Department of Defense, March 15, 2016; Combatant Status Review Board, Department of Defense, November 9, 2004; The author viewed numerous reports and the case file for this detainee. Pursuant to the prepublication review process, citations to those documents have been omitted.

Sanad al-Kazimi: Combatant Status Review Board, Department of Defense, November 10, 2004; The author viewed numerous reports and the case file for this detainee. Pursuant to the prepublication review process, citations to those documents have been omitted.

Transfer to Guantanamo Bay: The author viewed numerous reports regarding the transfer. Pursuant to the prepublication review process, citations to those documents have been omitted. Information surrounding the physical transfer of detainees to Guantanamo Bay were among the most censored documentation during the prepublication review process.

Chapter 14: Masters of the Earth

Marriott bombing: *See, e.g.,* Sworn Charge Sheet, Encep Nurjaman, Mohammed Nazir bin Lep, Mohammed Farik bin Amin, Guantanamo Bay Military Commissions, October 8, 2019; Majid Khan, "Unsworn Statement," read into court at Guantanamo Bay, October 28, 2021; Stipulation of Fact, *United States v. Majid Khan*, Guantanamo Bay Military Commission, February 15, 2012.

Explosives: Stipulation of Fact, *United States v. Majid Khan*, Guantanamo Bay Military Commission, February 15, 2012; Majid Khan, "Unsworn Statement," read into court at Guantanamo Bay, October 28, 2021; DIRECTOR [REDACTED] (181929Z JUN 03), disseminated as [REDACTED]; [REDACTED] 39239 (301600Z MAY 03); Senate Select Committee on Intelligence, "Study of the Central Intelligence Agency's Detention and Interrogation Program," December 3, 2014; [REDACTED] 13588 (171505Z JUL 03).

Uzair case: *US v. Uzair Paracha* (case documents); *Paracha v. Trump*, 453 F. Supp. 3d 168 (2020).

"Uzair is doing better than his father": "Interview with a Cousin of Uzair Paracha," *Cage International* (formerly *Cage Prisoners*), February 21, 2004.

Uzair's plea deal: *United States v. Paracha*, No. 03 CR. 1197 (S.D.N.Y. Jan. 3, 2006) (case documents); Saba Imtiaz, "Forever Prisoners: Were a father and son wrongfully ensnared by America's war on terror?" *The Guardian*, December 13, 2018.

"He did istikhara": Saba Imtiaz, "Forever Prisoners: Were a father and son wrongfully ensnared by America's war on terror?" *The Guardian*, December 13, 2018.

Uzair Paracha sentencing: *United States v. Paracha*, (case documents); Press Release, "Pakistani Man Convicted of Providing Material Support to al Qaeda Sentenced to 30 Years in Federal Prison," United States Attorney, Southern District of New York, July 20, 2006.

Two dirty bombs: For this section, see Government Accountability Office Report, "Border Security: Investigators Successfully Transported Radioactive Sources

Across Our Nation's Borders at Select Locations," *GAO-06-545R*, March 28, 2006.

"A wake-up call . . . Issues must be addressed": Associated Press, "Senators: Act fast to strengthen port security," NBC News, March 28, 2006.

"Sometimes he seems depressed": "Interview with Farhat Paracha," *Cage International* (formerly *Cage Prisoners*), February 21, 2004.

Special Administrative Measures: *See, e.g.,* Katherine Erickson, "This Is Still a Profession: Special Administrative Measures, the Sixth Amendment, and the Practice of Law," Columbia Human Rights Law Review, 2018 ("Uzair Paracha . . . was placed under SAMs shortly after he refused to accept a plea deal").

"About one in ten guards treated us like human beings": Uzair Paracha, "Innocent in the Eyes of the Law," *Hell Is a Very Small Place: Voices from Solitary Confinement*, 2016.

Indefinite detention: *Paracha v. Trump*, 453 F. Supp. 3d 168 (2020) (case documents); Summary of Administrative Review Board Proceedings for ISN 1094, Guantanamo Bay, December 2006; "Detainee Statement," "Periodic Review Board Initial Hearing, Saifullah Abdullah Paracha, ISN 1094", Guantanamo Bay, March 8, 2016; Combatant Status Review Tribunal for ISN 1094, November 2004.

"Gem of a man": "Interview with Farhat Paracha," *Cage International* (formerly *Cage Prisoners*), February 21, 2004; *Paracha v. Bush* (habeas corpus petition filed by Farhat Paracha) (November 17, 2004).

David Remes: *See, e.g.,* "Opening Statement of Private Counsel David Remes," Periodic Review Board, Saifullah Paracha, March 8, 2016; *Paracha v. Bush* (habeas corpus petition filed by Farhat Paracha) (November 17, 2004).

David Remes resignation from Covington & Burling: *See, e.g.,* Debra Cassens Weiss, "Covington Partner Reveals Resignation After Revealing Press Conference," *ABA Journal*, July 21, 2008.

"The reaction to what I did makes me very sad": Dan Slater, "David Remes, Who Dropped His Pants in Yemen, to Leave Covington," *Wall Street Journal*, July 21, 2008.

ICRC: "Interview with Farhat Paracha," *Cage International* (then called *Cage Prisoners*), December 14, 2003; "Interview with Zahra Paracha," *Cage International* (formerly *Cage Prisoners*), February 21, 2007; Huma Aamir Malik, "Father and Son Become Victims of the Global War on Terror," *Arab News*, February 25, 2006; Saba Imtiaz, "Forever Prisoners: Were a father and son wrongfully ensnared by America's war on terror?" *The Guardian*, December 13, 2018; FREEPARACHAS.ORG (a now defunct website run by the Paracha family that chronicled the events leading to his capture and its aftermath, available at http://web.archive.org/web/20080219151328/http://www.freeparachas.org/).

"Dear Mom, Farhat, Muneeza, Mustafa and Zahra": Saifullah Paracha, letter to his family transmitted through the International Committee for the Red Cross, March 24, 2003.

"Is it possible to loosen my handcuffs?": Sworn Detainee Statement, Combatant Status Review Tribunal, Guantanamo Bay, December 2004.

Paracha, December 2004 CSRT: Sworn Detainee Statement, Combatant Status Review Tribunal, Guantanamo Bay, December 2004; Review of Combatant Status Review Tribunal, Department of Defense, December 21, 2004.

"If I am allowed to tell a joke": Sworn Detainee Statement, Combatant Status Review Tribunal, Guantanamo Bay, December 2004.

CSRT back and forth: Sworn Detainee Statement, Combatant Status Review Tribunal, Guantanamo Bay, December 2004.

"That family": Saba Imtiaz, "Forever Prisoners: Were a father and son wrongfully ensnared by America's war on terror?" *The Guardian*, December 13, 2018.

"We don't know you": Saba Imtiaz, "Forever Prisoners: Were a father and son wrongfully ensnared by America's war on terror?" *The Guardian*, December 13, 2018.

"Medical counseling, psychiatric help, she was in depression": Zofeen Ebrahim, "Pakistan: 'Gitmo Is Like Being Alive in Your Own Grave,'" Inter Press Service, December 14, 2006.

Syed Abul Mahasin: Letter from Syed Mahasin to G. T. Hunt, "RE: MR. SAIFULLAH PARACHA," enclosed in a letter sent from Gaillard Hunt to Rear Admiral James McGarrah, Office of Administrative Review of Enemy Combatants, dated November 3, 2004.

Bakhtiar Ahmad, Pakistan Television Corporation: Letter from Bakhtiar Ahmad, Controller Special Productions, Pakistan TV Corporation, Ltd. "RE: Mr. Saifullah Paracha," enclosed in a letter sent from Gaillard Hunt to Rear Admiral James McGarrah, Office of Administrative Review of Enemy Combatants, dated November 11, 2004.

Khalid Khawaja: Letter from Khalid Khawaja, "To Whom It May Concern," enclosed in a letter sent from Gaillard Hunt to Rear Admiral James McGarrah, Office of Administrative Review of Enemy Combatants, dated November 11, 2004.

Khawaja Naveed Ahmed: Letter from Khawaja Naveed Ahmed, Advocate, Supreme Court of Pakistan, "To Whom It May Concern," enclosed in a letter sent from Gaillard Hunt to Rear Admiral James McGarrah, Office of Administrative Review of Enemy Combatants, dated November 12, 2004.

Character witnesses: Combatant Status Review Tribunal for ISN 1094, November 2004.

Hunt letter: Letter from Gailard Hunt, "Re. SAIFULLAH PARACHA," to Rear Admiral James McGarrah, Office of Administrative Review of Enemy Combatants, dated November 3, 2004.

"Gem of a man": "Interview with Farhat Paracha," *Cage International* (formerly *Cage Prisoners*), February 21, 2004; *Paracha v. Bush* (habeas corpus petition filed by Farhat Paracha) (November 17, 2004).

December 8, 2004, decision: Combatant Status Review Tribunal, Guantanamo Bay, December 2004.

Legal review: Memorandum from Legal Advisor to Director, Combatant Status Review Tribunal, December 20, 2004.

Rear Admiral McGarrah decision: Memorandum from Director, Combatant Status Review Tribunal, December 21, 2004.

Uzair trial: *US v. Uzair Paracha* (case documents).

Uzair testimony: *See, e.g.,* Karen Greenberg, "No Ordinary Pakistani: The Intertwined Stories of Saifullah and Uzair Paracha," *Lawfare*, January 5, 2023; *US v. Uzair Paracha* (case documents).

Uzair Paracha sentencing: *United States v. Paracha*, (case documents); Press Release, "Pakistani Man Convicted of Providing Material Support to al Qaeda Sentenced to 30 Years in Federal Prison," United States Attorney, Southern District of New York, July 20, 2006.

"Uzair was like any young twenty-something": Zofeen Ebrahim, "Pakistan: 'Gitmo Is Like Being Alive in Your Own Grave,'" *Inter Press Service*, December 14, 2006.

Majid Khan trajectory: *See, e.g.,* Majid Khan, "Unsworn Statement," read into court at Guantanamo Bay, October 28, 2021; Transcript of Combatant Status Review Tribunal Hearing for ISN 10020, March 10, 2007.

Majid Khan and Fox News: Transcript of Combatant Status Review Tribunal Hearing for ISN 10020, March 10, 2007.

"They gave me new wrong prescription eyeglasses to wear": Transcript of Combatant Status Review Tribunal Hearing for ISN 10020, March 10, 2007.

Responsible for the 9/11 attacks "from A to Z": Transcript of Combatant Status Review Tribunal Hearing for ISN 10024, March 10, 2007.

"I am an entrepreneur with many personal contacts": Transcript of Combatant Status Review Tribunal Hearing for ISN 10018, March 30, 2007.

Marwan al Shehhi: Transcript of Combatant Status Review Tribunal Hearing for ISN 10018, March 30, 2007.

Ramzi Binalshibh: Transcript of Combatant Status Review Tribunal Hearing for ISN 10018, March 30, 2007.

"Just a person": Transcript of Combatant Status Review Tribunal Hearing for ISN 10018, March 30, 2007.

"Export and import": Transcript of Combatant Status Review Tribunal Hearing for ISN 10018, March 30, 2007.

"I never knew Majid Khan was a member of al Qaeda": Transcript of Combatant Status Review Tribunal Hearing for ISN 10020, March 10, 2007.

Iyman Faris: Transcript of Combatant Status Review Tribunal Hearing for ISN 10020, March 10, 2007.

"You want to know whether my son is a terrorist": Transcript of Combatant Status Review Tribunal Hearing for ISN 10020, March 10, 2007.

Chapter 15: Lies, Schemes, and Betrayal

"Shitmo": Saba Imtiaz, "Forever Prisoners: Were a father and son wrongfully ensnared by America's war on terror?" *The Guardian*, December 13, 2018.

Saifullah Paracha medical issues: *See, e.g.,* Zofeen Ebrahim, "Pakistan: 'Gitmo Is Like Being Alive in Your Own Grave,'" *Inter Press Service*, December 14, 2006; SHC Directs Constitution of Medical Board: "Medical Treatment of Guantanamo Bay Detainee's Wife," APNAKARACHI.COM, June 2, 2010; Saba Imtiaz, "Forever Prisoners: Were a father and son wrongfully ensnared by America's war on terror?" *The Guardian*, December 13, 2018; *Paracha v. Trump*, 453 F. Supp. 3d 168 (2020); *Paracha v. Federation of Islamic Republic of Pakistan* (2003) Const. P. 926/2003 (D.B.) Principal Seat Karachi (Pak.). 40.

Cardiac catheterization: "Who Are the Guantanamo Detainees? Case Sheet 22," Amnesty International, October 2007; Joel Seidman, "Judge: Heart surgery must be at Guantanamo," NBC News, November 20, 2006.

$1 million to have an aircraft deliver a twenty-four-member team of cardiac specialists and equipment: Carol J. Williams, "Detainee refuses surgery," *Los Angeles Times*, November 23, 2006

Federal lawsuit: *Paracha v. Bush* (case documents).

Erroneous reporting: *See, e.g.,* "Lawyers Protest Medical Procedure on Gitmo Detainee's Heart," Fox News, November 16, 2006 ("Saifullah A. Paracha, a 69-year-old multimillionaire businessman from Karachi, Pakistan, already had one heart attack while in US custody . . ."); FREEPARACHAS.ORG (a now defunct website run by the Paracha family that chronicled the events leading to his capture and its aftermath, available at http://web.archive.org/web/20080219151328/http://www.freeparachas.org/) (the website erroneously stated that Saifullah Paracha suffered two heart attacks due to extremely harsh interrogations and torture. Unclassified documentation of FBI interviews with Saifullah Paracha reveal a less provocative picture of the situation).

Khawaja Khalid: Carol J. Williams, "Detainee refuses surgery," *Los Angeles Times*, November 23, 2006.

Court decision: Joel Seidman, "Judge: Heart surgery must be at Guantanamo," NBC News, November 20, 2006.

"Chacha": Saba Imtiaz, "Forever Prisoners: Were a father and son wrongfully ensnared by America's war on terror?" *The Guardian*, December 13, 2018.

Detainees verbally abused Saifullah / camp leader: The author viewed numerous reports regarding Saifullah Paracha's daily routine and behavior at Guantanamo Bay. Pursuant to the prepublication review process, citations to those documents have been omitted.

Saifullah Paracha as a camp sage: Saba Imtiaz, "Forever Prisoners: Were a father and son wrongfully ensnared by America's war on terror?" *The Guardian*, December 13, 2018.

VTC: Saba Imtiaz, "Forever Prisoners: Were a father and son wrongfully ensnared by America's war on terror?" *The Guardian*, December 13, 2018; Pascal Cuttat, "ICRC Pakistan Newsletter," *International Committee for the Red Cross*, November–December 2009.

Syed Abul Mahasin: Letter from Syed Mahasin to G. T. Hunt, "RE: MR. SAIFULLAH PARACHA," enclosed in a letter sent from Gaillard Hunt to Rear Admiral James McGarrah, Office of Administrative Review of Enemy Combatants, dated November 3, 2004.

Muneeza Paracha: Saba Imtiaz, "Forever Prisoners: Were a father and son wrongfully ensnared by America's war on terror?" *The Guardian*, December 13, 2018; "Interview with Farhat Paracha," *Cage International* (formerly *Cage Prisoners*), February 21, 2004.

Khalid Khawaja: Letter from Khalid Khawaja, "To Whom It May Concern," enclosed in a letter sent from Gaillard Hunt to Rear Admiral James McGarrah, Office of Administrative Review of Enemy Combatants, dated November 11,

2004; Huma Aamir Malik, "Saifullah Paracha Did Meet Bin Laden," Arab News, February 13, 2005 (describing a press conference with Farhat Paracha, her children, "and Khalid Khawaja, a close friend of her husband"); The author viewed numerous reports regarding Khalid Khawaja, Farhat Paracha, and the Paracha business. Pursuant to the prepublication review process, citations to those documents have been omitted.

Khawaja's death: *See, e.g.,* Bill Roggio, "Former ISI officer executed in northwestern Pakistan," *Long War Journal,* April 30, 2010.

Farhat Paracha success at Sindh High Court: *Paracha v. Federation of Islamic Republic of Pakistan* (2003) Const. P. 926/2003 (D.B.) Principal Seat Karachi (Pak.); SHC Directs Constitution of Medical Board: "Medical Treatment of Guantanamo Bay Detainee's Wife," APNAKARACHI.COM, June 2, 2010.

Pakistani Attorney General and Foreign Ministry Secretary in contempt: Tariq Siddiqui, "Remand Home shifted to Civil Defence building," *Dawn* (Pakistan), June 2, 2010.

Senator Hollings 2004 speech: "Congressional Record," United States Senate, July 22, 2004.

Mustafa Paracha: Saba Imtiaz, "Forever Prisoners: Were a father and son wrongfully ensnared by America's war on terror?" *The Guardian*, December 13, 2018.

John Cronan: *See, e.g.,* Staff Profile (archived), "Former Acting Assistant Attorney General John P. Cronan, Principal Deputy Attorney General John P. Cronan," Department of Justice, archived at justice.gov.

Obama Executive Order: Executive Order 13492, "Review and Disposition of Individuals Detained at the Guantanamo Bay Naval Base and Closure of Detention Facilities," January 22, 2009.

Eric Holder: "Attorney General Announced Forum Decisions for Guantanamo Detainees (archived)," Department of Justice, November 13, 2009.

David Raskin: Benjamin Weiser, "Top Terror Prosecutor Settles into a Familiar Role," *New York Times*, January 12, 2010; Martha Neil, "Meet David Raskin, Top Prosecutor Likely to Handle Case Against Accused 9/11 Mastermind," *ABA Journal*, January 12, 2010.

Umar Farouk Abdulmutallab: *See, e.g.,* Anahad O'Connor and Eric Schmitt, "Terror Attempt Seen as Man Tries to Ignite Device on Jet," *New York Times*, December 25, 2009; Paul Cruickshank and Tim Lister, "Al Qaeda in the Arabian Peninsula confirms links to underwear bomber," CNN, December 23, 2014; Press release, "Umar Farouk Abdulmutallab Indicted for Attempted Bombing of Flight 253 on Christmas Day," Department of Justice, January 6, 2010.

Ahmed Ghailani: *See, e.g., United States v. Ghailani*, No. S1098, 2010 WL 1839030 (S.D.N.Y. May 10, 2010); Press release, "Ahmed Ghailani Transferred from Guantanamo Bay to New York for Prosecution on Terror Charges" Department of Justice, June 9, 2009.

Ghailani verdict: "Guantanamo Detainee Ghailani Convicted on Just 1 Charge by N.Y. Jury," PBS News, November 17, 2010; John Yoo, "The Ghailani Verdict and the War on Terror," *Wall Street Journal*, November 20, 2010.

Guantanamo Review Task Force: "Final Report, Guantanamo Review Task Force," Department of Justice, Department of Defense, Department of State, Department of Homeland Security, Office of the Director of National Intelligence, Joint Chiefs of Staff, January 22, 2010.

Andy Patel: Joel Whitney, "The Terror Suspect's Advocate," *New York Magazine*, September 16, 2005; Benjamin Weiser, "Terrorism Law Is a Niche for Deepening Pool of Defenders in New York, *New York Times*, November 25, 2012.

Majid Khan CSRT: Transcript of Combatant Status Review Tribunal Hearing for ISN 10020, March 10, 2007.

Jemaah Islamiyah: *See, e.g.,* Sworn Charge Sheet, Encep Nurjaman, Mohammed Nazir bin Lep, Mohammed Farik bin Amin, Guantanamo Bay Military Commissions, October 8, 2019; Senate Select Committee on Intelligence, "Study of the Central Intelligence Agency's Detention and Interrogation Program," December 3, 2014.

Majid Khan accepting his fate: Stipulation of Fact, *United States v. Majid Khan*, Guantanamo Bay Military Commission, February 15, 2012; Majid Khan, "Unsworn Statement," read into court at Guantanamo Bay, October 28, 2021; "Majid Khan, at Guantanamo Bay, asks for forgiveness for role in al Qaeda terror," *Baltimore Sun*, September 14, 2016.

Eric Holder on 9/11 case: "Statement of the Attorney General on the Prosecution of the 9/11 Conspirators (archived)," Department of Justice, April 4, 2011.

Chapter 16: Who Did He Kill?

Captain John Murphy: *See, e.g.,* David Danzig, "Military Prosecutor: 66 Ready to be Tried at Guantanamo Bay," American Constitution Society, July 15, 2009.

Prosecution presentation and list of potential cases: The author prepared the prosecution presentation for Saifullah Paracha and viewed the potential list of cases. Pursuant to the prepublication review process, citations to those documents have been omitted.

Jeh Johnson: *See, e.g.,* Speech by Jeh Johnson, "The conflict against al Qaeda and its affiliates: how will it end," *Oxford University*, November 30, 2012.

Mark Martins: Peter Finn, "Pentagon names new Guantanamo prosecutor," *Washington Post*, June 23, 2011; Peter Finn, "Brig. Gen. Mark Martins, lead prosecutor in 9/11 case, in fight of his career," *Washington Post*, May 4, 2012.

Omar Khadr: "Canada to give apology, millions to compensate former Gitmo detainee," PBS News, July 5, 2017; "Omar Khadr: I don't wish people to love me," *al Jazeera*, May 31, 2015.

Material Support for Terrorism invalidated: *Hamdan v. United States, 696 F.3d 1238 (D.C. Cir. 2012).*

Aiding the Enemy: 10 USC 903b; 10 USC 948-50.

Chapter 17: McVindication

"I am not sure I would enjoy the company of my younger self": Saba Imtiaz, "Forever Prisoners: Were a father and son wrongfully ensnared by America's war on terror?" *The Guardian*, December 13, 2018.

New trial: *See, e.g.,* Benjamin Weiser, "Judge Orders New Trial in Al Qaeda Terror Case," *New York Times*, July 25, 2018; *United States v. Paracha*, 1:03-cr-01197, (S.D.N.Y.)

2007 CSRT: Transcript of Combatant Status Review Tribunal Hearing for ISN 10020, March 10, 2007.

9/11 charges: Sworn Charge Sheet, Khalid Sheikh Mohammad, Walid Muhammad Salih Mubarak bin Attash, Ramzi Binalshibh, Ali Abdul Aziz Ali, Mustafa Ahmed Adam al Hawsawi, *United States v. Khalid Sheikh Muhammad, et al*, Guantanamo Bay Military Commissions, April 4, 2012.

Jakarta Marriott bombing charges: Sworn Charge Sheet, Encep Nurjaman, Mohammad Nazir bin Lep, Mohammed Farik bin Amin, Guantanamo Bay Military Commissions, October 8, 2019.

Periodic Review Board: Executive Order 13567, March 7, 2011.

June 2016 PRB: "Guantanamo Detainee File Review," *Periodic Review Secretariate*, June 16, 2016.

David Remes letter to PRB: David Remes, "Personal Representative Statement," September 27, 2016.

"I deeply regret becoming involved with individuals who turned out to be al-Qaida": Saifullah Paracha, "Detainee Statement," Periodic Review Board Full Hearing, March 21, 2017.

"The detainee statements regarding his mindset and potential for re-engagement are not credible": "Guantanamo Detainee File Review," *Periodic Review Secretariate*, September 25, 2018.

Paracha family moved on: Saba Imtiaz, "Forever Prisoners: Were a father and son wrongfully ensnared by America's war on terror?" *The Guardian*, December 13, 2018.

War of the Worlds allegory: Al Horner, "How War of the Worlds became one of Spielberg's most controversial movies: 'He lost his sense of decency,'" *The Independent*, July 4, 2025.

Avoiding a second trial: Benjamin Weiser, "Once-Accused Al Qaeda Sympathizer Goes Home," *New York Times*, March 16, 2020.

Al Qaeda reconstituting in Africa: Shola Lawal, "Is Mali about to fall to al-Qaeda affiliate JNIM?" *Al Jazeera*, November 6, 2025; *see also* Michael Langley, "Digital Press Briefing on the New AFRICOM Strategy and US Military Cooperation in Africa," US Department of State, September 12, 2024.

PRB clearance: "Unclassified Summary of Final Determination," *Periodic Review Secretariate*, May 13, 2021.

Fighting ongoing detention in federal court: *See, e.g., Paracha v. Biden*, 21-CV-2567.

"A free and innocent man": Benjamin Weiser, "Once-Accused Al Qaeda Sympathizer Goes Home," *New York Times*, March 16, 2020.

First photograph: Karen Greenberg, "No Ordinary Pakistani: The Intertwined Stories of Saifullah and Uzair Paracha," *Lawfare*, January 5, 2023.

Pakistani government statement: Press Release, Ministry of Foreign Affairs, Government of Pakistan, October 29, 2022.

Chapter 18: Spiraling Toward the Next Attack

FBI Inspector General report: "A Review of the FBI's Handling of Intelligence Information Related to the September 11 Attacks, US Department of Justice, Office of the Inspector General, publicly released June 2006.

FBI reports losing more than 5,000 employees: Devlin Barrett and Adam Goldman, "F.B.I. Plans to Lower Recruiting Standards, Alarming Agents," *New York Times*, August 21, 2025.

Shutdown pay for intelligence analysts: Jenny Abamu, "It's supposed to be payday for many federal works. Instead, they're getting nothing," NPR, October 24, 2025.

FBI Agents Association concern: "FBI Agents Association Statement on Reports of FBI Agent Firings," FBI Agents Association, August 7, 2025.

FBI director announcement: Kash Patel, "Statement Before the US House Committee on the Judiciary," September 17, 2025.

Department of Justice Inspector General Report: Susan Landau, "The FBI's Dangerous Failure to Adapt to the Digital Age," *Lawfare Media,* July 7, 2025.

Refocusing on immigration: *See, e.g.,* "Under Patel, FBI heightens focus on violent crime, illegal immigration. Other threats abound, too," Associated Press, June 9, 2025.

Department of Justice Fiscal Year 2026 budget summary: "Fiscal Year 2026 Budget and Performance Summary," US Department of Justice, June 13, 2025.

NATO report: "Countering terrorism," North Atlantic Treaty Organization, August 6, 2025.

US National Counterterrorism Center memo: Kanishka Singh, "US National Counterterrorism Center warns of threat from al Qaeda," Reuters, September 19, 2025.

Chicago Council on Global Affairs report: Dina Smeltz and Emily Sullivan, "21 Years after 9/11, Americans are Less Concerned about Terrorism," Chicago Council on Global Affairs, September 7, 2022.

Qahtani's role: 9/11 Commission Report: Final Report of the National Commission on Terrorist Attacks Upon the United States," US Government, July 22, 2004.

Qahtani's Release Clearance: "Memorandum for the Record," *Periodic Review Secretariate*, June 9, 2021.

Qahtani Sent to Saudi Arabia: "Guantanamo Bay Detainee Transfer Announced," Department of Defense, March 7, 2022; *see also* "US repatriates suspected '20th hijacker' of 9/11 from Guantanamo Bay," BBC, March 8, 2022.

"Information relating to military chemical warfare agents": *Paracha v. Trump*, 453 F. Supp. 3d 168 (2020) (case documents).

Nuclear weapons: *Paracha v. Trump*, 453 F. Supp. 3d 168 (2020); Summary of Administrative Review Board Proceedings for ISN 1094, Guantanamo Bay, December 2006; "Detainee Statement," "Periodic Review Board Initial Hearing, Saifullah Abdullah Paracha, ISN 1094", Guantanamo Bay, March 8, 2016; Combatant Status Review Board, Department of Defense, November 12, 2004; *see also* Frank Davies, "Al-Qaeda nukes bid alleged," *Seattle Times*, February 11, 2005.

Raid evidence: ALEC [REDACTED] (222235Z DEC 02); DIRECTOR [REDACTED] (221835Z APR 02); DIRECTOR [REDACTED] (221835Z APR 02).

Ray Kelly: "Statement of Ray Kelly, Police Commissioner, City of New York," Subcommittee on Government Management, Finance, and Accountability of the House Committee on Government Reform, July 10, 2006.

2014 Senate Report: Senate Select Committee on Intelligence, "Study of the Central Intelligence Agency's Detention and Interrogation Program," December 3, 2014.

Thomas Pickard / John O'Neill: *See, e.g.,* Lawrence Wright, "The Looming Tower: Al-Qaeda and the Road to 9/11," *Vintage Books*, 2006; "Thomas Pickard statement to the House Subcommittee on Crime of the Committee on the Judiciary," May 3, 2001; "The Man Who Knew," *PBS Frontline*, October 3, 2002.

3,000 agents reassigned: Perry Stein, "A quarter of FBI agents are assigned to immigration enforcement, per FBI data," *Washington Post*, October 8, 2025.

Congressman Dan Donovan: *See* "Hearing Before the Subcommittee on Emergency Preparedness, Response, and Communications, of the Committee of Homeland Security," House of Representatives, March 15, 2016.

Homeland Security Grant Funding cuts to New York: Grace Ashford and Stefanos Chen, "Trump Cuts to Counterterrorism Funds for New York Reach $187 Million," *New York Times*, September 30, 2025.

Homeland Security Grant Funding cuts to Washington, DC: Katie Sheperd and Meagan Flynn, "Trump pledged to make D.C. 'safe and beautiful.' His administration cut $40M in homeland security funds," *Washington Post*, October 10, 2025.

Federal Emergency Management Agency funding cuts: Scott Dance, "FEMA Withholds $300 Million in Grants Until States Account for Deportations," *New York Times*, October 3, 2025.

DHS response: Katie Sheperd and Meagan Flynn, "Trump pledged to make D.C. 'safe and beautiful.' His administration cut $40M in homeland security funds," *Washington Post*, October 10, 2025.

DHS task forces: *See, e.g.,* "Department of Homeland Security: Additional Actions Needed to Improve Oversight of Joint Task Forces," Government Accountability Office, GAO-24-106855, February 7, 2024.

DHS Office of Intelligence and Analysis cuts: David DiMolfetta, "DHS intelligence office sent deferred resignation offers to shed staff in recent months," NEXTGOV, October 7, 2025.

Maritime security report: "Maritime Security, Government Accountability Office, GAO-25-108525, June 10, 2025.

Michael Ben' Ary: *See, e.g.,* Kelly O'Donnell and Zoe Richards, "Letter left on fired federal prosecutor's door warns Americans are less safe," NBC News, October 4, 2025.

Exodus of over 5,000: "Urgent Message from Recent DOJ Alumni Decrying Attacks on Justice Department," *Justice Connection*, October 6, 2025.

Chapter 19. "Five Republicans and Five Democrats"

NCTC list of terrorist groups: "Counterterrorism Guide," Office of the Director of National Intelligence, National Counterterrorism Center, 2026.

Palestinian groups: Matthew Levitt, "Hamas Plots in Europe: A Shift Toward External Operations?" *Combatting Terrorism Center at West Point*, October 2025.

Document intended as a guide for the second Trump administration: "Mandate for Leadership: The Conservative Promise," Heritage Foundation, 2023.

JNIM on the march: Shola Lawal, "Is Mali about to fall to al-Qaeda affiliate JNIM?" *Al Jazeera*, November 6, 2025; *see also* Michael Langley, "Digital Press Briefing on the New AFRICOM Strategy and US Military Cooperation in Africa, US Department of State, September 12, 2024.

9/11 Commission Report: "Final Report of the National Commission on Terrorist Attacks Upon the United States," US Government, July 22, 2004.

9/11 Commission 2004 testimony to Congress: Thomas H. Kean and Lee H. Hamilton, "Public Statement, Release of 9/11 Commission Report," July 22, 2004.

INDEX

ACKNOWLEDGMENTS

My goal over the years was to make this book unique in the annals of national security–related publishing, and I could not have accomplished that without many knowledgeable and generous contributions along the way. I'm unaware of any other nonfiction book involving national security that provides a blow-by-blow account of a rendition from conception of the plan for capture to its aftermath. Typically, the US government does not permit current or former officials from publishing that information. Without government approval, such accounts are often subject to the biases and interests of one side—usually the person rendered.

This book is different by intent. Through my experience and research into the Second Wave plot, I was able to collect insight from both sides—offering readers an objective and comprehensive account for the historical record. To that end, I am eternally grateful to the Department of Defense Office of Prepublication and Security Review (DOPSR), and the multitude of federal agencies that signed off on the information contained in these pages. The prepublication review process wasn't seamless. But in the end, the government largely approved the full story of the Second Wave.

On an individual basis, I could not have completed this book without the professionalism and candor of numerous federal law enforcement personnel and members of the intelligence community. These are the real experts—the ones who could recite the entire case file verbatim. Janelle Miller is the embodiment of the FBI's motto: Fidelity, Bravery, Integrity. The interview with David Raskin was particularly meaningful, as he represents the absolute pinnacle of what it means to be a national security prosecutor.

On the other side, attorneys for Saifullah Paracha were spectacularly gracious with their time and candor. G. T. Hunt and David Remes are quintessential defense lawyers. They care about their clients and sincerely want the system to work as intended. G. T. Hunt was the conduit to pass along information to Saifullah Paracha as the book was being completed.

I would be remiss in not acknowledging Saifullah Paracha's consent for his legal counsel to speak with me on his behalf.

As a lawyer who started out as a journalist, I have a special affinity for those reporters who doggedly investigated the post-9/11 maze of intrigue. For this book, I tried to separate true journalistic sources and reports from advocacy pieces disguised as journalism. For example, I did not use any information put out by Andy Worthington, a self-styled "investigative journalist" who prolifically wrote about Guantanamo Bay and its detainees. To me, his work was biased and advocacy-tainted. However, I did use interviews with the Paracha family from advocacy organizations such as *Cage International* to help tell the story. But with respect to facts gathered by journalists, I only trusted and used information from reputable media outlets or scholars. My respect for the *New York Times*' Carol Rosenberg—known as the Dean of Guantanamo Bay—knows no bounds. I wish I could have told her that in person while she was covering my work as a trial attorney at Guantanamo Bay.

I owe a special thanks to Jeff Schmidt, my agent who championed this book despite its initial draft being written in what he described as a "dear diary style of journalism." I also am immensely grateful to author Greg Lawrence for editing the manuscript so that it reads like an actual book instead of a really long newspaper article. Judy Katz read the book in its rawest form and provided valuable insight into making improvements. Keith Wallman and Scott Waxman from Diversion Books provided amazing feedback that transitioned this book from a moment in time into an enduring lesson from history that is relevant to 2026 and beyond. Finally, thanks so much to my wife, Jessica, who supported this project through its ups and downs.

ABOUT THE AUTHOR

Mike Lebowitz is one of America's few war-crimes prosecutors with frontline counterterrorism experience. A former senior attorney at the Department of Justice's National Security Division, he spent nearly a decade prosecuting cases at Guantanamo Bay, including the 9/11 and USS *Cole* cases, as well as trials of top al Qaeda commanders. A US Army combat veteran and former Pathfinder unit officer, Lebowitz also served as a senior legal advisor to US Army Cyber Command. He has been featured or quoted by the *Washington Post, Wall Street Journal,* NPR, and Associated Press. He lives in Washington, DC.